Shadow Man

THE LIFE OF

DASHIELL HAMMETT

Books by Richard Layman

Dashiell Hammett: A Descriptive Bibliography (1979)
Ring Lardner: A Descriptive Bibliography,
with Matthew J.Bruccoli (1976)

Editor

Some Champions: Sketches and Fiction by Ring Lardner, with
Matthew J. Bruccoli (1976)

Series editor

The Dictionary of Literary Biography (1978—   )

Shadow Man

THE LIFE OF

DASHIELL HAMMETT

BY
Richard Layman

A HARVEST/HBJ BOOK

HARCOURT BRACE JOVANOVICH, PUBLISHERS

BRUCCOLI CLARK

SAN DIEGO   NEW YORK   LONDON

For Abe
His Mother
and His Grandparents

Requests for permission to make copies of any part of the work should be mailed to:
Permissions, Harcourt Brace Jovanovich, Inc., 757 Third Avenue, New York, N.Y.
10017

Excerpts from "O, Look—A Good Book!" in *The Portable Dorothy Parker*, copyright
1931, © renewed 1959 by Dorothy Parker, originally appeared in *The New Yorker* and
are reprinted by permission of Viking Penguin, Inc. Excerpts from "Poor Scotland
Yard" in *Saturday Review*, copyright © 1927 by *Saturday Review*, are reprinted by
permission of *Saturday Review*. Excerpts from *Red Harvest*, *The Dain Curse*, *The Maltese
Falcon*, *The Glass Key*, and *The Thin Man* are reprinted by permission of Alfred A.
Knopf, Inc. All rights reserved.

Library of Congress Cataloging in Publication Data

Layman, Richard, 1947–
Shadow man.
(A Harvest/HBJ book)
Revision of: 1st ed., c1981.
Includes index.
1. Hammett, Dashiell, 1894–1961. 2. Authors,
American—20th century—Biography. 3. Detective
and mystery stories, American—History and criticism.
I. Title.
PS3515.A4347Z74 1984   813'.52 [B]   83-16645

ISBN 0-15-681400-5

Printed in the United States of America
First Harvest/HBJ edition 1984
A B C D E F G H I J

C O N T E N T S

P R E F A C E

Dashiell Hammett seemed, for most of his life, to crave privacy.
Unlike many literary celebrities, he never took his fame seriously.
He never relied on it, never expected it, and he was always contemptuous of those who treated him with deference because of his
literary reputation. When he was in certain moods, he delighted in
fooling interviewers, interested listeners, and sycophants with fabricated tales about his past and his future plans. More often, he
withdrew into his writing, his compulsive reading, or the melancholy
introspection that consumed him during the last years of his life. As
a result, Hammett has always been the most elusive of mystery
writers—an aura intensified by his extraordinary accomplishment
of elevating what had been regarded as a subliterary genre to the
level of art.

During the last thirty years of his life, Lillian Hellman was Hammett's most trusted friend, though they were by no means constant
companions. His will, made in 1952, expressed his wish that she
receive one fourth of what he owned at his death and that she be the
executrix of his estate. Hellman got that and more. In a legal action
she acquired control of all Hammett's copyrights after his death,
claiming that she had been asked to write his biography and that
literary control of his works would be useful to her if she undertook
that project. Six years later she announced in her first memoir, *An
Unfinished Woman*, that she would never write a full life of Hammett.

Since that time she has often written about him or spoken of him,
developing a clouded personal image of the man while discouraging

attempts at biographical research of his life—except for an "authorized biography" that has been under way for some years at this writing and is now on its second biographer. Hellman has stated in interviews that she does not wish her memory of Hammett to be violated, and she has insisted to at least one researcher that "no piece" on Hammett can be written without her assistance. This biography was written without her assistance and without hindrance from her.

There has been a trend in literary biographies of late to concentrate not on the facts of an author's life so much as on the recounting of something resembling his life story, filling the inevitable gaps with inferences and molding material to form a smooth tale. In some cases the rationale has been to get at the "truth" of an author's character, even at the expense of the facts. The argument is that sometimes evidence is misleading, and—as a respected biographer informed me while I was writing this book—an apocryphal anecdote may reveal a man's character better than any true story could. Hellman herself has been acclaimed for her discussions of the ephemeral nature of recollected and retold truth in her memoirs. Nevertheless, I have taken a more pedestrian view of the matter. Here truth is simply what happened. Facts are the important things. Research has taken precedence over invention or speculation.

The research for *Shadow Man* began in 1975, when I started work on *Dashiell Hammett: A Descriptive Bibliography* (Pittsburgh: University of Pittsburgh Press, 1979), though I did not plan a biography at that time. During the course of preparing my bibliography I discovered, among other useful information, forgotten products of his literary career, such as magazine publications in little-known pulps and a complete run of *The Adakian*, an army camp newspaper he edited from January 1944 until April 1945. When all the bibliographical information was organized, the shape of Hammett's curious life as a professional writer was revealed.

But more important, I established an association with others interested in Hammett's life, and learned in 1975 that there were at least three biographies of Hammett in progress—in addition to the "authorized" one—all hindered by the intimidating opposition, either real or imagined, of his literary executrix.

Chief among Hammett researchers were David Fechheimer, a detective in San Francisco who had applied his considerable skills as a private eye to gathering information about Hammett; William Godshalk, a professor of English at the University of Cincinnati who had located childhood acquaintances of Hammett's; and William F. Nolan, a professional writer who had done biographical and bibliographical research on Hammett for his *Dashiell Hammett: A Casebook* (Santa Barbara: McNally & Loftin, 1969) and who has become a sort of coordinator of Hammett investigation. When I announced this book in 1978, both Fechheimer and Godshalk abandoned plans for their books and shared all the information they had accumulated with me. *Shadow Man* would not have been possible without their conscientious research and remarkable generosity. William Nolan was similarly generous in sharing what he knew about Hammett. There was, then, the outline of a biography—many leads, many questions, many people to interview.

Shadow Man is the result of following the leads, finding the answers to as many questions as possible, and interviewing anyone I could who claimed to have known Hammett. The life story that took form in the process could never be the exclusive possession of any one person; instead, it is an amalgam of factual information, and the impressions of many people who knew Hammett. His army records, veteran's records, letters, FBI files, court proceedings, and the public record—newspaper articles and interviews—form one part of the story. Interviews with Hammett's childhood friends (conducted by William Godshalk), his wife, and his daughter Mary (conducted by David Fechheimer), his Pinkerton friends, business associates, writer acquaintances, lovers, and employees form another part. His writing itself is still another part of the story. Because a large portion of Hammett's literary works has long since gone out of print and is inaccessible due to its publication in magazines not considered worthy of preservation, even by the most conscientious libraries, a special effort has been made here to indicate the nature and something of the substance of each of Hammett's publications.

There are chinks in this life of Hammett, and they have not been disguised. Neither has information about Hammett been withheld or altered to cosmetize or remake the history of his life.

One realizes at the completion of a project such as this an enormous debt that can never be properly acknowledged by the listing of names, yet lists must suffice. These are some of the people to whom I am indebted: Muriel Alexander, W. T. Ballard, Tom Barensfeld, William Blackbeard, Melvin J. Bordley, Marianne Caratti, Cleveland State University Library staff, Robert Colodny, Pat Crawford, Ethel E. Dobiash, Ellen Dunlap, Rose Evans, David Fechheimer, Jean Gillmer, William Glackin, William Godshalk, Tom Goldwasser, Joe

PREFACE

Gores, J. S. Guy, Nancy V. Hammett, Gladys Hansen, Nils Hardin, Humanities Research Center staff at the University of Texas at Austin, Ralph Ingersoll, Doris Jones, Jack Kaplan, Judith K. Keys, Jack Kofoed, William C. Linn, Anita Luccioni, Susan Manakul, Jay Martin, Carolyn S. Mateer, Marjorie May, Irene McCarthy, Allen H. McCreight, R. G. McMaster, James S. Miller, Lena B. Miller, G. H. Mundell, Frederick T. Newbraugh, William F. Nolan, Mildred Norris, Herbert S. Nusbaum, Virginia Sparling, E. E. Spitzer, Tacoma Public Library staff, Thomas Cooper Library staff at the University of South Carolina, Strom Thurmond and his staff, Ben Wasson, William Wenders, Alden Whitman, Robert A. Wilson, Jane Yowaiski.

To those who worked on my manuscript I am particularly grateful—Carol J. Meyer, and the staff of BC Research, especially Joyce Fowler and Lynne Zeigler.

My greatest debt is to Matthew J. Bruccoli for his editorial assistance.

C H R O N O L O G Y

May 27, 1894. Samuel Dashiell Hammett is born in Saint Mary's County, Maryland, to Richard and Annie Bond Hammett.

1900. Richard Hammett moves his family to 2942 Poplar Street in Philadelphia, Pennsylvania. Later that year, the family moves to 419 North Sixtieth Street in Philadelphia.

1901. The Hammetts move to 212 North Stricker Street in Baltimore, Maryland, and Dashiell enters Public School No. 72.

September 1908. Dashiell Hammett enters Baltimore Polytechnic Institute, where he studies for one semester before quitting school permanently to help his father run a small business.

1909-1915. Hammett holds various odd jobs at such companies as the B & O Railroad and Poe and Davies Brokerage House.

1915. Hammett becomes an operative for Pinkerton's National Detective Service.

June 24, 1918. Hammett joins the U.S. Army, where he is a private in the Motor Ambulance Company at Camp Mead, Maryland.

October 6, 1918. Hammett suffers the first of a series of bronchial attacks, apparently related to the epidemic of Spanish influenza at the time.

May 29, 1919. Hammett, then a sergeant, is discharged honorably from the army. He returns to his father's house to live and works as an operative at Pinkerton's, probably part-time.

May 1920. Hammett moves to Spokane, Washington, where he works as a Pinkerton.

November 6, 1920. Hammett is hospitalized, 100 percent disabled with pulmonary tuberculosis, at U.S. Public Health Service Hospital Number 59, also called Cushman Hospital. He meets Jose Dolan, who is a nurse there.

February 21, 1921. Hammett leaves Cushman Hospital for USPHS Hospital Number 64 at Camp Kearny near San Diego.

May 15, 1921. Hammett is discharged from the hospital and goes to live briefly in Seattle at 1117 Third Avenue.

June 1921. Hammett moves to 120 Ellis Street in San Francisco.

July 7, 1921. Hammett marries Jose Dolan. He works as a Pinkerton operative. They live at 620 Eddy Street.

October 15, 1921. The Hammetts' daughter Mary is born.

December 1, 1921. The date Hammett claims to have quit detective work for good.

February 1922. Hammett begins a one-and-a-half-year vocational training course at Munson's Business College.

October 1922. Hammett's first publication—in *The Smart Set*.

October 1, 1923. "Arson Plus," the first op story, is published in *Black Mask*.

March 1926. Hammett quits writing to take a job as advertising manager at Samuels Jewelry Company in San Francisco.

May 24, 1926. The Hammetts' second daughter, Josephine, is born.

July 20, 1926. Hammett resigns from Samuels due to poor health.

October 1926. Hammett is advised by doctors to move away from his young daughter to keep from infecting her with tuberculosis. The family moves to 1309 Hyde Street and Hammett lives alone nearby, first at 20 Monroe Street, then at 891 Post, where his family joins him in fall 1927.

January 15, 1927. Hammett begins reviewing mystery books for *The Saturday Review of Literature*, which he continues to do until October 29, 1929.

February 1927. "The Big Knock-Over," Hammett's first story in eleven months, appears in *Black Mask*.

November 1927. The first of four parts of Hammett's first novel, later called *Red Harvest*, is published in *Black Mask*.

November 1928. The first of four parts of Hammett's second novel, later called *The Dain Curse*, is published in *Black Mask*.

February 1, 1929. *Red Harvest* is published by Knopf.

July 19, 1929. *The Dain Curse* is published by Knopf.

Fall 1929. Hammett lives briefly at 1155 Leavenworth Avenue in San Francisco before he leaves his family behind and moves in October to New York, where he lives at 155 East Thirtieth Street.

September 1929. The first of five parts of *The Maltese Falcon*, Hammett's third novel, is published in *Black Mask*.

February 14, 1930. *The Maltese Falcon* is published by Knopf.

February 1930. *Roadhouse Nights*, a movie based on *Red Harvest*, is released by Paramount.

March 1930. The first of four parts of *The Glass Key*, Hammett's fourth novel, is published in *Black Mask*.

April 5, 1930. Hammett begins a six-month stint as mystery book reviewer for the *New York Evening Post*.

Summer 1930. Hammett signs a contract with Paramount to write original screen stories. He moves to Hollywood.

Winter 1930-1931. Hammett meets Lillian Hellman in Hollywood.

January 1931. Hammett signs a contract with Warner Brothers to write a detective movie to star William Powell.

January 20, 1931. *The Glass Key* is published in London by Knopf.

April 1931. *City Streets*, a movie based on Hammett's original story, is released by Paramount.

April 28, 1931. Hammett's screen story "On the Make" is rejected by Warner Brothers. He is released from his contract and returns to New York, where he lives at 133 East Thirty-eighth Street.

Spring 1931. Hammett begins, then abandons, a novel called "The Thin Man."

May 1931. *The Maltese Falcon*, a movie based on Hammett's novel, is released by Warner Brothers.

October 8, 1931. *Creeps by Night*, an anthology of stories edited with an introduction by Hammett, is published.

Winter 1931. Hammett is charged with assaulting actress Elise De Vianne during a visit to Hollywood. He is found guilty on June 30, 1932, by default judgment. He lives at the Hotel Elysee at 60 East Fifty-fourth Street in New York and writes short stories.

Summer or Fall 1932. Hammett moves to the Hotel Pierre at Sixty-first Street and Fifth Avenue in New York City. He leaves without paying his bill at the end of September.

September 29, 1932. Hammett moves to Sutton Club Hotel at 330 East Fifty-Sixth Street in New York City to work on *The Thin Man*, which is completed in May 1933.

Winter 1933. Hammett and Hellman move to Homestead, Florida, where they stay until late spring or early summer 1934, when Hammett returns to New York.

December 1933. *The Thin Man* is published by *Redbook*.

January 8, 1934. *The Thin Man* is published by Knopf.

January 29, 1934. Syndication of *Secret Agent X-9*, a comic strip written by Hammett, is begun by King Features. Hammett is credited with writing the strip until April 27, 1935.

March 24, 1934. Hammett's last short story, "This Little Pig," is published in *Collier's*.

June 1934. MGM movie, *The Thin Man*, is released.

September 27, 1934. Universal buys Hammett's screen story "On the Make" and changes the title to *Mister Dynamite* for the film, released in May 1935.

October 29, 1934. Hammett begins working as a writer at MGM. He moves to Hollywood, where he lives at the Beverly Wilshire Hotel.

June 1935. The movie *The Glass Key* is released by Paramount. Hammett signs new contract with MGM.

January 1936. Hammett returns to New York where he is hospitalized at Lenox Hill Hospital for about two weeks. He then moves to the Hotel Madison on East Fifty-eighth Street.

July 1936. *Satan Met a Lady*, Warner Brothers' second movie version of *The Maltese Falcon* is released.

Fall 1936. Hammett moves to Princeton, New Jersey, where he rents a house at 90 Cleveland Lane.

December 25, 1936. *After the Thin Man*, a movie based on Hammett's original story, is released by MGM.

February 1937. Hammett sells MGM all rights to *The Thin Man* title and characters for $40,000.

March 1937. Hammett contributes to a fund for the Loyalists in the Spanish Civil War, the first indication of his political activism.

Spring 1937. Hammett is asked to leave Princeton by his neighbors, and he returns to Hollywood to work for MGM. He lives at the Beverly Wilshire Hotel.

August 31, 1937. A Mexican court grants Jose Hammett a divorce that has no legal standing in the United States.

Summer 1938. Hammett completes work on his second original story for the Thin Man series (*Another Thin Man*, the third in the series) and turns his attentions to politics and a new novel.

July 14, 1939. Hammett's contract with MGM is permanently terminated and he moves to 14 West Ninth Street in New York City.

May 1939. The first issue of *Equality* magazine is published under the direction of Equality Publishers, a seven-man group that included Hammett.

Fall 1939. Random House announces "There Was a Young Man," a new novel by Hammett, which never appears.

November 1939. *Another Thin Man* is released.

1940. Hammett is national chairman of the Committee on Election Rights—1940, a group to promote the political candidacy of Communist Party members.

July 2, 1941. The radio serial, "The Adventures of the Thin Man," based on Hammett's characters, begins. It runs, with a wartime interruption, until September 1950.

October 1941. Warner Brothers' third movie version of *The Maltese Falcon*, this one directed by John Huston and starring Humphrey Bogart, is released.

September 17, 1942. Hammett rejoins the army as a private, and is stationed at Fort Monmouth, New Jersey.

October 1942. The second movie version of *The Glass Key* is released by Paramount.

November 1942. *The Shadow of The Thin Man* is released by MGM.

August 1943. *Watch on the Rhine*, adapted by Hammett and Lillian Hellman from her play, is released by Warner Brothers.

September 8, 1943. Hammett arrives in Alaska, where he remains for the duration of the war.

January 19, 1944. The first trial issue of *The Adakian*, a daily newspaper edited by Hammett for army troops, is published.

1944. *The Battle of the Aleutians*, by Hammett and Robert Colodny, a history of the war against the Japanese on the Aleutian Chain in 1942 and 1943, is published for distribution to Adakian troops.

January 1945. *The Thin Man Goes Home* is released by MGM.

April 1945. Hammett leaves Adak and *The Adakian* for assignment at Fort Richardson in Anchorage, Alaska.

September 6, 1945. Hammett, now a sergeant, is honorably discharged from the army. He returns to New York where he lives briefly at 15 East Sixty-sixth Street before moving to 28 West Tenth Street.

1946. Hammett begins teaching courses in mystery writing at the Jefferson School of Social Science, which he continues until 1956. He serves as a member of the board of trustees for the school from 1949 to 1956.

January 21, 1946. "The Fat Man," a radio serial based on Hammett's Continental op, begins. It runs until 1950.

June 5, 1946. Hammett is elected president of the New York Civil Rights Congress, a position he holds until the mid-1950s.

July 12, 1946. "The Adventures of Sam Spade," a radio serial based on Hammett's character, begins. It runs until 1951.

May 28, 1948. Warner Brothers sues broadcaster, sponsor, director, and producer of "The Adventures of Sam Spade" for infringement of copyright. Hammett is later added to the suit, which is settled on December 28, 1951, in Hammett's favor.

Fall 1949. Hammett works as dramatic script consultant to stage producer Kermit Bloomgarden.

January 1950. Hammett goes to Hollywood as a screenwriter for Paramount. After six months he leaves Hollywood for good.

Fall 1950-Spring 1951. Hammett works with Hellman and Bloomgarden on producing her play *The Autumn Garden*.

July 9, 1951. Hammett testifies in United States District Court about the Civil Rights Congress bail fund. He is judged that evening to be an uncooperative witness in criminal contempt of court and is sentenced to six months in prison, beginning immediately at the Federal House of Detention in New York City.

September 28, 1951. Hammett is moved to the Federal Correctional Institute near Ashland, Kentucky.

December 9, 1951. Hammett is released from prison and returns briefly to his apartment at Tenth Street. His income is attached by the Internal Revenue Service in lieu of payment of back taxes amounting at that time to $111,008.60.

Spring (?) 1952. Hammett moves to the gatehouse on the estate of Dr. Samuel Rosen in Katonah, New York.

March 26, 1953. Hammett testifies before Joseph McCarthy's Senate subcommittee investigating the purchase of books written by Communists for State Department libraries overseas.

Ca. 1953. Hammett abandons the fragment "Tulip," his last attempt at writing a novel.

February 23, 1955. Hammett testifies before the New York State Joint Legislature Committee investigating charitable and philanthropic agencies and organizations.

August 1955. Hammett has a heart attack at Lillian Hellman's house on Martha's Vineyard.

January 1957. Hammett's federal income tax liability is set at $140,795.96 by civil court.

May 1959. Hammett is granted a pension of $131.10 per month by the Veteran's Administration.

January 10, 1961. Hammett dies at the Lenox Hill Hospital in New York City.

January 13, 1961. Hammett is buried at Arlington National Cemetery.

PART 1

The Early Years
1894-1922

CHAPTER 1

I was born in Maryland, between the Potomac and Patuxent rivers, on May 27, 1894, and was raised in Baltimore.

After a fraction of a year in high school–Baltimore Polytechnic Institute–I became the unsatisfactory and unsatisfied employee of various railroads, stock brokers, machine manufacturers, canners, and the like. Usually I was fired.

Dashiell Hammett
Black Mask, November 1924

The earliest record of the Hammett family in America is the death of Robert Hammett on July 13, 1719, in Saint Mary's County, Maryland.[1] The records do not show why or when Robert came to the New World, and family legend is clouded. The branch of the family that moved away from Saint Mary's County, the rural homestead, claims that the first American Hammett was an indentured servant, who diligently worked to repay his passage from England. The branch of the family that stayed in Saint Mary's County tells it more entertainingly. They say the first American Hammett was a scoundrel and a thief who was transported from England for stealing, probably to Virginia or the Carolinas. He had not been in America long when he got caught stealing again—it was the only skill he possessed—and after a speedy trial arrangements were made to return him to England for execution. But Robert Hammett escaped and fled to Saint Mary's County near what is now called Lexington Park, about forty miles southeast of Washington, D.C., where he prospered.

By the early nineteenth century Hammett was a respected if not entirely respectable name in southern Maryland. Samuel Biscoe Hammett, Dashiell's great-grandfather and Robert's great-grandson, owned a prosperous store at Millstone Landing on the banks of the Patuxent River, where the Patuxent Naval Base is presently located. Samuel Hammett's store was a two-story log building. The first floor was a combination trading post, community center, post office, and general store; the second floor was the family living quarters. The store and the area surrounding it were known as Hammettville.[2]

Business at Hammettville was good enough by 1827 for Samuel Hammett to buy a farm. On April 2 he paid $1,300 for a 197½-acre plot of land called "Hopewell and Aim"; but Samuel Hammett was a storekeeper, not a farmer, and his barren farm was a local standard by which agricultural failure was measured. By the time of his death twenty-seven years later in 1854, "Hopewell and Aim" was described as "void of fertility," and its value was set at five dollars an acre—nearly one-fourth less than Samuel had paid for it. He willed his farm to his children.

The store went to Samuel's oldest son, Samuel Biscoe Hammett, Jr., Dashiell's grandfather. In 1859, after five years as owner of Hammettville, Samuel Hammett married his first cousin, Ann Rebecca Hammett, and a year later his son Richard was born in a room over the store. Hammettville continued to prosper, largely due to its prime location at the mouth of the Patuxent River where it empties into Chesapeake Bay. The store was accessible from the river and to the residents of the county who traveled to the store by a well-worn dirt wagon road. In 1871 Samuel Hammett, Jr., bought for $750 the interest in "Hopewell and Aim" held by his brother Washington and his sister Janie Rebecca. He was then the leader of the family, a successful merchant and landowner. It was eighteen years before things went sour for him.

His wife died in the late 1880s and, because he had managed his money poorly, in 1889 Hammettville had to be sold. The transfer of the Hammettville inventory to Janie Rebecca was recorded at Leonardtown, the Saint Mary's county seat. Samuel agreed to satisfy his "long-standing debt" to her by transferring "the following property, to wit: one yoke of oxen; one ox cart; one hundred and thirty cords of pine wood; and my entire stock of goods in trade in my store known as Hammettville."[3]

Samuel Biscoe Hammett, Jr., took a new wife that year and moved into the three-story unpainted weatherboard house on "Hopewell and Aim." It was considered mildly scandalous when Samuel, then past fifty, married twenty-three-year-old Lucy E. Dyer, who was younger than his son and the same age as his daughter; but Samuel, being a Hammett, was accustomed to local gossip. Big as the house was, it was soon crowded. In 1892 Samuel's eldest son, Richard Thomas Hammett, who still lived with his father, married and moved his wife into the house. By 1896 Richard Hammett had a daughter and two sons—Aronica Rebecca (called Reba) born in 1893, Samuel Dashiell (called Dashiell or Dash) born in 1894, and Richard Thomas, Jr. (called Dick) born in 1896. Soon afterward Samuel and his wife further increased the size of the household with their two sons, George and Samuel, and a daughter, Lucy, born in quick succession.

Dashiell Hammett's father, Richard Hammett, Sr., was a big man—six feet tall and more than 200 pounds. He was handsome, with a local reputation as a ladies' man. Clothes were important to him, and his neighbors felt he always acted a little more prosperous than he really was. Those who knew him well called Richard a pure Hammett; that meant he drank more than his share of whiskey, never backed down from a fight, played a respectable game of poker, and had an inordinate appreciation for pretty women. He was stubborn, independent, and his ambition was tempered by a touch of laziness.

Richard Hammett was thirty-two when he married Annie Bond in 1892. He had served briefly as postmaster at Hammettville in 1882, and he had been a justice of the peace in Saint Mary's County since February 19, 1887. Like his father and grandfather, he called himself a farmer, but it was customary in southern Maryland for a man who owned land—or whose father did—to make such a claim, regardless of his true occupation. He was a Catholic, strong enough in his beliefs to convince Annie Bond to convert when they were married, but Richard Hammett's faith was stronger on Sunday morning than on Saturday night.

Annie Bond was an outsider in Saint Mary's County and in the Hammett family. Her parents had come recently to Maryland from Kentucky, and due to the influence of her father, who seems to have been a minister, she maintained an aloofness toward the rough socializing in the county that the Hammetts enjoyed. She was a proud woman who never approved of the drinking, the womanizing, and the undependability of the Hammett men. Known as

"Lady" in the family for her manners, her bearing, and her outspoken independence, Annie Hammett did not hesitate to criticize her husband for what she saw as the moral weakness inherent in his sex. She held one conviction firmly above all others: all men are no good.

Annie Hammett's health was poor during all her married life. She was tubercular, and her condition was aggravated by the damp air in Saint Mary's County. Yet despite her poor health, frequent pregnancies early in her marriage, and the burdens of childrearing, Annie Hammett worked as a private nurse when she could to help support the family.[4]

Samuel Dashiell Hammett was born in his grandfather's house at "Hopewell and Aim" on Sunday, May 27, 1894. His first name was for his grandfather, and his middle name was his maternal grandmother's maiden name. Annie Hammett, who held herself superior to her in-laws in all things, told stories of the bravery the French De Chiells showed in battle, and in honor of her ancestors' dignity—which she found so lacking in the Hammetts—she called her son Dashiell, insisting his name be pronounced properly with an accent on the second syllable (Da-sheel). When he was five weeks old, on July 5, 1894, Annie Hammett dressed her son for his christening and the family traveled in a wagon the two miles to Saint Nicholas Catholic Church. His godparents were David and Henrietta Hammett, his father's first cousin and his wife, and the baptism was conducted by Father J. M. Giroud, a Jesuit.[5]

Richard Hammett had visions of wealth and success. He first tried to realize those goals in politics, but he seriously misjudged the political climate in Saint Mary's County and lost forever his chances for a career in public office there. The county, the Hammetts included, had long been solidly Democratic before the 1896 presidential election, but 1896 was a prosperous year and voters rejected the Populist reforms of William Jennings Bryan, the Democratic nominee for president, in favor of Republican William McKinley, who advocated the conservative position of upholding the gold standard for U.S. currency. Local Republicans showed some strength in that election, and Richard Hammett saw a way to get on the ballot for public office. His chances of being chosen to run for office as a Democrat were limited because the field was too crowded, but with the Republican party he thought he might have an opportunity to run for state office. He switched parties, a mistake in a section of the country where political loyalty is held second in importance only to patriotism. No evidence has been found that Richard Hammett ever actually made the ballot, but he did pay the price for his disloyal notions. Family legend holds that he was "run out of the county, more or less on a rail."[6]

In 1900 Richard Hammett moved his family to Philadelphia and took a job as a manufacturer's agent. They lived first at 2942 Poplar Street and later moved to a small house at 419 North Sixtieth Street. But selling was not for Richard Hammett, and he felt he was too far away from his family in Saint Mary's County besides; so in 1901, when Dashiell was seven, Richard Hammett and his family left Philadelphia for Baltimore, where he took a job first as a streetcar conductor and then as a clerk.[7]

The Hammetts lived in a three-story row house at 212 North Stricker Street near Franklin Square in Baltimore. Theirs was a respectable middle-class address, about ten blocks west of the house where Edgar Allan Poe had lived and six blocks north of H. L. Mencken's house. There were two paved streets in the area then, and Stricker was not one of them. Plumbing was primitive. The Hammetts, like their neighbors, had an outdoor toilet; water from indoor sinks and tubs drained into gutters in the streets, until 1904 when sewers were installed.[8]

The three Hammett children were enrolled in Public School No. 72 and began to make friends in the neighborhood. Dashiell and his brother were never close; even during their childhood they went their separate ways. Dashiell was quiet, introspective, competitive, and temperamental. His friend Walter C. Polhous (whose last name Hammett used in 1929 for a policeman in *The Maltese Falcon*) remembers a hockey game he and Hammett played: "I was hitting the puck first all the time and it made him very angry. When we were playing the last game instead of hitting the puck he hit me with the stick and made a cut over my right eye. When he saw I was bleeding he got very upset and ran home."[9]

Polhous remembers that Hammett kept to himself more than the other boys in the neighborhood did; at a young age he discovered the West Lexington Library and read mysteries and swashbucklers late into the night. Annie Hammett had one complaint about her son when she visited her friends in Saint Mary's County: he stayed up reading too late at night and she often had to spend an entire morning getting him out of bed.

There was a special relationship between Annie Hammett and her elder son. He understood that hers was the strength that held the family together. She was a tragic figure, he felt, trapped in an unpleasant life by his father, a weak, self-centered man. He declared openly and often that he would never treat a woman the way his father treated his mother. Annie Hammett was not a woman to feel sorry for herself, though. She took a practical view of her problems and solved them with practical solutions, which she shared with her closest friends. Mrs. Hammett's views on how to hold a marriage together shocked her neighbors: she told them that if you can't hold a man with love, do it with sex.

Annie Hammett's children were proud, a quality they inherited in large quantities from both sides of their family and which Dashiell seemed to possess in abundance. When his mother's closest friend, who lived next door, went on vacation and sent Annie Hammett a postcard with the name Hammett misspelled, Dashiell took it upon himself to correct and reprimand her when she returned home. He believed in getting things right.[10]

In September 1908 Dashiell Hammett entered high school at Baltimore Polytechnic Institute, a public school which offered training in mechanics and engineering. Baltimore Poly was only twenty-five years old in 1908, but already it had a reputation as an outstanding school and was the only high school in Baltimore to provide sophomore college standing for its graduates. Hammett's first publisher, H. L. Mencken, attended Poly from 1892 to 1896 and was the school's most distinguished graduate.

Hammett took seven courses in his first semester: algebra, geometry, physics, history, English composition, American literature, and mechanical drawing. His best subject was history, his worst was algebra, and he ended the semester with an overall average of 78. Then he was forced to withdraw, ending his formal education.[11] As Dashiell's brother explained, "My father, who had a very small business, became ill and Dashiell was elected to pick up the pieces."[12]

The exact nature of Richard Hammett's business is unclear. He seems to have employed a few street peddlers, known in the area as Arabs (Ay-rabs), who sold seafood door to door. Whatever the business, neither Richard Hammett nor his thirteen-year-old son was able to save it, and the enterprise was abandoned in 1909 with at least one outstanding debt, which was settled only when a claim was filed against Richard Hammett's share of his father's estate after Samuel Hammett's death in 1911. The estate was $2,700, but after Samuel's debts were paid and the judgment against Richard was deducted from his one-fifth share, Richard Hammett inherited only $66.70.[13]

By 1911 Dashiell's brother Richard, the steadiest worker among the men in the family, had gotten a clerking job to help support the household. Dashiell, on the other hand, held at least a job a year between 1909 and 1915. Among his employers during that time were the B & O Railroad, where he worked as an office boy, and the stockbrokers Poe and Davies, where he noted market transactions on a chalkboard.[14]

Hammett was an enigmatic figure even then. He was reserved, yet self-assured; he was attractive to some and unimpressive to others; some saw him as ambitious, others as shiftless. Mildred Norris, a distant relative of Hammett's, remembers him coming back to Saint Mary's County as a teenager, along with a friend, to visit her sister. He was "long and lanky, just like a beanpole" she recalls. "I used to think he was the ugliest boy I ever saw in my life." Even to Mrs. Norris, who was six years Hammet's junior, he seemed shy and fidgety.[15]

Yet Hammett could be assertive as well. Later in his life he told the story of how he lost his job at the B & O Railroad after being late every day for a week. His boss called Hammett into his office and told him he was fired. Hammett acknowledged his termination with apparent unconcern and turned to leave. Having made his point, Hammett's boss called the boy back and offered him a second chance, but only if he would promise not to be late again. Hammett thanked him and politely refused; he knew he would be late again and his honor was more important than a job. The puzzled boss, impressed by Hammett's determined honesty, finally gave in and told him to keep the job anyway. Soon after, Hammett quit.[16]

But that is a story Hammett told later in life, when he typically made himself seem more self-reliant and nonchalant than he really had been. In fact, he was oddly dependent on his parents, living with them until he was twenty-six years old, even while fighting bitterly with his father much of the time. Richard Hammett objected to his son's companions, and he later maintained that he knew Dashiell was associating with Communists in Baltimore. But more probably, Richard Hammett's objections were simpler, an accumulation of complaints. At the age of twenty, in 1914, Dashiell had contracted gonorrhea; he was beginning to drink;[17] he would not hold a job; he had little respect for his father; and his life seemed directionless.

CHAPTER 2

An enigmatic want-ad took me into the employ of Pinkerton's National Detective Agency, and I stuck at that until early in 1922, when I chucked it to see what I could do with fiction writing.

In between, I spent an uneventful while in the army during the war, becoming a sergeant; and acquired a wife and daughter.

Dashiell Hammett
Black Mask, November 1924

In 1915, the year Hammett was twenty-one, he took a job as a Pinkerton detective that would influence him more than any other in his life.[1] The Pinkerton's National Detective Agency was the largest investigative agency in the country. Its logo was a single unblinking eye; its slogan, "We never sleep." The eye was meant to symbolize the methods of the Pinkerton detective, or operative as he was called in the agency, who saw everything, who solved crimes by his powers of observation, and who prevented crimes by recognizing criminal behavior. The agency boasted that none but a Pinkerton was worth counting on if detective work was called for. Though the agency had a distinguished history since its beginning in 1850, preventing presidential assassinations, solving sensational cases, and systematizing crime prevention for the first time, the turn of the century brought about a change in the nature of a Pinkerton agent's work. Municipal police forces were becoming more and more proficient in dealing with crime, and Pinkerton's became a source for hired policemen to supplement the efforts of local law enforcement agencies or to undertake work deemed improper for the local police or the U.S. Secret Service. When the labor movement in America began to gain a violent momentum early in the twentieth century, the business Pinkerton's had lost to municipal police forces was more than replaced by a new demand for the services of private policemen—as protectors of business property against damage by strikers. Pinkertons quickly became known as union busters for their frequent and prominent roles in labor disputes—breaking strikes, controlling strikers, and safeguarding scab workers who crossed picket lines. If Richard Hammett really believed his son was consorting with Communists, he must have been relieved to see him become a Pinkerton.[2]

A Pinkerton operative was on call twenty-four hours a day, and in 1915 his starting salary was twenty-one dollars a week.[3] Even with the changing nature of Pinkerton's business, the basic work of an operative was still surveillance. A detective who lacked the ability to shadow a suspect inconspicuously was considered incomplete, and a man who could not sit quietly for hours at a time watching or listening for evidence could never be a detective. Dashiell Hammett was a very good operative; despite his size—he was 6´ 1½" and weighed about 160 at the time—he could follow a suspect all day without being observed.

Pinkerton's Baltimore office was in the Continental Building. The territory of the Baltimore branch was broad and the operatives often worked out of the city, as far away as southern Florida. Though there were twenty Pinkerton's offices in 1915, there was only the New Orleans office in the South, and no eastern office farther south than Baltimore. Hammett was taught his job by the assistant manager of the Baltimore office, a short, squat, tough-talking operative named James Wright. Wright's expertise was legendary, and his adventures were impressive enough to Hammett that he used Wright as the model for his Continental op when he began writing detective stories seven years later.[4]

While James Wright was teaching Hammett the rudiments of private investigation, he instilled in him not only a set of procedural principles and a romanticized concept of his work, but also a detective's code, an amalgam of Pinkerton's regulations, professional ethics, and rules for self-protection, which Hammett embraced enthusiastically and adhered to with an almost religious devotion for the rest of his life. The code was pragmatic and unwritten; it provided an operative with an approach to his job that would allow him to do it well with as little physical and emotional risk as possible. Essentially, the code was built around three elements: anonymity, morality, and objectivity.

A good detective must be anonymous, because the less known about him, the less his chances are of having personal information used against him. A good detective neither seeks publicity nor accepts it easily if it comes his way. Accordingly, a Pinkerton operative's reports were anonymous. He was identified by number; one copy of his report was filed at the branch office and another, perhaps abridged or rewritten, was supplied to the client. A Pinkerton was expected to be closemouthed and secretive about his job. Hammett, for instance, gave his occupation as "clerk" in the city directory while he was a detective in Baltimore. Later, while working as a part-time operative in San Francisco, he described himself as a "broker."

The morality of a private detective is based on a personal sense of right and wrong only incidentally connected with religious or civil law. In the simplest terms, his job is to protect good people from exploitation by bad people, and the means to that end require no justification. Since the detective takes it upon himself to track down and confront criminals, who do not conduct their lives in accordance with any rules of fair play, he realizes that to be successful he too must ignore the rules of conventional behavior. He will disguise himself, misrepresent himself, lie, cheat, steal, or blackmail if that is what it takes to get his man. And if he is good, he will do it skillfully enough to avoid getting caught—by the police or by his agency supervisor. The private detective must maintain a carefully ordered sense of priorities. He is hired by a client, and if he accepts his client's money, he owes him a certain loyalty. But that loyalty never supersedes the detective's personal ethics.

The essential quality which a detective must develop to avoid being consumed by his job is objectivity—an emotional distance from the people with whom he deals. If he becomes emotionally involved with a client, he will forfeit the objectivity required to gather all the available information and observe all the pertinent clues relating to the case. If he allows himself to hate a criminal, he will lose the emotional equilibrium required to protect himself and to make all his decisions coolly and logically.

Perhaps partly as a result of his assimilation of the detective's code, there is very little information available about the cases Hammett worked on in Baltimore. None of his case reports survives;

Pinkerton's maintains that they were destroyed by fire.[5] Their loss is all the more distressing because Hammett bragged late in his life about the "literary quality" of his reports. In his earliest published writing, though, he did refer briefly to isolated incidents: the time he was dispatched to find a man who had stolen a Ferris wheel; the time he was hired to discharge a woman's housekeeper. Lillian Hellman has written that Hammett told her he was asked to assassinate the International Workers of the World (IWW) labor leader Frank Little during this time and declined. Little, a member of the executive council of the radical and often violent IWW, was lynched in Anaconda, Montana, in August 1917. That story of Hammett's peripheral involvement is implausible, though his telling such a tale is likely. Hammett's accounts of his days as a detective are always suspect, because he was writing these accounts, describing his adventures in interviews, and telling friends stories about his past after he had changed occupations. He was by then a writer with experience and considerable interest in advertising. He knew that people liked his writing because it was realistic, made to seem more so by his firsthand experience as an operative. In a half self-serving, half playful manner, he characteristically amplified his stories, rewriting, revising, even inventing accounts of his experiences.

If the exact nature of Hammett's work as a Pinkerton is unknown, that experience cannot be overemphasized in its importance to his work and his life. Pinkerton's gave Hammett a code that he took as his own and shaped his life by. He learned a method of observation that he later used to give his work a sense of stark reality. And he came away with stories to tell.

On June 24, 1918, fifteen months after the United States declared war on Germany, Hammett left his job to enlist in the army. He took his basic training with the 34th Company, 9th Training Battalion, 154th Depot Brigade at Camp Mead, Maryland; and on July 12, 1918, he received his permanent assignment to the Motor Ambulance Company at Camp Mead, about fifteen miles from his home on Stricker Street.[7]

Hammett was in the army for not quite a year. He left his ambulance company with a resolve, which he apparently broke only rarely, never to drive again and with a crippling illness that remained with him the rest of his life. He explained that his aversion to driving resulted from the trauma of his turning over an ambulance full of wounded men returned to the States for medical attention.

That incident does not appear on his service record. What does appear is a history of chronic respiratory disease. Nineteen eighteen was the year of the worldwide Spanish influenza epidemic. The influenza, apparently transmitted by soldiers returning from Europe, swept United States military camps and ultimately caused more deaths of American soldiers than military action during the war. Some estimates of deaths attributable to the epidemic of 1918-1919 are as high as five hundred thousand people in the United States alone.

Hammett first complained of flu-like symptoms on October 6, 1918, when he reported to field hospital number 241, unable to work and with a temperature of 103 degrees. He was immediately transferred to the base hospital, where he remained bedfast for twelve days, eight of which he could not sit up. The diagnosis was bronchopneumonia, concentrated at the base of his right lung. After twenty days in the hospital Hammett was released and returned to active duty.

On Valentine's Day 1919, Hammett was promoted to private first class. Nine days later he was back in the hospital, complaining of a sore throat in the mornings and a nagging cough. Under the direction of Dr. R. S. Freid, Hammett was given a battery of tests. The diagnosis this time was "Acute bronchitis, catarrhal, bilateral"— inflammation of the bronchial tubes and mucous membranes in both lungs. He remained in the hospital for four days before Dr. Freid judged him to be cured and able to resume active duty.

Hammett left the hospital on February 27 and performed his duties well enough to get promoted to sergeant on April 23, 1919. But he was not cured, and he was back in the infirmary on May 29. This time his illness was diagnosed as untreatable; he had disabling tuberculosis, the doctors said, contracted in the line of duty. (They were apparently unaware that Hammett's mother was tubercular and that he had been exposed to the illness since he was a child.) He was declared 25 percent disabled, given a statutory award of $50 for his disability, and his immediate discharge was recommended and processed that day.

When Hammett left the army he was a very sick twenty-five-year-old man, given no hope that his condition would improve. He had always been thin, but he had lost about twenty pounds in that year and weighed barely 140 at the time of his discharge. His symptoms were dizziness, sore throat, coughing, shortness of breath, and physical weakness caused by a diminished supply of oxygen to his muscles. But Hammett was determined to return to his prewar profession as a private detective.

He was unsure enough about the future that he moved back into his father's house after his discharge. His disability pension, granted on May 31, 1919, was only $7.50 a week, hardly enough to support himself if he found he could not work steadily. When he went to Pinkerton's to ask for his old job back, he was rehired for $105 a month.[8] Hammett tried to pick up his life where it left off before the war, and he failed.

Though he had not seen battle—in fact he had never been more than twenty miles from home as a soldier—Hammett was a war casualty, a disabled veteran. He was unable to climb a flight of stairs without paralyzing breathlessness. He no longer had the endurance to work for more than a few hours without bedrest. He coughed and he hemorrhaged. He tried to make himself well, giving up drinking altogether and attempting to control his smoking. Yet his health continued to worsen and exactly six months after he resumed his job at Pinkerton's, Hammett was back in the hospital again. On December 26, 1919, Hammett's disability and his pension were reviewed by the Bureau of War Risk Insurance. He was now officially 50 percent disabled, and his pension was set at forty dollars a month. Army doctors advised him to resume his former occupation, and he tried, but he apparently was able to perform only part-time as a detective.

The Hammett residence resembled a boardinghouse in 1920. The family had moved around the corner from Stricker Street to 1419 West Lexington Street while Hammett was in the army. Richard and Annie's children all had jobs: Hammett's sister Reba, 27, was a stenographer; his brother Dick, 24, was still a clerk; Dashiell, 26, was a part-time Pinkerton; and they all lived at home. While Hammett was very close to his sister and his mother, his relations with his brother and his father only deteriorated. Hammett was beginning finally to feel the need for independence, so in May 1920 when his health and his finances permitted, he left his family behind, cutting nearly all ties with the men in his family and staying in touch with Reba and his mother by letter only.

He went across the country to Spokane, Washington, perhaps partly because there was a Pinkerton's office there. The damp cold climate of the Northwest would not seem to be an improvement over humid Baltimore, but Washington was good for Hammett at first. He began working as a detective again; his weight increased to 155, the highest it had been since he entered the army; and he liked his work, which took him to Idaho and Montana where the I.W.W. was continuing its by then nearly ten-year-long fight to organize ore miners.

Hammett later had pleasant memories of his days as a Pinkerton working out of the Spokane office. He said that his most exciting work as a detective came during the Anaconda strike of 1920-1921 when the huge mining corporation finally broke the I.W.W. attempts to unionize the miners.[9] He liked to tell about the prisoner he was transferring from Gilt Edge to Lewistown, Montana, who began the trip insisting on his innocence, but who confessed after Hammett's car broke down and they had to spend the night on a cold, deserted Montana highway. Or about the Montana gandy dancer (railroad track worker) named Tony whom Hammett was instructed to arrest. Tony was a big man who inspired fear even when he did not have a pick in his hands, especially in the heart of the local sheriff who dared Hammett to arrest Tony at work with a crew of other gandy dancers to support him. Hammett walked to the boss's station and called Tony over in a friendly way. When the big man dropped his pick and moved unsuspectingly away from his friends, his arrest was easy. Or about Blackjack Jerome, the strike-breaker Hammett worked with who would go into the city early in the morning with a flatbed wagon and round up drunks, promising them a hot breakfast and a few bucks for a little work. He would then take them across picket lines and dare them to try to go back across alone before he safely escorted them to the city after a full day's hard work.[10]

He liked to tell about a man in northern Washington dubbed the Midget Bandit who was incensed when he read in a news account of one of his robberies the statement of a victim, bragging what he would do to the Midget Bandit if he ever showed up again. When the cocky little thief went back the next day to give him the chance he had publicly asked for, agents—Hammett presumably among them—were waiting, and the Midget Bandit was arrested. And about the time he tried to get information from an Oregon Chapter of the Women's Christian Temperance Union by introducing himself as the secretary of the Butte Civic Purity League, only to get a lecture on erotic consequences of smoking cigarettes.[11]

In a 1936 syndicated interview for King Features, Hammett recounted one of his close calls when he went with a group of Pinkertons to arrest a gang of blacks who had been stealing dynamite: "Everybody thought it was the Germans . . . and there was quite a scare. When I got inside this house men were being knocked around in fine shape. In the excitement I had a feeling something was wrong but I could not figure what it was till I happened to look down and saw this negro whittling away at my leg."[12]

But the good, adventurous times were short-lived. By October 4, Hammett's weight had fallen to 132, and one month later, on November 6, 1920, he was admitted to Cushman Hospital, also known as United States Public Health Service Hospital Number 59, in Tacoma, Washington. He was considered 100 percent disabled, and his hospitalization would last six and a half months.

Cushman sanatorium opened on September 13, 1920, at the site of the former Cushman School for the Puyallup Indians, which was established in 1860 and closed for lack of funds in 1917. The sanatorium used the old school buildings, converting classrooms into laboratories or patients' rooms, and a blacksmith shop and a log jail into storerooms. The hospital was staffed initially with four medical officers and seven army nurses; in January 1921 a vocational education department was added with four staff members.

Cushman Hospital was directed by Maj. George B. Story, a man who had an unenviable job. He had to organize a hospital from scratch in unsuitable quarters; he had to convince the people of Tacoma that the sanatorium, which was to house patients with respiratory ailments at first and shell-shock victims later, was not a threat to the health nor safety of the community; and, with a small staff, he had to arrange care for two hundred patients.[13] Early on the patients learned that rules could be broken at Cushman without penalty.

Tuberculosis is by nature an erratic disease. A patient may be bedfast one month and energetic the next, a circumstance that compounded disciplinary problems for Major Story. He had to keep his patients, all men and all veterans, occupied. The vocational training program helped, but it was a minor diversion which included, besides basic high-school classes, instruction in basket weaving, beadwork, and belt knotting. Hammett remembered Cushman as a disorderly place where patients were more interested in manly pursuits: poker, smuggling liquor into the hospital, and flirting with the nurses and female vocational instructors, nine women in all, of whom eight were unmarried. He later wrote about a patient called Snohomish Whitey who used a blackjack to commit strong-arm robberies near the hospital and retreated to his sickbed after the crimes.[14]

Hammett found his own diversion at the hospital with a twenty-three-year-old nurse named Josephine Dolan. Miss Dolan, known as Jose (pronounced Josie), was a pretty, petite woman with auburn hair and an ingratiating smile. She had come to Cushman from Anaconda, Montana, where she was raised by an uncle. Her Irish father had deserted the family soon after her birth, and her mother had died when she was three. Jose Dolan had spent two years in an orphanage, so she knew the feeling of loneliness and emptiness that came with calling an institution home. At the age of fifteen, in 1912, Jose Dolan entered nurse's training at Saint James Hospital in Anaconda, and after working as a nurse for a short time at Saint Ann's Hospital there, she enlisted in the army when the United States entered World War I. She came to Cushman with the rank of second lieutenant.

After some fifty-five years, Jose Dolan Hammett recalled her first impression of Dashiell Hammett. He stood out from all the rest, she remembered; he was different from the others who were "country boys and all." Hammett had that air of pride that characterized his family. He was strikingly handsome, with a full head of light-colored hair combed in a pompadour, dark brown eyes, and boyish smile. He dressed meticulously, even when he was so sick he could only manage to wear a neat pair of pajamas. Above all, Hammett was intelligent, with an insatiable intellectual curiosity. He was using his convalescence to get the education that had been denied him in his youth, taking vocational classes and reading every book he could get.[15]

Hammett was infatuated with Jose Dolan. He helped her out around the ward, performing an orderly's duties to make her job easier, and when he asked her for a date, she accepted. It was easy for patients to obtain passes for visits into Tacoma or even for overnight trips to Seattle, where, sometime during his hospitalization, Hammett took an apartment so he would have a private place to go. Hammett used his passes to court Jose Dolan. They liked to go out to eat at good restaurants, or to a local park where they could sit quietly and talk, or to Seattle for longer respites from hospital routine. In a short time, they fell in love.

Hammett wrote twice about a courtship between a nurse and a

patient in a hospital, though neither account has been published, perhaps because they are too close to autobiography, which Hammett characteristically avoided. The two pieces are similar: one is part of a short work titled "Seven Pages"; the other, a bolder and ruder version, is called "Women Are a Lot of Fun, Too." That story is narrated by Slim (a hospital nickname of Hammett's) who remembers a nurse named Evelyn, "a small-bodied wiry girl with a freckled round face that went easily to smiling." In "Seven Pages" Hammett wrote that the narrator and Evelyn would go together in the early evening into a small canyon to lie under a group of four trees. They would stay there together, he wrote, until late at night, gazing at the stars and enjoying the smell of the night-damp earth. "Our love seemed dependent on not being phrased. It seemed if one of us had said 'I love you,' the next instant it would have been a lie. So we loved and cursed one another merrily, ribaldly, she usually stopping her ears in the end because I knew more words."[16]

Hammett stayed at Cushman for just less than four months. In February 1921 it was decided that the damp weather of Tacoma might be inhibiting the recovery of the tubercular patients and the more serious cases were transferred to Camp Kearny, California, just outside of San Diego, where Public Health Service Hospital Number 64 was located. On February 21, 1921, Hammett left Cushman—and Jose Dolan—for the trip by train to San Diego. He did not know that she was pregnant. When she discovered her condition, Jose Dolan quit her job and went home to Anaconda. From there she corresponded with Hammett, and from that distance they arranged their marriage.

The facilities at Camp Kearny were better suited to the treatment of patients with respiratory ailments than those at Cushman. The Camp Kearny hospital was much more businesslike in its operation and the rules were strictly enforced: no drinking, no late hours, limited passes to leave the hospital grounds. That atmosphere plus Hammett's new incentive to get well so he could prepare for his new family contributed to the temporary remission of his symptoms. At the beginning of April, Hammett's disability was still set at 100 percent. By mid-May, however, he had recovered enough that his request for dismissal was granted. The Bureau of War Risk Insurance provided Hammett a train ticket from the hospital to his home. He asked for a ticket to Seattle.

He lived in Seattle at 1117 Third Avenue for a month, during which it became clear that his release from Camp Kearny had been premature. He twice reported to the hospital there as an outpatient. On May 31, he complained of being underweight at 135 pounds, and on June 2 he returned, this time with abscessed teeth. When a hospital employee asked his occupation, Hammett responded "former detective."

C H A P T E R 3

For the rest, I am long and lean and gray-headed, and very lazy. I have no ambition at all in the usual sense of the word; like to live as nearly as possible in the center of large cities, and have no recreations or hobbies.

> Dashiell Hammett
> *Black Mask*, November 1924

In mid-June 1921 Hammett left Seattle for San Francisco. He was twenty-seven, unable to work, with an eighty-dollar-a-month pension from the Bureau of War Risk Insurance as his only income. Jose Dolan was five months pregnant and he wanted to marry her. He had a promise to uphold—that he would never treat a woman the way his father had treated his mother.

Hammett took a room at 120 Ellis Street, two blocks from the St. Francis Hotel, and he wrote Jose Dolan asking her to come to San Francisco. She arrived in early July and Hammett got her a room at the Golden West Hotel, just around the corner from his apartment. On Thursday, July 7, 1921, he met her with a bouquet of flowers. They took a cab to Saint Mary's Cathedral, where they were married by Father Maurice J. O'Keefe before two witnesses, John A. Lally and Eugene Lynch, both living at 1100 Franklin Street near Hammett's apartment. Jose Dolan was an observant Catholic who believed that their marriage had to be a religious ceremony in order to have any legitimacy. Because Hammett professed no religion, they had to be married in the rectory rather than at the altar; the church stance on marriages between Catholics and non-Catholics was that they are always mistakes and therefore could not be held in the church proper, but such a marriage could be legitimized in the church's view if it were performed by a priest away from the altar.[1] Only after the ceremony was over did Hammett tell his wife that he had been baptized a Catholic as an infant and therefore would have qualified for a full church wedding. To him the distinction between marriage in the rectory and at the altar was more curious than significant.

The Hammetts' first apartment was at 620 Eddy Street, about four blocks from the San Francisco Public Library. It had three rooms, with a large hallway; the rent was forty-five dollars a month. Hammett's disability rating had been revised from 100 percent, which was worth an eighty-dollar monthly pension, to 50 percent, at forty dollars. He needed supplementary income, so he returned to the only work he knew—as a private investigator for Pinkerton's.

Hammett's illness was cyclical. He felt good, even healthy, for periods of two to six months, but his health always failed, and each low ebb left him weaker and sicker than the last. There were times when he could work comfortably, but only for a short while. An experienced operative could always get part-time detective work, paid by the hour, which is apparently what Hammett did with Pinkerton's in the fall and winter of 1921.

The San Francisco Pinkerton's office was in the Flood Building, Room 314. The supervisor was Phil Geauque, later a U.S. Secret Service agent; his staff of full-time operatives numbered five or six.[2] San Francisco was a wide-open town in the early twenties and Pinkerton's had its share of work. The Volstead Act was a joke and a boon to the local economy. Speakeasies operated freely if they were willing to buy the consent of local authorities. Prostitutes were considered a necessary evil for young men and a deserved pleasure for old ones; they protected the innocence of young ladies in the city by diverting the lusts of those who would threaten their virtue. As a port city San Francisco attracted its share of wealth and more than its share of transients on the make. Chinatown, with its closed society and its criminal gangs, added another facet to the excitement of what was one of the most lawless big cities in the country at the time. Part-time or full-time, detective work in San Francisco was a dangerous, exciting occupation.

Hammett could not have worked as a San Francisco detective for longer than eight months—half that length of time is more likely. Yet much more is known about that portion of his career as a detective than about his active days in Baltimore. More people are still alive who knew Hammett in San Francisco than who knew him five years earlier in Baltimore; but still Hammett himself is the primary source of most of the stories about his San Francisco detective adventures. The anecdotes about his experiences that he told his friends and his reading audience became grander, more exciting, less accurately detailed, and less plausible as time passed.

Being a detective was rough, hard work for Hammett. Jose Hammett remembers the night he was shadowing a man without knowing the man had a partner. Hammett was led by his suspect into an alley where the partner slammed him over the head with a brick. He refused to go to a hospital; instead, he went home where he sat stonelike for two full days. On another occasion, Hammett operated undercover as a prisoner in the San Francisco City Jail to get information from a suspect being held there. Whether he came away after his two-day stay with the information he sought is unknown, but he did carry an infestation of lice home with him. Those were the day-to-day hazards of detective work, the part of the job that lacked glamour and made detectives seem less heroic than Hammett liked.[3] He preferred to talk about cases—particularly the big ones—which carried with them an air of romance, adventure, and importance.

There were four big cases Hammett associated himself with. Each of them was investigated, at least in part, at about the time when Hammett was doing detective work for the San Francisco Pinkerton's office, probably part-time. And his involvement in each case is suspect.

Among the most sensational criminal trials of the 1920s, a decade when public interest in lurid crime was high and yellow journalism was reaching its peak in America, was the Fatty Arbuckle rape case. Hammett called it "The funniest case I ever worked on. . . . In trying to convict him everybody framed everybody else."[4] In "Seven Pages" Hammett wrote: "I sat in the lobby of the Plaza, in San Francisco. It was the day before the opening of the second absurd attempt to convict Roscoe Arbuckle of something. . . . He looked at me and I at him. . . . I made my gaze as contemptuous as I could. . . . It was amusing. I was working for his attorneys at the time, gathering information for his defense."

Arbuckle was among the leading film comedians of his day, and his fans were shocked when it was reported that during a Labor Day orgy in Arbuckle's suite at the Saint Francis Hotel in San Francisco, he raped a would-be actress named Virginia Rappe, killing her when the pressure of his fat torso on top of her ruptured her bladder. Arbuckle was charged with rape and murder in two trials which became focal points for a movement to impose a moral standard on the movie industry. Arbuckle's first trial, held in San Francisco, was the most sensationalistic. His defense hired Pinkerton's to assist in their investigations, and Hammett claimed to be among the operatives assigned to the case, though he never made his duties clear. At the first trial, which lasted from September 22 to December 4, 1921, a superabundance of evidence and exhibits was entered, including the door to one of the rooms in Arbuckle's suite at the Saint Francis at which a maid claimed she overheard a conversation inside while polishing a doorknob. The defense effectively countered the sensationalism surrounding the trial with the argument that the charges against Arbuckle were an extortion scheme, and the trial ended with a hung jury. The second trial, which ran from January 11 to February 3, 1922, resulted in Arbuckle's acquittal. It was finally revealed during the trials that Virginia Rappe had a long history of immoral conduct, and her bladder ailments were caused by venereal disease and a careless abortion.[5] By then, Hammett was out of the detective business.

While Hammett probably had some small role in the Arbuckle case, his claims that he worked on the Arnstein bond theft case are highly questionable. When he went to Hollywood in the early 1930s, Hammett became friendly with comedy actress Fanny Brice, a former Ziegfeld Follies star who had married gambler Jules Nicky Arnstein. Hammett liked to tell his friends how he had followed Arnstein as a detective in 1921 when Arnstein was charged with masterminding the theft of $1.5 million in securities from a Wall Street brokerage house and planning the theft of $5 million more. He always ended his story with an admonition not to tell Fanny, because she might get mad. The theft and the trials—for robbery and then for conspiracy to smuggle the stolen bonds into Washington, D.C.—took place on the East Coast. Hammett is not known to have left the West Coast during that year, and with Nicky Arnstein on bail and prohibited from leaving the area from the time of his arrest until after the trial (from February 1921 to spring 1922), it is difficult to see how Hammett could have been involved in the case except as an interested reader of newspaper accounts.[6]

There is conflicting evidence about Hammett's role in the apprehension of Gloomy Gus Schaefer, a crook of a more conventional sort who was the subject of headlines in San Francisco newspapers during the winter of 1921-1922. In December 1921, Schaefer and two other men robbed the Shapiro Jewel Company in Saint Paul, Minnesota, of $130,000 in silver and gems. After the robbery they fled to Vallejo, California, about thirty miles from San Francisco, where they holed up in a two-story roadhouse. Pinkerton's had been called in on the case and had followed a trail which had led to the roadhouse, but they could find no evidence of the loot from the robbery and held off making an arrest in the hope of recovering the stolen goods. Hammett, by his own account, was assigned to the case and began frequenting the roadhouse in the role of a wealthy businessman. He discovered that Schaefer and his partners were, in fact, hiding out there and that on one particular night they were meeting in a second-story room. He climbed onto a porch roof to eavesdrop. The meeting had just begun when the floor gave way. Hammett crashed to the ground, twisting his ankle, and Schaefer, suspicious of the ruckus, fled with his friends.

Promotional releases by King Features Syndicate for Hammett's comic strip *Secret Agent X-9* twelve years later claimed he continued on the case. Schaefer had stowed his share of the Shapiro take in an Oakland bank deposit box, and he was reluctant to leave the area until he felt it was safe to take the money with him. A short time after Hammett's noisy fall, Schaefer was spotted on a street in Vallejo by a Pinkerton—perhaps, as the King Features advertisement reported, Hammett. Schaefer was shadowed until he led the authorities to his safe deposit box where he was arrested, on March 9, 1922, with the loot in hand.[7]

But as with the Arbuckle and Arnstein cases, the dates of the Schaefer case conflict with the story he told most often about his last Pinkerton assignment, investigating the robbery of gold coins (specie) on board the freighter *Sonoma*. This case was solved on December 1, 1921, the day Hammett said he quit Pinkerton's for good. That was one day after Nicky Arnstein's trial for conspiracy to transport stolen bonds began in Washington, D.C., three days before the first Arbuckle trial had ended, and before Schaefer had committed his robbery of the Shapiro Jewel Company. Moreover, by the time the Arnstein and Arbuckle cases had been tried and Schaefer had been arrested, Hammett was bedridden.

The *Sonoma* gold specie robbery case offered Hammett, he said, the possibility of a trip to Hawaii. He claims he quit the detective business for good in his disappointment over not getting to make the trip when he solved the case one day too early, depriving himself of the job working undercover as a crewman on the *Sonoma*'s next cruise. The *Sonoma*'s route took her from San Francisco to Hawaii, to Pago Pago, to Sydney, and back. During a return trip to San Francisco in late fall 1921, $125,000 in gold English sovereigns was stolen. Since discovery of the theft came at sea and the gold was on board ship at the last port, it was assumed that a crewman had taken the gold and hidden it somewhere on the ship. When the *Sonoma* docked in San Francisco on November 23, the San Francisco Police and dock authorities sealed off the ship and began their unsuccessful search for the missing gold. A nervous insurance company hired Pinkerton's to help, and Hammett claimed he was assigned to the case, posing as a deckhand hired to help maintain the freighter while the regular crew was under ship's arrest. After a careful search for the stolen gold had been conducted unsuccessfully, it was decided that the *Sonoma* would be allowed to leave for Hawaii with undercover operatives aboard, Hammett apparently among them, posing as crewmen, on the off-chance that the thief would try to retrieve the gold and escape at a foreign port. On November 29, one week before the *Sonoma* was to leave San Francisco (not one day, as Hammett claimed), a check was made of areas that had already been searched, and most of the gold was found—some in fire hoses, some suspended overboard in chests supported by stout ropes. The remainder of the stolen coins was located on December 1.

There were conflicting reports of who discovered the *Sonoma* gold. Two San Francisco plainclothesmen took the credit in one newspaper story; a ship's engineer named Carl Knudsen received credit in other reports; and Pinkerton agents got the credit in still other accounts.[8] When Hammett was telling the story, the find was his. Though he may very well have found the *Sonoma* gold specie, he quit Pinkerton's for a different reason than he gave publicly. He was sicker than he had ever been. By January 1922, Hammett's weight fell to 126 pounds, and he was suffering from a debilitating bronchial infection. Within a month, he was too weak to walk four blocks to the public library. There were days when he could not get from his bedroom to the bathroom unassisted; he lined the hall of his apartment with chairs so he could rest along the way.[9] The Bureau of War Risk Insurance reviewed Hammett's claim and confirmed his 50 percent disability. In fact, he was an invalid who could not possibly have worked regularly as a detective. If Hammett had attempted to sail to Hawaii on the *Sonoma*, he might well have died aboard ship.

In the early days of their marriage, the Hammetts lived a simple life punctuated by the struggle to meet their monthly bills. Jose Hammett, pregnant at first, then with an infant to care for, could not work, so money was very tight. She kept running accounts at the neighborhood grocer's and butcher's and managed the family budget very carefully. Hammett did the cooking. Hamburgers were a special treat, a favorite of his, but many meals were meatless because meat was too expensive. The Hammetts kept to themselves. They had few friends and they did not go out much. When there was a special occasion to celebrate, they had a meal brought in rather than go to a restaurant. Movies and plays were uncommon diversions for them. Hammett was often too sick to sit comfortably in a theater for two hours and besides, health permitting, his interests ran more to the fights at the Winter Garden or to the nearby public library where he could read the daily newspapers and check out as many books as he wished.[10] Like Thomas Wolfe, who bragged that he wanted to read every book in the Widener Library at Harvard, Hammett made up his mind to read a large share of the books at the San Francisco Public Library. He read hungrily on a wide range of subjects with the zeal of a mature man trying to get the education he had missed in his youth. Science (particularly criminology), biography, medieval history, contemporary popular fiction, classic literature, the occult: all were subjects of Hammett's reading in the early 1920s. It was as if realizing that he was physically limited, he turned to intellectual pursuits expecting to find a way to justify his Hammett pride.

On the afternoon of October 15, 1921, the Hammetts' daughter was born at Saint Francis Hospital in San Francisco. She was named Mary Jane. Hammett was advised to limit his contact with her to avoid infecting her with his tuberculosis, and he began sleeping in a Murphy bed in the large hall of their three-room apartment; Jose Hammett slept with the baby in the bedroom. When Hammett became unable to work, no more than four months after the baby's birth, he had a second blow to his role as father: not only was he a threat to his daughter's health, but he had no means to support her except an inadequate disability pension. Reluctantly, he turned to his own family. Without letting the opportunity for remonstration pass, Richard Hammett sent his son some money, enough to see him through the worst time in February 1922 when the future was most uncertain.[11]

Later that month Hammett took advantage of a vocational training program offered by the newly formed Veterans Bureau. He entered Munson's Business College in San Francisco where he began taking courses in stenography and writing, apparently with the intention of training himself as a newspaper reporter. Hammett studied at Munson's for a very difficult year and a half. During that time, his weight stayed between 130 and 135, and he was rarely out of bed for more than four hours a day.[12] He spent a large portion of his twenty bedfast hours each day reading, writing, studying, and planning. He soon decided that advertising, not reporting, was the career he preferred, and that in any case he wanted to write.

Hammett began his career in advertising modestly. He was a free-lancer whose services included writing ads, designing them, and providing art. His method was to work on speculation. He would go to a business with an ad already prepared for them and try to sell it. Sometimes he bartered—his ad in exchange for a suit or a pair of shoes—as he did with the San Francisco shoe store that bought his first ad.[13]

C H A P T E R 4

I know a man who once stole a Ferris-wheel.

Dashiell Hammett
"Memoirs of a Private Detective," 1923

At the same time, in the fall of 1922, Hammett, at age twenty-eight, was beginning to write for publication—more successfully than he was selling ads. It is revealing that he chose *The Smart Set*, the self-proclaimed "aristocrat among magazines," for his first fiction. *The Smart Set* reflected the iconoclasm, the irreverence, and the intellectual snobbery of its coeditors, H. L. Mencken and George Jean Nathan. Yet, while Eugene O'Neill, Maxwell Anderson, Stephen Vincent Benét, F. Scott Fitzgerald, Sinclair Lewis, Aldous Huxley, and Somerset Maugham had been published in that magazine, its authors were more likely to be undistinguished; the official editorial policy, prompted by a very tight budget, was to provide a forum for "new and unknown writers with something new and interesting to say and a fresh way of saying it." For Hammett—self-educated, hardly aristocratic, a member of no set, much less the smart set—the choice of Mencken and Nathan's irreverent magazine for his first stories was more a matter of image making than anything else. He could point to his publication there and his correspondence with H. L. Mencken as proof to his family and friends on the East Coast, and even to his wife, that he was not without ability, that he was on the road to success, and that he was not a helpless invalid.[1]

The Smart Set paid among the lowest rates in magazine publishing for their material—little more than a penny a word. Hammett's first appearance in those pages was a 100-word anecdote called "The Parthian Shot," published in October 1922. It is about Paulette Key who dislikes her husband for his "stupid obstinacy" and realizes that her six-month-old son is like his father. Her Parthian shot comes when, before leaving her family, she has the boy christened Don. The reader is left to realize that the boy's name is Don Key.

Encouraged by his first success, Hammett submitted another piece which *The Smart Set* published in the November 1922 issue. "The Great Lovers" is a highly affected nonfiction piece which celebrates the arrogance of twelve historical figures from Charles IV of Spain to Thomas Hart Benton by quoting their self-admiring remarks. The quotes are prefaced by Hammett's curious explanation:

Now that the meek and the humble have inherited the earth and it were arrogance to look down upon any man—the apologetic being the mode in lives—I should like to go monthly to some hidden gallery and, behind drawn curtains, burn perfumed candles before [these] images. . .

Hammett appreciated and even admired the arrogance of the twelve great lovers of themselves he quoted. He had something in common with them—an enormous pride that slipped easily into aloofness. His pride was not based on accomplishment but on what he felt he could accomplish. It was the necessary ingredient of his later success, and, more important at the time, it was the quality that kept him out of a sanatorium, scraping out a living.

As a result of his early acceptances, in the fall of 1922 Hammett began to devote a major part of his energies to writing. He worked on his ads and his fiction with equal zeal, always allotting a portion of the day to reading and researching. He did not drink excessively then, and he stayed at home with his family at night. His worst habit was that he smoked, as he had since he was a teenager—Camels were his brand then, Murads later—despite the warnings from doctors that recovery from his respiratory disease was inhibited by smoking.

In the early days of his marriage, Hammett bought an Underwood typewriter, which he used to type his stories. He wrote at the kitchen table in the cramped apartment at 620 Eddy; when the family moved to a larger apartment in the same building, he made a desk for himself in the living room. His method at first was to make notes, often in pencil on scrap paper; then to write a draft by hand;

to revise his draft; and finally to type his story for submission to a publisher. Later, when he became more accustomed to the type-writer, he typed his first draft.[2] Initially the process was very slow. Hammett had many story ideas by late 1922 but very few finished stories about which he felt confident. He stuck to short pieces; it was a full year before he tried a story as long as three thousand words. Early on, he was guided in the selection of his material and in his writing style by a knowledge of the writers' markets gained by a careful survey of popular magazines, their editorial policies, and their audiences. In Hammett's first year as a writer, beginning in October 1922 with his first story in *The Smart Set*, he saw twelve of his pieces published in five different magazines. He finished that first year with a valid claim to only minor achievement as a writer.

After his first publication in *The Smart Set*, Hammett had four other short pieces accepted there before the end of October 1923. By the close of his first writing year, he had largely abandoned the sophisticated, cleverly ironic, "smart" writing style for a type of writing very different; but as long as he wrote, Hammett never gave up entirely his attempts to write at least minor pieces for the audience *The Smart Set* claimed to reach. He was most successful in that attempt with "The Master Mind" (*The Smart Set*, January 1923) and "The Crusader" (*The Smart Set*, August 1923). Minor successes, to be sure—each is less than five hundred words long—they are clear advances in Hammett's ability as a writer. "The Master Mind" is a short, ironic description of a detective whose abilities at ferreting out criminals had won him worldwide respect, but who had invested his retirement money in worthless, even fraudulent, stocks—one hundred sixty thousand shares in such companies as the New Era Fuelless Motor Company. The piece achieves the irony that Hammett tried for in all his early work, usually with mixed results.

He was similarly successful in "The Crusader," about a Walter Mitty-like man whose wife is fitting him in his Ku Klux Klan robe as he imagines himself a medieval Crusader. But his romantic spell is broken when his young child comes into the room and thinks her father in his ceremonial robe is playing a game of peekaboo. Hammett manages to make his crusader seem human and to make his misguided romantic quest seem silly and childish.

Very different in every way from his other contributions to *The Smart Set* is "From the Memoirs of a Private Detective" (March 1923), a remarkable short piece of nonfiction which set the tone and staked out the material for Hammett's most successful fiction.

"From the Memoirs of a Private Detective" consists of twenty-nine separate descriptions, none longer than a paragraph, of unusual things that happened to him during his career as a Pinkerton operative. The supercilious tone and the sometimes cloying verbiage of his earlier contributions to *The Smart Set* are gone. Here, Hammett was writing about a subject he knew in a style that seemed natural. Although it would be misleading to compare "Memoirs" to Ernest Hemingway's early vignettes written in search of one true sentence, there are similarities.[3] Hammett's statements in "Memoirs," like Hemingway's in that they are pared-down observations of events reported without subjective comment, provided what would be the key to his development as a writer and the formula for his most successful work: tell the story from firsthand experience, tell it simply, and tell it objectively.

Hammett's "Memoirs" is notable for its candid realism and understated irony: "I was once falsely accused of perjury and had to perjure myself to escape arrest."

"I was once engaged to discharge a woman's housekeeper."

"I know a forger who left his wife because she had learned to smoke cigarettes while he was serving a term in prison."

"In 1917 in Washington, D. C., I met a young woman who did not remark that my work must be very interesting."[4] "Memoirs" is authoritative and self-confident. The tone is aloof and smart-alecky, anticipating the wisecracking quality of his later detective stories.

Hammett was clearly looking to his own experiences to provide material for his fiction, but he was a private man who instinctively resisted the impulse to reveal too much of himself. "Holiday" (*The New Pearson's*, July 1923), an autobiographical story, is an exception. It is a two-thousand-word melancholy vignette about Paul Hetherwick, a tubercular patient at United States Public Health Service Hospital Number 64 at Camp Kearny, California, who takes a twelve-hour leave to go to Tijuana. After he loses most of his eighty-dollar monthly pension check at the racetrack, Hetherwick passes the remaining time of his leave at seedy bars where he is hustled by B-girls. When his time is up and his resources are gone, he goes back to the hospital, leaving the world of cold, sordid sex and staring at lovers on the way like a voyeur. He is a proud and lonesome man who lives only for the present. "Holiday" is sensitive, yet unsentimental. It is perhaps the finest story of Hammett's first year as a writer. Nonetheless, it was too personal for him, and he turned in his fiction away from himself as a subject, focusing instead on his former profession. Stories about crime and about detectives dominated Hammett's work beginning in mid-1923. The material was successful for him, and he never abandoned it while he was active as a writer.

His last publication in *The Smart Set*, "The Green Elephant" (October 1923), was his longest up to that time, a twenty-five-hundred-word story about "an unskilled laborer in the world of crime," who by happenstance gets possession of $250,000 in stolen money and finally collapses under the burden of his newfound wealth. Though "The Green Elephant" is calculated to achieve the irony characteristic of Hammett's early fiction, it is not a *Smart Set* story in the sense that his first stories were. He had taken a major stride in his writing when instead of catering his work in each of its elements to the audience he imagined read *The Smart Set*, he began to tell his stories as he himself thought they ought to be told. The stories Hammett had to tell were about detective work, and despite *The Smart Set*'s acceptance of "The Memoirs of a Private Detective" and "The Green Elephant," he had to find a new publisher in order to gain the freedom to write his fiction naturally and to experiment without feeling the need to affect a sophistication he did not then possess.

While the detective story found its primary audience at that time among unsophisticated readers, it was also considered a sort of gentleman's diversion, though rarely did anyone take detective fiction seriously as literature. The form is widely held to have been introduced with Edgar Allan Poe's "The Murders in the Rue Morgue" (April 1841), the first of three stories featuring C. Auguste Dupin, an amateur investigator who is able to solve crimes through his prodigious ability for analytical thinking. It was another fifty years, however, before detective fiction blossomed when Arthur Conan Doyle tried his hand at the form which had become a common pastime for amateur writers. Doyle's sixty Sherlock Holmes novels and stories, the first of which, *A Study in Scarlet*, was published in 1887, marked the beginning of the modern era for detective fiction and set new standards for ingenuity in plot and complexity in characterization.

Doyle notwithstanding, late nineteenth- and early twentieth-century detective fiction tended toward the melodramatic and proved to be a genre in which women writers were particularly proficient. Among the most popular mystery writers of the time were Anna Katherine Green, whose *Leavenworth Case* (1878) is said to be the first detective novel by a woman; Mrs. Belloc Lowndes, who liked to draw on historical fact for her works, as she did with *The Lodger* (1913), based on the Jack the Ripper murders; the Baroness Orczy, whose title character in *The Old Man in the Corner* unraveled a series of cases reported by a female journalist while he habitually knotted string; and Mary Roberts Rinehart, the American writer who developed the type of story Ogden Nash called the "Had-I-But-Known" type, in which a muddle-headed heroine blunders repeatedly into situations that could have been avoided had she but known.

Meanwhile, E. C. Bentley, whose *Trent's Last Case* (1913) is considered a classic that reestablished the long novel of detective fiction, and G. K. Chesterton, whose witty, exquisitely stylized Father Brown stories concentrated not so much on detection as on the morals of his tales, foreshadowed the development of the mystery story that took place in the 1920s. By the time Hammett was ready to try his hand at detective fiction, the classical mystery tale was near the peak of accomplishment in what literary historian Howard Haycraft called its Golden Age. Such writers as Agatha Christie, J. S. Fletcher, Dorothy Sayers, A. A. Milne, Philip MacDonald, and Monsignor Ronald Knox brought the form a sophistication of tone and characterization it had not previously had with any consistency.

The Golden Age was typified in America by the novels of S. S. Van Dine. Van Dine was a pseudonym adopted by Willard Huntington Wright to protect his family name from association with what he considered a low type of literature. Wright was a distinguished literary man, a former editor-in-chief of *The Smart Set* and a friend of Mencken's and Nathan's. The first of his twelve novels as S. S. Van Dine was *The Benson Murder Case* (1926). Wright's detective, Philo Vance, was a pompous amateur with an encyclopedic knowledge and a propensity for long discourses on ephemeral subjects. He was the paradigm of the detective in the Golden Age.

In 1926 the erudite Wright summed up for the majority of readers and writers alike what, properly, detective stories attempted to accomplish. Their purpose was plot—to provide the reader with a puzzle, to provide as well clues to the solution, and finally to provide the answer. He said that emotions had no more place in a detective story than in a crossword puzzle, that violence should be minimized, and that a detective story should have a unity of mood—a single tone, or aura, developed throughout the story. It was Wright's intention to elevate and refine the form, and though Philo Vance seems a silly character today, he was the most popular fictional detective in America during the late 1920s and 1930s.[5]

Philo Vance stories were published in the respectable but low-paying *Scribner's Magazine* (Charles Scribner's Sons published the Van Dine novels), but generally detective fiction was considered unsuitable for such publications. The market for magazine fiction was more open sixty years ago than it is today, however. In the 1920s a proficient writer could aspire to a comfortable living writing magazine stories alone. If he could break into the slick-paper mass-circulation magazines—the *Saturday Evening Post*, *Cosmopolitan*, *Redbook*, or *Liberty*, for instance—a writer could hope for as much as a dollar a word for his writing and to reach an audience counted in seven figures. But magazine publishing sixty years ago was not limited to the slicks. There were some twenty thousand periodicals, exclusive of newspapers, published in the United States in 1922, aimed at all readerships, providing a forum for a wide range of writers.[6]

At the other end of the spectrum from the slicks were the pulp magazines or the "grey paper" publications, so known for the cheap paper on which they were printed. The pulps were the primary publishers of detective fiction, and it was for this market that Hammett produced virtually all of his fiction in the 1920s. There were some seventy pulps published at any one time in America during the twenties, specializing in stories of romance and adventure, Westerns, flying stories, or detective stories—with titles like *The Parisienne*, *Saucy Stories*, and *Black Mask* (these three founded by Mencken and Nathan) or *True Detective Stories*, *10 Story Book*, *Brief Stories*, *Detective Fiction Weekly*, *Action Stories*, *Mystery Stories*, and *Argosy All-Story*, to name some that published Hammett. The pulps were aimed directly at a lowbrow audience who liked their plots simple, their characters heroic, and their writers unpretentious. One could get about one hundred fifty pages of stories for ten or twenty cents an issue in the early twenties, in magazines published weekly, biweekly, or monthly. Pulp writers got a standard fee for their work—a penny a word—but even at that low rate some managed a decent income writing for the pulps alone, because the formula for the stories was easily mastered and an accomplished writer could crank out words at a furious pace.[7]

One detective magazine stood out among the ten or so pulps devoted primarily to mystery and detective fiction. That was *Black Mask*, founded in 1920 by Mencken and Nathan as a money-making scheme to subsidize their work on the magazine they cared about, *The Smart Set*. Mencken and Nathan tired of editing what they called one of their "louses" after less than six months and sold *Black Mask* for $12,250 to the owners and publishers of *The Smart Set*, Eugene Crowe and Eltinge Warner.[8] The new owners appointed Francis M. Osborne editor. *Black Mask* began to publish the stories that not only revitalized the tired detective story genre but influenced an entire generation of mainstream writers under Osborne's successor, George Sutton, Jr. (October 1922-March 1924), and his associate editor, Harry North (October 1922-September 1925). By the end of 1923, Hammett was almost exclusively a *Black Mask* author, and Sutton and North were the men most responsible for nurturing his talents as a short-story writer.

Hammett's near total commitment to the pulps after mid-1923, with their paltry pay and lowbrow audience, is puzzling after such a self-consciously pretentious beginning to his career in the pages of *The Smart Set*. His correspondence with *The Smart Set* editors does not survive, but the common ownership of that magazine and the *Black Mask* and the unpromising quality of his first writing efforts make it tempting to speculate that Hammett was advised by *The Smart Set* editors to lower his sights and write for an easier, less demanding market. Hammett's version is different. He told his family and friends that he picked up a detective story pulp one day and was appalled at the inaccuracy and the ineptness of the contents. He knew he could write better detective stories than those, and he decided to prove it.[9]

The energy with which Hammett pursued his writing career is indicated by his publishing record. From November 1922 through June 1924, a period of twenty months, twenty-five of Hammett's stories were published in pulp magazines—those in addition to the two articles and two stories in *The Smart Set* and one story in *The New Pearson's*, already mentioned. About half of these stories were longer than twenty-five hundred words.

Hammett's first pulp story, "Immortality" in *10 Story Book*, has not been located.[10] His next four pulp stories published in his first year as a writer are dissimilar, but there are the kernels of themes that interested him for the rest of his writing career. In two of these stories women reject their doltish husbands, and characters are destroyed by their foolish pride. "The Barber and His Wife" (*Brief Stories*, December 1922) is about a narcissistic man who loses his wife because he ignores her for masculine company; and in "The Joke on

Eloise Morey" (*Brief Stories*, June 1923), a woman drives her husband to suicide, then implicates herself as his murderess when she destroys his suicide note because she feels it would embarrass her. "The Road Home" (*Black Mask*, December 1922) introduces the detective's code, illustrated by a detective who tracks his man from New York to the jungles of Burma, then saves the man's life during his desperate escape through crocodile-infested waters. "The Sardonic Star of Tom Doody" (*Brief Stories*, February 1923) is a humorous story that exemplifies the wry, clever twists with which Hammett tried to end his early stories. After his parole a petty con-man makes the best of his unjust imprisonment for robbery by playing the role of a reformed criminal lecturing to church groups. His con is exposed when he is exonerated by the deathbed confession of the real robber, and outraged lecture organizers threaten to charge the imposter with accepting money under false pretenses.

All these works depend for their effect on an ironic turn of events, handled with various degrees of skill. In his early pulp stories Hammett was learning something about characterization and a great deal about plot. He was experimenting with a light, humorous tone in "The Barber and His Wife" and "The Sardonic Star of Tom Doody," with a serious moralistic one in "The Road Home," and with a wry, objective narrative voice in "The Joke on Eloise Morey."

Hammett was uncertain at first about these writing experiments he was conducting in the pulps, enough so that he protected his name and his pride by writing under the pseudonym Peter Collinson. (In turn-of-the-century carnival and theater slang, Peter Collins is the name for a nonexistent person, taken from a prank played on gullible novices who would be told to "Ask Peter Collins for a green-handled rake.") Pseudonyms were common among writers for the pulps. Many were amateurs, like their fictional detectives, and they wanted to protect their names from association with the somewhat disreputable magazines in which they were published. Others wrote professionally at such an extraordinary rate that they adopted pseudonyms in order to get two stories published in the same magazine or to get published simultaneously in two or more pulps. Still other writers adopted one pseudonym for mystery stories, another for Westerns, and still another for science fiction.

Between December 1922 and January 1924, Hammett used his Collinson pseudonym eight times, and his daughter's name, Mary Jane Hammett, once for a story in *The Smart Set*. He used a pseudonym only once later in his career, when he signed "The

Diamond Wager," a very poorly written story in the October 19, 1929, issue of *Detective Fiction Weekly*, as Samuel Dashiell. The purpose for Hammett's pseudonym seems to have been to protect his name at first, to avoid having more than one piece published under his own name in an issue of *Black Mask* later, and finally to use for publications in magazines other than *Black Mask*.

But the practice was short-lived. Hammett liked to see his name in print. He first identified himself to his pulp audience in *Black Mask* in a letter to the editor in which he claimed "The Vicious Circle" (June 15, 1923), published under the Collinson pseudonym. It was his fifth pulp story, and certainly the worst among his early work. "The Vicious Circle" is an implausible story about a senator with presidential aspirations who is being blackmailed by a man who knew the senator when the politician was serving time under a different name in San Quentin. The senator hires a friend, Gene Inch, to murder the blackmailer, which Inch does efficiently. But Inch teaches the senator a valuable lesson: criminals cannot be trusted. Inch takes over where the previous blackmailer left off, demanding a monthly check for his silence. Although Hammett usually managed to match tone and content in his stories very well, here he seems to have confused his *Smart Set* audience with pulp readers. The result is a pompously written, awkwardly plotted tale marred by writing like the description of the senator's speech: "He talked desultorily, letting his sentences lose themselves half-formed, their logical endings being replaced by irrelevancies or not at all." The single virtue of "The Vicious Circle" is that Gene Inch acts like a real criminal.

It was common for *Black Mask* to solicit comments from authors about their work in a section of the magazine called "Our Readers' Private Corner." In his comments about "The Vicious Circle" in the next issue, Hammett took the opportunity to brag a little about his past, to bask in his newfound recognition, and to explain his story energetically.

I have been out of town for a couple of weeks—I have to go up in the hills to see some real snow at least once each winter—which is why I haven't answered your letter before this.

About the story: None of the characters is real in a literal sense, though I doubt that it would be possible to build a character without putting into it at least something of someone the writer has known. The plot, however, is closer to earth. In the years during which I tried my hand at "private detecting" I ran across several cases where the "friend" called in to dispose of a blackmailer either went into partnership with him or took over his business after getting him out of the way. And I know of at least one case where a blackmailer was disposed of just as "Inch" disposed of "Bush."[11]

Throughout 1923 and 1924 Hammett practiced his skills on insignificant pieces. There were short anecdotes: "Itchy" (*Brief Stories*, January 1924) is about a crook who attempts to make an image for himself as a gentleman rogue and assures his arrest by making himself unmistakably identifiable; or "The New Racket" (*Black Mask*, February 15, 1924), in which an old ex-con tells about the time he almost beat the law by claiming he had not robbed a series of stores but had begged money from employees and was thus subject to a charge of vagrancy, not theft. But the judge changed the charge from theft to receiving stolen property, since store employees had given away money not theirs. Other of Hammett's stories were mood pieces, like "The Dimple" (*Saucy Stories*, October 15, 1923), in which a writer finishes his night's work and discovers his wife has not returned from the theater. When he learns the theater burned during the performance his wife attended, he calls on the police commissioner, his friend with an "unsavory reputation for numerous affairs with numerous women," to help him find her. After they learn she is not in the hospital, they visit the morgue, where the police commissioner is able to identify the horribly disfigured body of the writer's wife by the dimple on her leg. In "The Man Who Killed Dan Odams" (*Black Mask*, January 15, 1924), a murderer escapes from jail and takes temporary refuge in the home of a widow and her son. She treats him tenderly to hold his attention while she secretly sends her son for the authorities, for, it is revealed at the end of the story, she is Dan Odams's widow, and she is assuring that her husband's murderer is caught. And in "Esther Entertains" (*Brief Stories*, February 1924), a cavalier businessman's attraction to his lover Esther, along with his distaste for her, is exposed in an internal monologue.

"Afraid of a Gun" (*Black Mask*, March 1, 1924), a longer story, is a character study of Owen Sack, a man with an obsessive fear of guns. "No matter where he had gone, he had sooner or later found himself looking into the muzzle of a threatening gun. It was as if his very fear attracted the thing he feared." As a result he had spent his life running like a coward from one place to the next until he is finally shot by a drunk who thinks Sack has informed the police of his family's liquor smuggling operation. When Sack finds that the bullet does not hurt in the way he had imagined it would, he stands fearlessly as the drunk empties his gun at him, and he then kills the drunk. As he is apparently dying in a doctor's office, Sack busily makes plans to get himself a pistol so he can retrace his life and redress all the wrongs he has suffered as a result of his former fear of guns.

Another of Hammett's longer stories is more interesting than his other early works. "The Second-Story Angel" (*Black Mask*, November 15, 1923) is a light satire on pulp writers. The angel of the title is Angel Grace Cardigan, a con-woman who clumsily breaks into writer Carter Webright Brigham's apartment, is caught, and tells a sorrowful tale of her life. Taken by her beauty, friendliness, and potential as story material, Brigham bribes a policeman who claims to have seen her entering his apartment to let her go free. After she has spent the night, Angel Grace leaves for a rendezvous with Brigham at a distant town, where she will be safe from police harassment, but when he goes to meet her, she is not there. After he writes her story, based on the information she gave him the night they spent together, Brigham finds he is one of five writers who have been conned by the lady burglar and her "policeman" accomplice. But Brigham's only worry is "Lord! I wonder if she kissed this whole bunch, too!" Carter Brigham rationalizes the bribe he paid for Angel Grace's freedom as an investment: "The things you can tell me will fairly write themselves and the magazines will eat 'em up!" he tells her. Other writers were also convinced that they could regain an investment of $500 to $1,000 because they had realistic material for a good story. The irony is, of course, that the writers had been victimized by a more capable storyteller than themselves, because she had firsthand knowledge of her story material—like Hammett did.

PART 2

The Work

1922-1933

CHAPTER 5

I doubt that Hammett had any deliberate artistic aims whatever; he was trying to make a living by writing something he had firsthand information about. He made some of it up; all writers do; but it had a basis in fact; it was made up out of real things.

Raymond Chandler
"The Simple Art of Murder," 1944

For a two-year period beginning in the summer of 1923, Hammett's life was consumed by his fiction. He was too ill to work steadily for anyone else, and he had no social inclinations, so he stayed home and he wrote. The story of Hammett's life during that time is his own stories, for he devoted himself fully to developing his talents as a writer.

In 1922 a new type of fiction had begun appearing in *Black Mask*. It was notable for its lack of literary affectations, for its emphasis on accurately rendered dialogue, for its focus on the underside of life, usually in American cities, and for its toughness—its narrative objectivity. Like the naturalistic fiction of Stephen Crane, Frank Norris, and Theodore Dreiser in that it attempted to infuse stories with a new level of reality and an awareness of the lower strata of society, the so-called hard-boiled fiction in *Black Mask* departed from naturalism in its lack of sympathy for people in the miserable, pitiful, and horrible circumstances it described. At its worst, hard-boiled fiction was action stories distorted by self-conscious toughness into self-parodies. At its best, it reflected the moral ambivalence of post-war America and emphasized the need for personal codes of behavior in a time when civil and religious institutions were faltering.

Carroll John Daly is acknowledged as the earliest of the hard-boiled mystery writers. "Dolly," his first story in *Black Mask*, appeared in the October 1922 issue (also the first issue edited by George Sutton) and initiated a new feature in the magazine—the "Daytime Story." George Sutton explained that *Black Mask* would "continue to print fascinating clever detective and mystery tales, which have proved so popular with readers. In addition it will use other stories—like "Dolly" and several others in this issue—that are founded on the deepest human emotions. These awesome tales are called DAYTIME STORIES because they are not to be read at night by people with weak nerves." "Dolly," a story told by a psychotic admirer about a deceptive woman, shows the influence of Poe, and it is anything but hard-boiled. Daly's next contribution to the magazine, however, marks the beginning of the hard-boiled story in *Black Mask*. "The False Burton Combs," which appeared in the same issue as Hammett's "The Road Home," is about a tough-talking, tough-acting adventurer who never reveals his name: "I ain't a crook; just a gentleman adventurer and make my living working against the law breakers. Not that I work with the police—no, not me. I'm no knight errant, either. It just came to me that the simplest people in the world are crooks. They are so set on their own plans to fleece others that they never imagine that they are the simplest sort to do."

When he gets in a jam, he gets out his gun: "For just the fraction of a second he took his eyes off me—just a glance down at the door with a curse on his lips.

"And with that curse on his lips he died.

"For as he turned the handle I give it to him right through the heart. I don't miss at that range—no—not me. The door flew open and he tumbled out on the road—dead."

Daly developed an array of enormously popular characters in *Black Mask*, with names like Terry Mack ("Three Gun Terry") and Satan Hall. His most popular character was Race Williams, another fast-shooting, rough-talking "gentleman adventurer," introduced in spring 1923. It has been reported that the announcement of a Race Williams story on the cover of *Black Mask* increased the sales of that issue by 20 percent.[1]

Daly was a hack writer who in many ways epitomizes the excesses of the hard-boiled school. His prose is unpolished; his use of the vernacular is inexact; the violence in his stories is gratuitous and exaggerated well beyond the bounds of plausibility. While the Golden Age detectives—such as Arthur Conan Doyle's Sherlock Holmes, and later Dorothy Sayer's Lord Peter Wimsey and S. S. Van Dine's Philo Vance—were savants engaged in highly specialized approaches to crimes which often resembled intricate puzzles more closely than any real-life criminal activity, Race Williams and the many so-called hard-boiled heroes who were created in his image were super heroes of a different sort operating in an equally implausible world of exaggerated violence.

Hammett's achievement as a writer came in his introduction of plausibility into the detective story. For him hard-boiled did not mean insensitivity in the face of gore. Rather, that term expressed the hard realism of his characters, who accepted the fact of criminality without excessive emotion as real detectives would who are at once hardened to the fact of crime and appalled by it. Hammett took conventional detective story plots, peopled them with realistic criminals and realistic detectives, and solved the puzzles he created as they would have been solved had they actually occurred. His stories are hard-boiled in the same sense that Ernest Hemingway's are.

It took time for the *Black Mask* movement toward hard-boiled detective stories to catch on. In the early twenties, Hammett and Daly were virtually alone in writing tough detective stories of any quality. By the end of the decade Raoul Whitfield, Frederick Nebel, Erle Stanley Gardner, and Tod Ballard had become regular contributors of hard-boiled stories to *Black Mask*. In the thirties, Raymond Chandler, Paul Cain, Norbert Davis, George Harmon Coxe, and Lester Dent joined the *Black Mask* circle. By that time the hard-boiled movement was conscious of its brief history and, under the promotion and organization of Joseph Shaw, then the editor of *Black Mask*, began to have some cohesion. When the history of the movement was discussed, Hammett was acknowledged as the first (despite Daly's priority) and usually the best of them. Raymond Chandler wrote:

Hammett took murder out of the Venetian vase and dropped it into the alley; it doesn't have to stay there forever, but it looked like a good idea to get as far as possible from Emily Post's idea of how a well-bred debutante gnaws a chicken wing.

Hammett wrote at first (and almost to the end) for people with a sharp, aggressive attitude to life. They were not afraid of the seamy side of things; they lived there. Violence did not dismay them; it was right down their street. Hammett gave murder back to the kind of people that commit it for reasons, not just to provide a corpse; and with the means at hand, not hand-wrought dueling pistols, curare, and tropical fish. He put these people down on paper as they were, and he made them talk and think in the language they customarily used for these purposes.

. . . He was spare, frugal, hard-boiled, but he did over and over again what only the best writers can ever do at all. He wrote scenes that seemed never to have been written before.[2]

Hammett's first hard-boiled story, "Arson Plus," was published in *Black Mask* on October 1, 1923. He introduced a character in that story who would serve him well over the next five years—a fat, nameless, middle-aged operative for the Continental Detective Agency. Some twenty-five years later, Hammett confided to Frederic Dannay, one half of the writing team who called themselves Ellery Queen, that he had based his Continental op on Jimmy Wright, the assistant supervisor of the Baltimore Pinkerton's office. But that may have been Hammett responding to a common question with an answer his friend wanted to hear. In a letter to the editor at *Black Mask* in the same issue as "Arson Plus," Hammett described more credibly how the op took on his character:

This detective of mine: I didn't deliberately keep him nameless, but he got through "Slippery Fingers" and "Arson Plus"*without needing one, so I suppose I may well let him run along that way. I'm not sure that he's entitled to a name, anyhow. He's more or less of a type: the private detective who oftenest is successful: neither the derby-hatted and broad-toed blockhead of one school of fiction, nor the all-knowing, infallible genius of another. I've worked with several of him.[3]

Between October 1, 1923, and November 1930 there were twenty-six stories, two related novelettes, and two novels about the op's adventures, all of them told by him in the first person. He was tough, but not so tough he was distorted; his stories were action packed, but still plausible; most of all, as he developed in Hammett's stories he became more and more realistic with human faults and human merits.

It is conventional for authors of mystery fiction to develop a

---

*"Slippery Fingers" was published in the next *Black Mask* issue after "Arson Plus" appeared, though the two stories may have been submitted together.

strong detective and to build stories or novels around him, usually narrated in the first person by the detective or a close associate of his. There are several reasons for this tradition, most of them pragmatic. Readers appreciate the recognition of reading about the adventures of a character they are familiar with. The process of invention is simplified for a writer if he can start a story with an already developed central character and a set of circumstances. Moreover, the problem of repetition is solved when a writer of detective fiction can tell the various adventures of a single detective rather than invent a new, different detective for each story. If a character is successful he can achieve a following of readers, ensuring to some degree the success of each new story that features him.

From the beginning, Hammett's Continental op was successful. The op is unlike other fictional detectives in that he belongs to an agency, but he is not a policeman. Though he is bound by agency rules, he has a certain freedom from civil law, which he is not sworn to uphold. Hammett's op is not a genius like the Golden Age detectives nor is he a cold-blooded killer like Carroll John Daly's Race Williams. He is merely a fat, middle-aged man who goes about his job as a professional. When he conducts an investigation, he does so with businesslike precision. He follows all the leads, promising or not, and he reports his findings to the reader faithfully and fully.

When asked about the op in a newspaper interview, Hammett said, "I see in him a little man going forward day after day through mud and blood and death and deceit—as callous and brutal and cynical as necessary—towards a dim goal, with nothing to push or pull him towards it except he's been hired to reach it."[4]

During the course of "Arson Plus," the reader learns where the action of the story is located (between Tavender and Sacramento on the old county road that parallels the state road); where each principal of the story is at the time of the fire that draws the op's attention; when, as precisely as it is known, the fire occurred; how much insurance money was involved; and who held the policies. A reclusive man named Thornburgh is supposed to have died when his house burned. There are three witnesses: the Coomses, a man and wife pair of live-in domestics, and Howard Henderson, a traveling salesman. The op is investigating because some $200,000 worth of insurance had been purchased recently on the deceased (with his niece as beneficiary) and because the house had been doused with gasoline. He uncovers a plot by the domestics, the salesman, and Evelyn Towbridge, a woman posing as the niece of the dead man, to defraud the insurance company by staging the death of an imaginary person. When Thornburgh had to show himself, it was Henderson in disguise who played the part. Otherwise, only the Coomses claimed to have seen him, and they could fabricate tales of his actions. "Arson Plus" moves swiftly and surely. The characters and their dialogue are American and real.

In the November 1923 issue of *Action Stories*, a story by Hammett appeared which more closely resembled Daly's Race Williams stories. It does not feature the op, it did not appear in *Black Mask*, and it is not up to the quality of the first op stories. "Laughing Masks" is an awkward thirteen-thousand-word story, yet among Hammett's more interesting early publications in light of his later achievement. The main character is Phil Truax, a tough adventurer, if not a gentleman, who stumbles onto a mystery and pursues it to its end. On his way home from a poker game, Truax hears a woman screaming and cautiously goes to her aid. He is unsuccessful. When he regains consciousness from a blow on his head, he realizes the woman and her assailants are gone, and only her pocketbook, containing $350 and a "rumpled sheet of note-paper covered with strange, exotic characters," is left behind. At length, Truax learns that the paper contains an important message. The pocketbook belongs to Romaine, niece of a Russian nobleman named Kapaloff who was exiled after the fall of the czarist government. Romaine is beautiful and clearly distressed, so Truax takes it upon himself to help her. After a short imprisonment in Kapaloff's house that reaches a bloody climax, Truax learns that the Russian was a murderer who lost his property in Russia then killed Romaine's father to gain control of his estate until Romaine was of age. The letter was a blackmail threat to Kapaloff from a Russian friend. After having solved the mystery and rescued Romaine from exploitation by an evil man, Truax hints at an honorable, if improbable, intention. He will get Romaine an honest lawyer to handle her estate and then see if he can settle down and be a good husband to her.

The basic plot elements of *The Maltese Falcon*, written four years later, are present in "Laughing Masks." There is a beautiful woman (who lacks the villainy of Brigid O'Shaughnessy), a tough, relentless man who loves her (Truax is not a detective by profession, but he plays the role of one), an evil genius consumed by greed, and an illusive object of great value. What is lacking from "Laughing Masks" is a careful plot, plausibility, and a sense of human values being tested. In 1923 Hammett had not yet achieved that state of his art. He had assembled the pieces; he was fumbling with them for the right combination; but he was still years away from solid achievement. When that achievement would come, it would be in the pages of *Black Mask* magazine, using characters he introduced and developed there.

From October 1923 to October 1924, twenty of Hammett's stories were published in five different magazines, and six of those stories were shorter than twenty-five hundred words. Of the fourteen remaining stories of substantial length, the eleven about the Continental op were all published in *Black Mask*.

Some of the op stories were simply hackwork. "Slippery Fingers" (October 15, 1923), published under the Peter Collinson pseudonym, is about a blackmailer who attempts to avoid punishment for murder by having a set of manufactured fingerprints laminated to his fingertips. In "Bodies Piled Up" (December 1, 1923) a hired murderer mistakenly assassinates three men when he goes to the wrong hotel room. The criminal of "Night Shots" (February 1, 1924) is a rich, cranky old man who fears that while deliriously ill he has babbled the truth about murdering his wife, and then plots to murder his nurse to protect the secret. "One Hour" (April 1, 1924) is the story of a group of Dutch counterfeiters who work in a print shop and run off sheets of Dutch currency when their chronically ill boss is home sick.

These four stories are lethargic; the plots revolve around one unusual circumstance, which the op must discover and explain at the end. The characters are one-dimensional. Here Hammett was at his worst—not a beginner struggling to learn his craft and exhibiting his shortcomings along the way; but a lazy writer, producing facile intrigues on schedule.

He did not often sink to the level of stories such as "One Hour," although his imitators and colleagues writing for the pulps at that time rarely rose above that standard. More often Hammett wrote solid, competent adventure stories about the op, such as "Arson Plus." There was "Crooked Souls" (October 15, 1923), about the runaway daughter of a rich, tyrannical father. She pretends to be kidnapped, hoping to provide a stake for herself and her crooked boyfriend. Hammett hints at some reasons for the girl's plan, some attraction of low-life, which he developed in his later stories, but that vein is unmined here.

"It" (November 1, 1923) is a light murder mystery with a clever plot, interesting as the first of Hammett's op stories to use a characteristic plot device in which the guilty party hires the op to make himself seem innocent by initiating an investigation of his own crime. Here the op is hired by a man to investigate the disappearance of his business partner. He learns that the partners had planned to rob one another of co-owned bonds in a company safe. The missing partner had gotten there first, but not by much. The op's client had caught him before he could get out of town and murdered him.

"Zigzags of Treachery" (March 1, 1924) is narrated by the op in a mood to explain his occupation. It is the story of a disgraced doctor who buys the license and identity of another doctor, moves to San Francisco, and makes good. But his past haunts him in the form of a blackmailer and the doctor ultimately chooses suicide to protect his wife from the embarrassment of his past. The complication is that his wife is accused of murdering the doctor. The op is hired to clear the innocent wife of the charges against her. He does his job expertly, concentrating in the telling of it on his method. He recites the four rules of shadowing: stay behind your man as much as possible; do not ever try to hide from him; act naturally, regardless of what happens; and never look him in the eye. Then, as if to illustrate, Hammett introduces a character shadowing the blackmailer. The shadow man breaks all the rules and gets a broken neck for his ignorance. The op describes the methods and uses of surveillance and his working relationship with the management of certain hotels; he even assumes a disguise. But as thoroughly as he seemed to be describing how a detective worked, Hammett backed off when it came time to test his op's code.

The blackmailer, Jake Ledwich, has a suicide note sent him by the doctor. It is the only piece of evidence to prove Mrs. Estep, the doctor's widow, innocent of his murder. The op knows Ledwich to be a murderer whose capacity for treachery is enormous, and he is in the position of bargaining with Ledwich—the suicide note for the murderer's freedom. If the op takes the deal, a murderer goes free; if he refuses it, an innocent woman either dies of grief or is convicted of murder; if he double-crosses Ledwich, the op has sunk to his level. The op agrees to the deal, but Ledwich, as he is about to make his getaway, breaks his part of the bargain by attempting to take the suicide note with him, and the op then feels free to call in the police, who kill Ledwich as he attempts to escape.

It is an evasive ending to a story that raises questions about the ethical complexities of the detective's code, the more disappointing because "Zigzags of Treachery" demonstrates that Hammett was on the verge of real literary accomplishment—but the time had not yet come. He dealt squarely with the same problem in *Red Harvest* four years later. There the op is not burdened with excessive moral baggage that Hammett was unprepared to handle.

"Zigzags of Treachery" also illustrates the realistic quality of Hammett's stories that distinguishes them from other pulp detective fiction. He explained in his letter to the editor of *Black Mask* on March 1, 1924:

I'll have another story riding your way in a day or two; one for the customers who don't like their sleuths to do too much brain-work. [Apparently "One Hour."]

The four rules for shadowing that I gave in "Zigzags" are the first and last words on the subject. There are no other tricks to learn. Follow them, and, once you get the hang of it, shadowing is the easiest of detective work, except, perhaps, to an extremely nervous man. You simply saunter along somewhere within sight of your subject; and, barring bad breaks, the only thing that can make you lose him is over-anxiety on your own part.

Even a clever criminal may be shadowed for weeks without suspecting it. I know one operative who shadowed a forger—a wily old hand—for more than three months without arousing his suspicion. I myself trailed one for six weeks, riding trains and making half a dozen small towns with him; and I'm not exactly inconspicuous—standing an inch or so over six feet.

Another thing: a detective may shadow a man for days and in the end have but the haziest idea of the man's features. Tricks of carriage, ways of wearing clothes, general outline, individual mannerisms—all as seen from the rear—are much more important to the shadow than faces. They can be recognized at a greater distance, and do not necessitate his getting in front of his subject at any time.

Back—and it's only a couple years back—in the days before I decided that there was more fun in writing about manhunting than in that hunting, I wasn't especially fond of shadowing, though I had plenty of it to do. But I worked under one superintendent who needed only the flimsiest of excuses to desert his desk and get out on the street behind some suspect.

Sincerely,
Dashiell Hammett
San Francisco, Cal.

The editorial reply simply underscores the point of Hammett's letter, which was that his stories drew from his own experiences as a detective:

It is a complete surprise to us to learn that Mr. Hammett comes by his information regarding detectives and criminals through actual experience. We are sure that our readers will find added interest in his yarns, now that they know they are written by a former detective.[5]

The editor must not have been paying attention, because Hammett pointedly referred to his days as a detective in his first letter to *Black Mask* on June 15, 1923.

Hammett convincingly showed his rapid growth as a writer in his three best op stories in 1924. "The Tenth Clew" (January 1, 1924) is a twelve-thousand-word story, longer than average for him during the period, and in it he achieves as well as he ever did a confident ease in narration and naturalness in diction. The narrative voice is the op's, and as Raymond Chandler observed about Hammett's diction, "He had a literary style, but his audience didn't know it, because it was in a language not supposed to be capable of such refinements. They thought they were getting a good meaty melodrama written in the kind of lingo they imagined they spoke themselves. It was, in a sense, but it was much more. All language begins with speech, and the speech of common men at that, but when it develops to the point of becoming a literary medium it only looks like speech."[6]

"The Tenth Clew" begins at the house of Leopold Gantvoort who has been threatened and has asked the op to come see him. Gantvoort is not at home, and the op waits as Gantvoort's son is informed by phone that his father has been murdered. The op describes in a characteristic manner what happens next:

Neither of us spoke during the ride to the Hall of Justice. Gantvoort bent over the wheel of his car, sending it through the streets at a terrific speed. There were several questions that needed answers, but all his attention was required for his driving if he was to maintain the pace at which he was driving without piling us into something. So I didn't disturb him, but hung on and kept quiet.

Half a dozen police detectives were waiting for us when we reached the detective bureau. O'Gar—a bullet-headed detective-sergeant who dresses like the village constable in a movie, wide-brimmed black hat and all, but who isn't to be put out of the reckoning on that account—was in charge of the investigation. He and I had worked on two or three jobs together before, and hit it off excellently.

He led us into one of the small offices below the assembly room. Spread out on the flat top of a desk there were a dozen or more objects.

"I want you to look these things over carefully," the detective-sergeant told Gantvoort, "and pick out the ones that belonged to your father."

"But where is he?"

"Do this first," O'Gar insisted, "and then you can see him."[7]

As the title suggests, there is a profusion of clues; nine strong ones lead nowhere, but the tenth clue is the important one: there are too many clues, too obvious. So the op decides to ignore them all. By industry and accident he discovers the murderer, a jealous con-man whose girl friend had been about to marry his mark, the man now dead.

Near the conclusion of his case, the op's investigation takes him on a ferryboat with the murderer and his accomplice. In a desperate attempt to escape arrest, the two criminals throw the op off the boat into San Francisco Bay, where he must swim for his life, semi-conscious from a blow to his head. The op's description of his swim is a splendid piece of writing, foreshadowing a scene in *Red Harvest* when the op has taken laudanum. Here he is torn between the desire to succumb to the water and the annoyance of reality, suggested by foghorns that prevent him from enjoying the "comfortable, sooth-ing numbness" he felt overtaking him. Finally, it is the foghorns, harshly moaning their warnings to traffic in the night, that save the op's life. They will not let him sleep; they demand his attention until he regains full consciousness. It is just such annoying, persistent moans from his clients in the city that call the op to the drudgery of his life's work. Such skillful use of imagery and of near-metaphor characterizes Hammett's best writing.

Early in 1924 Hammett was beginning to have the confidence to try longer works, and he was beginning to understand that in order to accomplish certain effects, to establish a pattern of imagery, and to be effective in his characterization, stories longer than the six thousand words that had been his limit would be necessary. With "The House in Turk Street" (April 15, 1924) he began, probably unintentionally, a two-part serial, each part running close to ten thousand words. It was his most ambitious writing project up to that time, and it shows the extent of his development as a writer.

In "The House in Turk Street" the op's narrative begins quietly enough: he is canvassing a block on Turk Street for a missing person. At one house he is invited inside by a kindly old couple who graciously entertain him until a gunman pokes a revolver at his neck and orders him tied up. The op has stumbled onto a gang that steals bonds in a manner similar to the thefts Nicky Arnstein was accused of in 1921. The gang consists of a Chinaman named Tai, the brains of the operation; an impetuous gunman, Hook; Elvira, a beautiful, dangerous redhead; and the elderly Quarres, Thomas and his wife. They have just stolen $100,000 in a Los Angeles job typical of their operation. Elvira seduced a bank messenger, convincing him to make a pickup from the bank and to skip town with her and the bank's money. The night after the theft, Hook showed up pretending to be her irate husband. Elvira, seemingly distraught, fled with Hook and the money, intending to leave the bank messenger to fend for himself; but this boy showed too much spunk, so Hook killed him.

Now, confronted by the op, whom they mistakenly believe to be looking for them, the gang begins to lose its cohesion. Hook and Tai are both in love with Elvira. Hook despises Tai; the Quarres distrust the Chinaman; and Elvira, out only for herself, will ruthlessly use anyone she can for her own gain. She encourages Hook in his plan to double-cross Tai, using the confrontation between the two as a distraction while she takes the bonds from Tai's bag, hides them, and substitutes magazines for weight. She plans to return after they make their getaway to claim the entire bundle for herself. But the op sees through her plot. Meanwhile, Tai devises a plan to rid himself of Hook. He will loosen the ropes that bind the op, leave a gun loaded with one bullet within his reach, and warn him that Hook will be in to kill him; then after the gang leaves the house, Tai will send Hook back to kill the op—by now armed and waiting.

When Hook returns to the house alone, Elvira fears he saw her hide the bonds and tells Tai that Hook took the bonds; so they too return to the house, but not before the op has killed Hook and hidden the bonds himself so that he is in a bargaining position. At the climax, the op, Elvira, and Tai are negotiating—the op for their arrests, the others for the money—when the Quarres come in, armed and thinking they are being sold out. A gunfight begins in which the Quarres are killed and the op overcomes Tai. Elvira escapes. The story ends with the op promising himself to find her.

For a short story, there are too many characters to manage and a

DASHIELL HAMMETT

too complicated plot, but Hammett obscured those faults by the sheer force of his story. In "The House in Turk Street" one can find elements of Hammett's first three novels, in addition to half a dozen typical plot situations and characters that appear throughout his work. The plot of the story involves the op being held captive, so that he must rely on his savvy, not just his gun, to escape and to arrest his criminals. He manages this task by creating dissent among his captors and having them kill off one another until he can step in and manage the situation by himself. That plot situation, typical of Hammett's stories, is refined in *Red Harvest*, *The Maltese Falcon*, and to a lesser extent in his other three novels.

Elvira, the temptress who is all the more dangerous because of her beauty, foreshadows Brigid O'Shaughnessy in *The Maltese Falcon*. She is described as having "little sharp animal-teeth," anticipating the description of Gabrielle Leggett in *The Dain Curse*, who becomes convinced of her inherent evil because of her animal-like characteristics, including her "white, small, pointed" teeth. And Elvira's seduction of the bank messenger suggests Dinah Brand's romance with the bank teller in *Red Harvest* during which she unknowingly induces the boy to steal for her and finally to commit murder out of jealousy.

Tai is a prototype of Gutman in *The Maltese Falcon*; he is smart, smooth, and cold-blooded, but he prefers finesse to gunplay. Tai particularly resembles Gutman in his obsession with the $100,000 in stolen money, and in his position of bargaining with a detective whom he holds captive for loot that the detective has hidden.

In the sequel "The Girl with the Silver Eyes" (June 1924) the op tries again to capture Elvira, who has changed her name to Jeanne Delano. She has also changed the color of her hair and let it grow long, but she is still dangerously beautiful and the price of falling in love with her is still death. The op is hired by Burke Pangborn, a poet and a brother-in-law of multimillionaire R. F. Axford. Pangborn has fallen in love with a beautiful woman who has mysteriously disappeared, and he wants the op to find her. She is Jeanne Delano. The op discovers that before Jeanne Delano disappeared, she withdrew $20,000 that had been deposited in Pangborn's account in the form of a check forged with his brother-in-law's signature. Then Pangborn disappears too. He is seen several days later at a roadhouse in a situation that recalls the Schaefer gang hideout Hammett had watched as a Pinkerton in 1921. When the op goes to the roadhouse, he finds Pangborn dead in front, just then shot by an unknown gunman. Jeanne Delano and her boyfriend Kilcourse escape and there is a chase which results in two more deaths before the op captures Jeanne Delano. After stoically resisting her attempt to seduce him and gain her freedom, the op sends Jeanne Delano to the gallows.

"The Girl with the Silver Eyes" is a much more successful story than "The House in Turk Street." In his second attempt to write about Elvira / Jeanne Delano, Hammett described her ruthlessness not by words, but by illustrating her effects on others. There is a minor character in the story, an informant named Porky Grunt, "whose name was a synonym for cowardice the full length of the Pacific Coast."[8] Porky falls under Jeanne Delano's spell and at the end of the story stands solidly in front of the op's speeding car emptying his gun at it in an attempt to save Jeanne Delano from arrest. The effect of that scared little man taking a firm, fatal stand for a woman he loves and who is cold-bloodedly using him to save her own neck transcends any simple description of her character.

Hammett establishes the importance of the op's work. He is more than merely a private policeman. He is a man—the only man in the story—who can withstand the temptation of Jeanne Delano. He apprehends her because of his self-discipline, because he has a purpose that he never loses sight of, and because he is as hard and tough and pragmatic as she is.

CHAPTER 6

If I stick to the stuff that I want to write—the stuff I enjoy writing—I can make a go of it, but when I try to grind out a yarn because I think there is a market for it, then I flop.

Dashiell Hammett
Letter to the editor, *Black Mask*, 1924

Creatively, 1922 to 1924 were years of accomplishment, energy, and experimentation for Hammett; physically and emotionally, however, that period took its toll on him, and even so was only a prelude to a very difficult decade. His vocational training at Munson's Business College ended in late May 1923, but Hammett was unable to embark on a vocation that would allow him to provide well for his family. His health had broken again; in October he went to the hospital where his illness was diagnosed as active pulmonary tuberculosis. His pension, suspended while he was at Munson's, was restored, and his disability was fixed at 50 percent. He weighed 131 pounds, a near low during his mature lifetime. On February 9, 1924, a United States Public Health nurse who visited Hammett at home found him to be poorly nourished and unmuscular.

It is unclear exactly when the warnings from the public health officials became strong enough or threatening enough to cause him to act, but sometime during 1924 or early 1925, Hammett became sufficiently convinced that his poor health might affect his daughter Mary, three years old in October 1924, that he sent her and his wife to live with Jose Hammett's family in Anaconda, Montana. The separation lasted about six months, during which Hammett secured a larger apartment in the same building at 620 Eddy Street that he prepared for their homecoming.[1] The 1924 World War Veteran's Act provided a permanent 50 percent disability rating for veterans suffering from or recovered from tuberculosis. So even if Hammett could not manage to secure a salaried job, he was guaranteed a pension sufficient to cover most of his rent, and as long as he could produce eighteen to twenty stories a year for the pulps, averaging, say, thirty-five hundred words apiece, he could add an extra $50 or so a month to his income. In order to earn $1,000 a year in the early twenties, Hammett had to struggle.

It was in the midst of that struggle to churn out words that paid a penny apiece while maintaining some claim to pride in his accomplishment that a remarkable exchange took place in "Our Readers' Private Corner" of *Black Mask*. In August 1924, directly after publication of Hammett's two most ambitious and most promising stories, "The House in Turk Street" and "The Girl with the Silver Eyes," Phil Cody, who had succeeded George Sutton, Jr., as editor of *Black Mask* in April 1924, publicly rejected two of Hammett's stories. Cody's explanation and Hammett's response to the rejection were published under the title "Our Own Short Story Course":

We recently were obliged to reject two of Mr. Hammett's detective stories. We didn't like to do it, for Mr. Hammett and his Continental Detective Agency had become more or less fixtures in *Black Mask*. But in our opinion the stories were not up to the standard of Mr. Hammett's own work—so they had to go back.

In returning the manuscripts, we inclosed the "Tragedy in One Act," referred to in the letter which follows. The "Tragedy" was simply a verbatim report of the discussion in this office, which led to the rejection of the stories.

We are printing Mr. Hammett's letter below; first, to show the difference between a good author and a poor one; and secondly, as a primary course in short story writing. We believe that authors—especially young authors, and also old authors who have fallen into the rut—can learn more about successful writing from the hundred or so words following, than they could possibly learn from several volumes of so-called short story instruction. Mr. Hammett has gone straight to the heart of the whole subject of writing—or of painting, singing, acting. . . or of just living for that matter. As the advertising gentry would say, here is the 'Secret' of success.

Hammett's letter was apparently addressed to Harry North, associate editor to Cody, as he had been to Sutton.

I don't like that "tragedy in one act" at all; it's too damned true-to-life. The theater, to amuse me, must be a bit artificial.

I don't think I shall send "Women, Politics, and Murder" back to you—not in time for the July issue anyway. The trouble is that this sleuth of mine has degenerated into a meal-ticket. I liked him at first and used to enjoy putting him through his tricks; but recently I've fallen into the habit of bringing him out and running him around whenever the landlord, or the butcher, or the grocer shows signs of nervousness.

There are men who can write like that, but I am not one of them. If I stick to the stuff that I want to write—the stuff I enjoy writing—I can make a go of it, but when I try to grind out a yarn because I think there is a market for it, then I flop.

Whenever, from now on, I get hold of a story that fits my sleuth, I shall put him to work, but I'm through with trying to run him on a schedule.

Possibly I could patch up "The Question's One Answer" and "Women, Politics, and Murder" enough to get by with them, but my frank opinion of them is that neither of them is worth the trouble. I have a liking for honest work, and honest work as I see it is work that is done for the worker's enjoyment as much as for the profit it will bring him. And henceforth that's my work.

I want to thank both you and Mr. Cody for jolting me into wakefulness. There's no telling how much good this will do me. And you may be sure that whenever you get a story from me hereafter,—frequently, I hope,—it will be one that I enjoyed writing.

DASHIELL HAMMETT[2]
San Francisco, Cal.

Public confessions were never Hammett's style and "Our Own Short Story Course" is unique in all of his written work for its apparent ingenuousness. But Hammett's statement simply does not ring true; the tone is all wrong, patronizing, and solicitous. Moreover, Hammett's next op story, "Women, Politics and Murder," the story he says in his letter is not worth fixing, was published in *Black Mask*; the other rejected story was apparently retitled "Who Killed Bob Teal?" and published the next month under his own name in *True Detective Stories*. Far from keeping his resolution not to write on schedule, op stories appeared regularly in every other issue of *Black Mask*—in September and November 1924, and January, March, and May 1925.

If the version of "Women, Politics and Murder" published in the September 1924 *Black Mask* is "patched up," it is easy to understand Cody's rejection of the original version. The story is a lazy and implausible attempt at a corruption theme; the characters are flat and the plot leads the op in several interesting directions before diverting him and the reader's attention with an insignificant conclusion. The op is hired by Mrs. Bernard Gilmore, the wife of a crooked building contractor who is often out late at night either arranging fixed city contracts with corrupt officials or cheating on his wife. One night his wife, irrational with jealousy, follows her husband, and that night he is shot on Pine Street near the apartment of Stanley Tenant, the assistant city engineer who is known to be on the take. Also involved is Gilmore's girl friend, a pretty, cold-blooded tart named Cara Kenbrook. Hammett had gathered all of the elements for an interesting story, the op's first exposure to political corruption, but he backed away from it. Instead Gilmore is killed accidentally by a beat cop who mistakes him for a prowler then covers up by leading others to believe Gilmore was murdered. After he is framed and beaten by Tenant and Kenbrook, the op is content to settle the score by punching Tenant in the mouth. That is all there is to "Women, Politics and Murder"—not much. But as before, even in this failure there is the hint of things to come. Hammett introduced a theme that he would return to with a firmer resolve of purpose and sharpened skill. Political corruption plays a part in a handful of Hammett's stories written in 1924 and 1925, and it is the cornerstone of *Red Harvest* and *The Glass Key*.

It is virtually certain that "The Question's One Answer" was the story slightly revised and published as "Who Killed Bob Teal?" in *True Detective Stories* (November 1924). The original title is echoed as the op begins to explain the overcomplicated plot: "Well, first off, I knew that the question *Who killed Bob Teal?* could have only one answer."[3] Moreover, the story exaggerates the faults of Hammett's worst work of the period and illustrates the need for Cody's "Tragedy in One Act." "Who Killed Bob Teal?" is credited to "Dashiell Hammett of the Continental Detective Agency" and the story is presented as a true case of Hammett's. There was, of course, no Continental Detective Agency and there is no evidence whatsoever that the story Hammett told ever happened—except in Hammett's previous fiction. The story bears certain similarities to a number of op stories that had appeared in *Black Mask* over the past year. Ogburn and Whitacre are business partners in a land options swindle. Ogburn comes to the Continental Detective Agency complaining that his partner is mishandling the company books, and he requests an investigation. Two days later, the agency investigator, Bob Teal, is murdered. The op learns that Ogburn fell in love with Whitacre's girl friend and that they plotted to make away with all the proceeds from the land swindle while ridding themselves of Whitacre. They hired Teal and told Whitacre he was a postal inspector on to their swindle. The frightened Whitacre wanted to get out of town immediately, but he was convinced by Ogburn to stay. One night Ogburn took Whitacre out to try to discover whether in fact someone was shadowing them and, of course, Teal was. Ogburn told Whitacre he would bribe this postal inspector to leave them alone. He approached Teal, who trusted him, and shot the op twice through the heart, claiming to Whitacre it had been accidental. When the frightened Whitacre bolted, the frame was complete. All the journal entries in the company books were in Whitacre's hand; since he was an ex-con, no one would believe his testimony against Ogburn; and Ogburn could claim Whitacre had taken all the money they had realized from their land option business. But as a result of the op's detective work Ogburn is hanged, his girl friend gets fifteen years, and Whitacre gets a suspended sentence.

Hammett's public admission that he was embarrassed as a writer by this story, then his submission of it for publication within sixty days, under his own name, indicates the extent to which he needed money at the time; but more important, the publication of "Who Killed Bob Teal?" reveals for the first time in his professional life Hammett's tendency to disregard his readers, to play them for suckers who would accept his worst work as readily as his best. That attitude, amplified over the next fifteen years, finally caused Hammett to quit writing altogether. "Who Killed Bob Teal?" has an element of the private joke about it. First, he was letting Cody know that "Our Own Short Story Course" was a disingenuous response to what he saw as a naive criticism. Second, he was proving that the level of the pulp audience was so low that he could write down to them, repeating formulas he had devised in his earlier fiction, and even passing his fiction off as truth. Third, he was indicating to Cody that Dashiell Hammett did not need *Black Mask*; he could find publication elsewhere. Nevertheless, in the end, "Tragedy in One Act" had its effect. The first new story Hammett wrote after Cody's reprimand is very good, and over the next fifteen months Hammett wrote fewer stories and they were longer and better.

In "The Golden Horseshoe" (November 1924) the op is called to find a runaway husband who has left his wealthy wife after she unjustly accused him of being unfaithful to her. When she discovered her mistake, she tried to find him. After three years he wrote her but refused to come back, claiming to be addicted to drugs and unwilling to have her see him in that condition. For the past year she has sent him money each month. Now she wants him found. The op has an easy time finding where Mrs. Ashcraft's monthly payment is going. He traces it to an Englishman named Bohannon, whose mailing address is the Golden Horseshoe Cafe in Tijuana. He goes to investigate and finds Bohannon claiming to be Ashcraft and to have changed his name to avoid his wife. He seems inclined to return to her now, since his drug habit seems controllable. So the op returns with an optimistic report for Mrs. Ashcraft. When he goes to her house to tell her the news, he finds her and two of her servants murdered. His instincts lead him back to Tijuana. There he learns that Bohannon is not Ashcraft, but a petty crook who got lucky.

Bohannon was burglarizing Ashcraft's hotel room some years earlier when he heard someone coming and hid in a closet. It was Ashcraft, despondent and preparing to commit suicide. He wrote a note and shot himself in the head. The gunshot brought people to the room, so, to avoid being accused of murder, Bohannon, who bore a resemblance to Ashcraft, pocketed the suicide note, switched roles, and claimed he had shot the dead man, who had broken into his room. Ashcraft's suicide note explained his relationship with his wife, and Bohannon, seeing a way to provide himself a monthly stipend, began forging letters to Mrs. Ashcraft.

After a year he got greedy for the entire estate and, as the op knows but cannot prove, he sent a thug to San Francisco to murder Mrs. Ashcraft during the op's first visit to Tijuana. Though the op lacks proof that Bohannon is guilty of the three murders in San Francisco, he does have the evidence to prove him guilty of the murder he did not commit—Ashcraft's—since Bohannon had destroyed the suicide note that was his only protection (a plot twist similar to "The Joke on Eloise Morey"). So the op bends the law, breaks some rules, and sees that the guilty man hangs, even if for the wrong murder. In contrast to his code in "The Zigzags of Treachery," written nine months earlier when the op treated unfair men fairly, the op now has a more pragmatic attitude. For him the end does indeed justify the means and that concept is debated only by fools and victims.

"Mike, Alec or Rufus" (January 1925) is a good, solid story which plows no new ground but cultivates old fields well. It is the story of a robbery committed in an apartment building under circumstances that would make escape seem impossible—a variation on the conventional locked-room mystery. Hammett unravels his tale almost entirely with dialogue—believable, distinctive, and tough—and he designs his puzzle, traditional as the structure is, with modern twists.

The Toplins have been robbed of $100,000 in jewels in their fifth-floor apartment by a short, thin, boyish, fuzzy-faced thief. After the robbery the thief runs upstairs to the seventh-floor apartment of an athletic-looking woman named Eveleth. By that time the commotion had aroused enough interest that all exits from the building were being watched. Without leaving the building, the op solves the case. Eveleth is a transvestite who rented the apartment as a woman, let his beard grow for the robbery, and then used a depilatory before receiving the police and the op for questions. "Mike, Alec or Rufus" is a clever story well told, in the style Hammett was growing more and more proficient at. It had become a pattern for him by 1925 to try an ambitious story and then to follow it with an easy one; he tested his skill then sharpened it.

"The Whosis Kid" (March 1925), his next op story, is a testing story and it ranks with his best attempts, though it is only partly successful. The length of a Hammett story is usually an indication of how ambitiously he approached it—the longer the story, the better it is. His style was lean and spare; rarely did he overwrite his material or pad his stories while he was regarding his career as a writer seriously. "The Whosis Kid" is about thirteen thousand words long and it was Hammett's attempt once again to portray the femme fatale he had first attempted in "The House in Turk Street" ten months earlier. Hammett frequently recast material; he often retold an old story for a quick buck. But he was up to something different here: he was struggling with what he knew to be the stuff of fine fiction. He had all the elements, but he could not quite fit them together properly.

The basic plot of "The Whosis Kid" is simple: beautiful and dangerous Inez Almad seduced the employee of a jewelry store and convinced him to steal the choicest stones in the store. His theft was to be covered up with a fake robbery by Inez's friends The Whosis Kid and Edouard Maurois, who expected along with Inez to double-cross the store employee and keep the stones for themselves. Inez's idea of double-cross went further. She seductively made separate deals with Maurois and the Kid, each to double-cross the other. The plan called for her to take the stones and meet the pair in Chicago; but she led Maurois to believe she would meet him in New Orleans instead and split the stones two ways; The Whosis Kid expected to meet Inez in Saint Louis. Inez, however, went alone to San Francisco, planning to keep all the loot for herself. The action of the story takes place there, when Maurois and The Whosis Kid catch up with her. As in "The House in Turk Street" and "The Girl with the Silver Eyes" every man who falls prey to Inez's seductions loses his life as a result. The op is able to solve his case precisely because he resists her allure.

"The Whosis Kid" illustrates Hammett's growing awareness of his audience, which craved action in their stories, and his struggle to meet those demands while maintaining some integrity as a writer. He was becoming very good at dramatic action—at building to an action-filled climax slowly so that he could keep his audience interested without sacrificing plausibility. Four people are killed in "The Whosis Kid," all in one climactic gunbattle which the reader knows is inevitable from the beginning of the story. But finally, much as it shows Hammett's progress as a writer, "The Whosis Kid" is not as good as it could have been, and Hammett knew it. "I had failed to make the most of a situation I liked," he remarked nine years later.

A typical structural difficulty in Hammett's stories (and in mystery stories in general) arose from his complex plots. It was necessary for the op to explain the plot—to unravel the mystery for the reader—at the end. Very often, the result was an awkward, anticlimactic monologue in which the reader for the first time got the information necessary to understand the action. In "The Whosis Kid" that flaw is particularly apparent: the story trails off with a lackluster speech by the op that detracts from the story's effectiveness. Moreover, understatement in the story is imperfectly managed. Much of the impact of hard-boiled fiction depends on understated emotions or terse, laconic descriptions. But that device fails if it is used too subtly. The reader must know the full extent of a character's treachery, for instance, to understand the irony of understatement. Hammett is too subtle in his characterization of Inez, the most dangerous criminal in the story, partly because the focus of the story vacillates between her and "The Whosis Kid."

He followed "The Whosis Kid" with a story that came closer to its mark. "The Scorched Face" (May 1925) is clearly an early treatment of the material that would later be used in *The Dain Curse*. Unlike his earlier stories in which he was experimenting with themes and characters and plot situations, "The Scorched Face" has a smooth finish, a polished style, and a structure that even his best fiction had lacked until then.

"The Scorched Face" unravels gradually and when the end comes, the reader knows all he has to. The op is called in to locate the missing daughters of his wealthy client in an opening that recalls "Crooked Souls" (October 1923). Dogged, routine detective work, rather than brilliant insights, leads him to expose a hedonistic religious cult that caters to rich women and secretly photographs them in licentious poses during drug-induced reveries. While the women were members of the cult, its leaders were supported by their contributions; when a member dropped out, she was blackmailed with such embarrassing photographs that suicide was frequently the result.

The most notable feature of "The Scorched Face" is the characterization of the op. Hammett had changed his concept of the fat detective in the nineteen months since he had described him in a letter to *Black Mask* as "more or less of a type." In "The Scorched Face" the op's feelings are expressed more fully than they ever had been. Beginning with "The House in Turk Street," the op had begun to battle against his emotions in order to do his work, but the battles had always been brief and he had ultimately shown no concern other than catching his criminal. Here Hammett explores the way the op's humanity affects his job. Early in the story he is questioning the husband of a suicide. "I felt sorry for this young man," the op concedes. "Apart from that, I had work to do. I tightened the screws."[4] Later, when he discovers the blackmailers' file of embarrassing photos, he convinces the police department detective on the case to burn them rather than save them as evidence to be used in a trial, thus exposing publicly the materials that had already caused a number of suicides. And finally, the op withstands a barrage of curses and insults from his policeman partner—a difficult thing for a man as proud as he to do—while stoically, even heroically, withholding one last piece of evidence—that one of the photos burned was of the policeman's wife. Hammett had added to his story the element that finally distinguishes good hard-boiled fiction from tough-guy nonsense—feelings.

The hard-boiled detective movement was well under way by 1925. The detective pulps devoted monthly issues to stories about wisecracking misfits who packed well-used weapons.[5] Their guns "spewed metal," their victims fell like toy soldiers bowled over by a child's marble, they drank hard, slept sparingly, and spurned the affections of female sycophants. Hammett had helped create the mold for these stories, and he showed his talent as a writer by variations he was able to introduce.

"Corkscrew" (September 1925) is partly a reaction to the distortions hack writers were making of the detective story. It has the Hammett brand: the op goes to lawless Arizona border country to make it safe for civilized people. He is hired by the landowners who want to stop the smuggling of illegal aliens from Mexico and impose law and order on a group of people who have never known it. The op succeeds by turning one lawless element against another and picking up the pieces after they fight it out. The deaths in the story are uncountable. There are gunfights, ambushes, fistfights, and prairie battles, yet through it all, the op is the voice of reason. "The proper place for guns is after talk has failed,"[6] he preaches; and still he is most effective in his work when he does not talk, when he withholds a crucial piece of information in order to cause one bad man to turn against another. The story clearly anticipates *Red Harvest*, which Hammett began writing two years later.

In "Corkscrew" the two forces the op manipulates are those of Peery and the Circle HAR Ranch who oppose Big Nacio the Mexican and his partner Bardell, a Corkscrew saloon owner. The code of the Old West is preserved in this 1925 desert country, and when one of the Circle HAR hands is killed, apparently by a gambler friend of Bardell's, Peery and his men feel obliged to retaliate. They kill the gambler, and Bardell's men, in turn, are compelled to react. Finally, the op orchestrates a range battle in which the two gangs shoot it out.

Throughout, the story borders on parody, as if Hammett were testing his ability to make exaggerated actions believable. He includes the stock situations of a Western—as when the greenhorn op proves his manhood to the cowboys by trying to ride a wild bronco, or when the op and his local assistant face a group of Peery's gunmen and, against unlikely odds, kill Peery and convince his gang to give up the fight. Even for a pulp detective story the amount of violent action is excessive; and yet, Hammett's increasing skill at characterization gives "Corkscrew" a measure of plausibility.

"Dead Yellow Women" (November 1925), a long story of twenty thousand words, is another step in the progression of Hammett's style that led two years later to his first novel. It is a well-made story, told with comfortable ease. Once again, the resolution comes when the op turns two criminal forces against each other, and once again the op arranges the murder of a dangerous crook by framing him. The best quality of the story is Hammett's development of the op's character. The most difficult problem with writing about a hardboiled detective is that he will become a caricature, and indeed, in Hammett's least successful stories, the op becomes a parody of himself. But when Hammett was at his best, the op was tough and competent, yet fallible, vulnerable, and sometimes even sensitive.

"Dead Yellow Women" reflects Hammett's interest in international politics and particularly in things foreign. The action is centered in Chinatown at the mazelike house of Chang Li Ching, a Chinese national who is a leader in the anti-Japanese movement headed by Sun Yat-sen before his death in March 1925. Chang has joined forces with a smuggler known as The Whistler, who uses his boats to take Chang's guns to China and loads them for the return trip with coolies whom he can sell for $1,000 or so apiece in the United States.

The op is employed by Lillian Sheen, wealthy daughter of a Manchu provincial leader who fled when the Manchu rule was overthrown. Her house, in a protected cove, was ideal as a center for The Whistler's smuggling activities, and he was trying to buy it from her when she let it be known she was leaving for the East for several months. Without her knowledge, her property was used as the unloading point for a boatful of coolies, and in the process two of her servants were killed. When she returned home early and found their bodies, she went to the Continental Detective Agency. When guilt for the murders falls on Lillian Sheen in a blackmail scheme to get her to give up her house for Chang's use, the op has a final confrontation with the inscrutable Chang. By presenting a false piece of evidence, the op convinces Chang that The Whistler is selling the guns intended for the Chinese nationals to the Japanese, their enemy. In gratitude Chang clears Lillian Sheen and turns over to the op the Chinamen—all of them from Whistler's gang—responsible for the murders. After the case has been solved, Chang learns he has been tricked. "I don't mind admitting that I've stopped eating in Chinese restaurants," the op confesses, "and that if I never have to visit Chinatown again it'll be soon enough."[7]

Along with "Corkscrew," "Dead Yellow Women" introduces a new element into Hammett's stories. Both involve murder on a large scale. Previously, Hammett had observed the dictum that detective fiction should involve murder because that is the only crime sufficiently serious to sustain a lengthy explanation of the detective's method. Throughout 1925, however, the violence of Hammett's stories increased until in "Corkscrew" and "Dead Yellow Women" murders are common occurrences. *Black Mask* readers wanted violence on a grand scale, and that is what Hammett gave them.

"The Gutting of Couffignal" (December 1925), his next story, features the sacking of an entire island by a band of clever criminals armed with machine guns. It is at best a mediocre story, notable for one scene with splendid possibilities that Hammett mishandled this time but which he later tried again at the end of *The Maltese Falcon* when it became the most memorable scene in all his work.

The op is on a routine assignment, guarding wedding presents at the house of the wealthiest resident on the island of Couffignal, about two hours from San Francisco in San Pablo Bay. The night of the wedding the entire island comes under siege by a band of heavily armed crooks who move from business to business, house to house, sacking the island.

In the process of detection which is thoroughly explained, but which Hammett fails to dramatize, the op learns that the crooks are prominent wedding guests. These Russian aristocrats, exiled from their homeland during the Bolshevik Revolution and now at the end of their resources, had decided to replenish their coffers by gutting Couffignal. The climactic scene comes when the op confronts Princess Zhukouski, one of the leaders of the assault on the island. He tries to explain to her why he is a detective and turns down her bribes of wealth and sex. Then, when she tests him further, thinking to avoid arrest by simply walking away, gambling that the op would never harm a woman who was not assaulting him, he shoots her in the leg.

"I like being a detective, like the work. And liking work makes you want to do it as well as you can. Otherwise there'd be no sense to it. That's the fix I am in. I don't know anything else, don't enjoy anything else, don't want to know or enjoy anything else. You can't weigh that against any sum of money. Money is good stuff. I haven't anything against it. But in the past eighteen years I've been getting my fun out of chasing crooks and tackling puzzles, my satisfaction out of catching crooks and solving riddles. It's the only kind of sport I know anything about, and I can't imagine a pleasanter future than twenty-some years more of it. I'm not going to blow that up!"

She shook her head slowly, lowering it, so that now her dark eyes looked up at me under the thin arcs of her brows.

"You speak only of money," she said. "I said you may have whatever you ask."

That was out. I don't know where these women get their ideas.

"You're still all twisted up," I said brusquely, standing now and adjusting my borrowed crutch. "You think I'm a man and you're a woman. That's wrong. I'm a manhunter and you're something that has been running in front of me. There's nothing human about it. You might just as well expect a hound to play tiddly-winks with the fox he's caught."[8]

Despite its promise, "The Gutting of Couffignal" is not carefully written. There are too many loose ends, and the plot is carelessly planned. The same is true of Hammett's next story, "The Creeping Siamese" (March 1926), a short piece that reads more like a story outline than a finished piece of work. Half the story is spent explaining the murder of a man who stumbles into the Continental Detective Agency office and utters two meaningless words before he dies. Because he had staunched his fatal stab wound with an expensive sarong, the op and the police, in an implausible bit of deduction, go looking for a Siamese as the murderer. Instead they discover that the man was double-crossed by his wife and his former partner during the theft of Burmese gem caches. When he returned to the States after some years for revenge on them, his wife stabbed him. There are hints, again, at certain minor elements of the plot in *The Maltese Falcon*, but the story is disappointing. Since the quality of Hammett's recent op stories had been so high, it is tempting to attribute the drop-off in the quality to either health problems, laziness, a lack of interest, or the possibility that "The Creeping Siamese" is a story written earlier in his career, and that he simply pulled it out of a drawer for publication in March 1926, when his thoughts were turning to advertising work.

Hammett had a full drawer of unpublished stories mostly accumulated during the mid-1920s.[9] Virtually all of these stories, which he tried to place and failed, have one thing in common—they are not mysteries and they have no detective hero. Hammett had been typed as a pulp detective-story writer. Although that typing eventually made him a wealthy man, he was barely getting by in 1925, and he resented being categorized for two reasons: his income was limited because he could not break out of the low-paying pulp-story market; and his pride was damaged because pulp magazines and detective stories were decidedly lowbrow diversions in the mid-1920s. When Hammett described himself as a writer, the unspoken qualification that he was a *pulp mystery writer* always irritated him. He strained to maintain his dignity as an author, to let it be known that he was not just another pulp hack.

In June 1924 he wrote a letter to *The Writer's Digest* responding to an article by H. Bedford-Jones, a very prolific Canadian poet and writer of popular adventure fiction, attacking "sex stories." In his second paragraph, Hammett declared much more than his opposition to Bedford-Jones. He let the seriousness of his art be known: "Literature, as I see it, is good to the extent that it is art, and bad to the extent that it isn't. . . .

"If you have a story that seems worth telling, and you think you can tell it worthily, then the thing for you to do is to tell it, regardless of whether it has to do with sex, sailors, or mounted police-men"[10]—or detectives, he might have added. In making his argument, Hammett invoked the names of Casanova, Anatole France, Shakespeare, and Jack London, demonstrating to his readers that he was a well-read man—as he most certainly was.

Six months later, he contributed his first of three book reviews to *Forum*, a respected magazine with a literary bent that concerned itself with contemporary problems. *Forum* paid fifteen cents a line for reviews, most of which were unsolicited. Hammett was driven to those pages by the same impulse that led him to *The Smart Set*: he wanted to establish his credentials as an intellectual. His style in these book reviews is pedantic and laconic, as in his thirty-line, $4.50 review captioned "The Cabell Epitome":

Illustrated with eight woodcuts from the knife of Leon Underwood, printed by William Edwin Rudge, under the direction of Byron J. Musser, from Garamond type on Vidalon Vélin paper in an edition limited to three thousand copies, James Branch Cabell's BEHIND THE MOON [*sic*] (John Day, $6.00), tells of young Madoc who was not a very good minstrel; and of how he got a large quill pen fashioned out of a feather which had fallen from the black wings of Lucifer, the Father of All Lies; and of the eminently successful lays Madoc wrote therewith; and of his unrest because of the tune Ettarre had brought from behind the moon to haunt him; and of how with a punctuation mark from his quill's black nib he cogged the Gray Three, turned history back seven hundred seventeen and three-quarter years, and gained

Ettarre and a great content; and of what came after that: and in the telling is summed all Cabell has said since the first page of *Beyond Life*.

Half a hundred pages hold the fable. It is the beautiful attainment of a perfection in prose not hitherto reached by Cabell, nor, with those pages warm in memory it is easily believed, ever by anyone else.[11]

In March 1925, *Sunset Magazine*, a pulp, published one of the very few full-length stories by Hammett which does not have a detective and is not a mystery. The story is "Ber-Bulu," and it was a source of gratification for Hammett because he was asked by *The Editor* ("A Journal of Information for Literary Workers, A Weekly Service for Authors") to explain his story in their column "Contemporary Writers and Their Work." He wrote: " 'Ber-Bulu' grew out of wondering what sort of man Samson was if he was neither inspired Judge of Israel nor solar myth, if he was simply a rugged old warrior, nowise supra-human, whose peculiar adventures formed the nucleus of the familiar legend."[12]

"Ber-Bulu" is a first-rate story about a Moro named Jeffol who loses his favorite wife Dinihari to a hairy giant named Levison when he disposes of his harem after converting to Christianity. Jeffol divorces his first wife so, under Christian law, he can legally marry Dinihari, the woman he most loves. But while the divorce is being arranged, she lives with Levison, and when Jeffol tries to get her back, he is abused by the bearded intruder. So Jeffol makes Christianity work for him. He reads in his Bible the story of Samson and, gun in hand, goes to Levison's hut, where he shaves the giant's body clean, exposing him as a chinless, pink-bodied man, so funny looking he inspires old women to laugh. Levison's power—his self-esteem—is gone, and Jeffol takes Dinihari home.

At the end of "Vamping Samson," Hammett's explanatory article in *The Editor*, he summed up his writing career so far: "about half of the fiction I have written has had to do with crime, though, curiously, I was some time getting the hang of the detective story. And while, with the connivance of The Black Mask, that type of story has paid most of my rent and grocery bills during the past two years, I have sold at least one or two specimens of most of the other types to a list of magazines, varied enough if not so extensive."[13] In fact, of the thirty-three publications Hammett had produced in the two years preceding May 1925, only five short-short stories, three book reviews, and "In Defence of the Sex Story" do not deal with crime. The truth is that Hammett had difficulty selling full-length stories about anything else, and when he did succeed—as in "Nightmare Town" (*Argosy All-Story Weekly*, December 1924), about a beautiful young woman who attempts to break her wealthy boyfriend's possessive hold on her, or "Ruffian's Wife" (*Sunset Magazine*, October 1925), a set piece about a rough soldier of fortune named Guy Tharp who is unable to understand his wife's need for tenderness—raw violence dominates the action, just as in the hard-boiled detective stories of that period.

Hammett had already begun to resent his association with the op, and he showed some signs of trying to break away from that character. In January 1926 "The Nails in Mr. Cayterer" was published with a new detective, Robin Thin, a bumbling, egocentric, effeminate pseudointellectual who is an embarrassment to his father's detective agency. The story is a satire in which Robin Thin is the antithesis of the pulp hero. (Thin appears in one other story, "A Man Named Thin," published in *Ellery Queen's Mystery Magazine* in March 1961, two months after Hammett's death.) He followed "The Nails in Mr. Cayterer" with "The Assistant Murderer" (*Black Mask*, February 1926), a straight detective story that introduces a new detective, Alexander Rush, an ugly ex-policeman who left the force in disgrace and is now a private eye. The character is an interesting one, foreshadowing Sam Spade, but the story is a sloppy rehash of earlier material that was none too good the first time and grew stale with age.

CHAPTER 7

Each dollar invested in diamonds buys more lasting beauty, value and satisfaction than any dollar spent for anything else you can wear.

Copy from 1926 advertisement
of Albert S. Samuels Company

March 1926 marks the beginning of an interruption in Hammett's writing career and the end of his short-story-writing apprenticeship. The nineteen months since "Our Own Short Story Course" had been productive ones during which Hammett produced his best short works. Only the last four stories of the period, "The Gutting of Couffignal," "The Nails in Mr. Cayterer," "The Assistant Murderer," and "The Creeping Siamese," are disappointing, but by then Hammett had his mind on other things.

In September 1925 Jose Hammett became pregnant with their second child. Hammett's income was barely sufficient to support a three-person family and he did not see how he could feed another child on his writer's income. So he decided to give up writing for a more lucrative, if less satisfying, career.

Sometime in the winter of 1925 or early spring of 1926, Hammett placed a classified ad in the "positions wanted" section of the *San Francisco Chronicle*. He offered his services in almost any line of work and added at the end that he could write.[1] Hammett had a local reputation as a writer by that time and his work was known to San Francisco jeweler Albert Samuels. Samuels liked writers (he came to like Hammett especially) and he hired Hammett to be his advertising manager. It was the first full-time salaried job Hammett had held in eight years, since June 1918.

The Albert S. Samuels Company was the oldest jewelry business in San Francisco. In 1926 Samuels had three stores in San Francisco and one in Oakland. The company was known for its aggressive advertising. Samuels called his stores "The House of Lucky Wedding Rings," and once gave a party for all married couples in the Bay Area who had bought their wedding rings from him. Samuels's son, Albert Samuels, Jr., summed up the image Samuels Jewelry Company attempted to establish: "It was a store where Mrs. Vanderbilt—and her maid—could shop comfortably."[2]

As advertising manager, Hammett worked from eight to six, Monday through Saturday, in an office above the store at 895 Market Street, and made about $350 per month, a 50 percent increase over his recent income as a writer. He had part-time secretarial help, but other than that, Hammett was the advertising department—writing copy and providing art for Samuels's weekly newspaper ads, which were a tradition with him.[3] As they ran in the *San Francisco Examiner*, for example, the ads were large, about one-third of a page, and typically consisted of a three-hundred-word anecdote signed by Samuels, demonstrating the desirability of a quality Samuels diamond. Before Hammett was hired, Samuels had taken great pride in writing all his ads himself, and it is a measure of his respect for Hammett's ability that Samuels would turn that work over to him.

Hammett's ads tended to be much more visual than Samuels's had been, emphasizing a simple message, as in the following, set in large display type:

DIAMONDS *of* ETERNAL BEAUTY
in GOLD *or* PLATINUM
RINGS // BRACELETS // BROOCHES
FASHIONED BY
THE ABLEST MODERN CRAFTSMEN
↜ *MONTHLY PAYMENTS.*

Another of Hammett's advertisements consisted simply of a silver fork and knife, illustrated without comment.[4]

Hammett did not totally abandon Samuels's method of the story ad. At graduation time, Hammett struck a moralizing tone:

The Graduate Should Get
Something Out of It ↶

74

His parents enjoy every last bit of the pride to which the great event entitles them. The local celebrities have an opportunity to repeat their last year speeches. Teachers and school officials congratulate themselves on having turned out another batch of literates. Empty-headed editorial writers and despairing cartoonists seize on the graduate as a topic that will keep them from being fired for lack of ideas for at least another month.

And what of him who is the center, the cause, of all this hubbub—the graduate himself?

His has been the toil of study and the torture of the examinations' third degree. He is the uncomfortable target of parental boasting, of celebrities' eloquence, of preaching editorials, of insulting cartoons.

And, as if all that weren't enough, when it's all over the chances are he'll have to go out and hunt for a job.

Surely he is entitled to some reward for submitting to all this misery so those others can have their fun. Is there anything in a jeweler's stock too good for him? Is there any gift you can give him that will pay him in full?

Probably not—but you might do what you can.

Monthly or weekly payments
without added cost.[5]

Hammett's new, dependable source of income had an unsettling effect on his family life. Jose Hammett believed the job at Samuels marked a turning point in his life. He met so many people there, she said; that was when he got confused. She thought he probably started to drink heavily at that time.

Albert Samuels was a staunch Catholic, and he expected his employees to behave respectably. He was protective toward his female workers, and if a man was known to be a drinker, he was fired. Hammett, however, seems to have been exempt from the rules. While he was at Samuels, he carried on an affair with a secretary, and his drinking began to cause problems for the first time in his life. He had a little money, but he also had the compulsion to spend it—on clothes, on women, on liquor, and on gambling.[6] Dashiell Hammett was Richard Hammett's son, as he proved in the summer of 1926—but he did not have his father's endurance. On Tuesday, July 20, 1926, Hammett collapsed at work and was found lying in a pool of blood. He had been hemorrhaging from the lungs. At his medical examination, it was learned that Hammett also had hepatitis.

After eight weeks off the job it became clear that Hammett's recovery would be very slow and that he would not be able to return soon. On September 23 Albert Samuels wrote a notarized letter to the Veterans Bureau: "This is to certify that Samuel Dashiell Hammett resigned his postition as advertising manager of Albert S. Samuels Company on July 20, 1926, because ill health had made it impossible for him to perform his duties." Hammett's full-time employment at Samuels's had lasted about half a year.

Josephine Rebecca Hammett, named for her mother and her paternal aunt, had been born on the afternoon of May 24, 1926, minutes after her mother arrived at Saint Francis Hospital by taxi.[7] She was not quite two months old when her father had his breakdown, and the Veterans Bureau took a dim view of an infant living with a tubercular patient in a cramped apartment. Once again Hammett was forced to move away from his family because of his health.

Briefly, he lived in a furnished room at 20 Monroe Street while he and Jose Hammett arranged for the family to move to a larger apartment. In October the Hammetts, Dashiell included, moved to 1309 Hyde Street. He stayed with the family for one week before he took a two-room apartment within walking distance at 891 Post Street. He lived alone and tried to salvage for himself a career in advertising. He had been on 100 percent disability since July, and it was hard to put food on the table.

In spring 1927 Jose Hammett took her two children to San Anselmo, north of San Francisco, to live in the country. It was a move made for the sake of economy and to allow Hammett to regain his health and reorder his life. His daughter Mary was withdrawn from Charity Cross Nursery School, but she would be back in time to begin the first grade at a San Francisco public school.[8]

Although Hammett lived with his family off and on for the next two years, the marriage was over. He became increasingly undependable in observing his responsibilities as a father and a husband, simply turning his attentions away from his family. As he became more social, Hammett had a succession of girl friends in San Francisco, including recently widowed piano player and music teacher Nell Martin, to whom he later dedicated his fourth novel, *The Glass Key*.

Hammett was reluctant at first to turn to writing full time again. He had made considerably more money working for Samuels than he ever had writing, though he had been on the job for only a short time. A career in advertising looked promising, and he devoted his full energy to that goal in the fall of 1926, studying the field thoroughly and trying to establish his reputation as an authority on the writing of ad copy. Between October 1926 and March 1928 he contributed five articles to *Western Advertising*, a monthly trade journal that described itself as "A Magazine for the Buyer and Seller of Advertising." In his articles, he took a very serious view of advertising as a profession. "The Advertisement IS Literature" (October 1926) and "Advertising Art Isn't ART—It's Literature" (December 1927) argue that the selection and arrangement of words in an advertisement are just as important as in a novel; the desired effect is simply different, and the good ad writer must learn to "use everything that art has learned, but must learn to use it in its own way for its own purposes."[9] To support his case, Hammett invoked Aristotle, Joseph Conrad, John Galsworthy, and Anatole France. In "Have You Tried Meiosis?" (January 1928), Hammett explained the use of rhetorical understatement in ad copy as carefully as a composition instructor. "The Literature of Advertising—1927" (February 1928) is a running review of forty books published during the year on advertising and related subjects. Hammett's last article in *Western Advertising* is charged with implications about his writing career. "The Editor Knows His Audience" (March 1928) advises ad writers to examine carefully the editorial content of magazines in which they expect to place ads and to write their copy in a tone consistent with the magazine's contents. Hammett's statement in "The Advertisement IS Literature" may be taken as his general feeling about writing for publication: "Whether he likes it or not, every man who works with words for effects is a literary worker. His only liberty is in deciding how adept he shall be."[10]

Hammett proved himself very adept at judging an audience and writing for it. In 1926 he had been published four times—three stories in *Black Mask* and one article in *Western Advertising*. In 1927 Hammett published book reviews, articles, a short parody, poems, stories, and the first two installments of a novel, seventeen appearances in all, in seven different magazines: *The Forum*, *The Saturday Review of Literature*, *Judge*, *Black Mask*, *Stratford Magazine*, *The Bookman*, and *Western Advertising*. That year Hammett renewed his commitment as a writer, at least partly due to the encouragement of the new editor at *Black Mask*, Joseph T. Shaw, who bought a financial interest in *Black Mask* when he became editor. His job, as he saw it, was to make the magazine bigger and better by building on the base of writers who had first made the magazine successful. Shaw rounded up as many of the former contributors to *Black Mask* as he could and urged them to join what he regarded as a select group of writers who would make *Black Mask* the best magazine of its kind. Among the writers he contacted was Hammett, who agreed to write a new op story. In the January 1927 issue of *Black Mask* Shaw proudly announced: "Dashiell Hammett has called back the Continental detective from his long retirement and is setting him to work anew."

In a 1946 anthology of stories from *Black Mask*, Shaw misremembered his takeover of the magazine. He wrote:

We meditated on the possibility of creating a new type of detective story differing from that accredited to the Chaldeans and employed more recently by Gaborieau, Poe, Conan Doyle—in fact, universally by detective story writers; that is, the deductive type, the cross-word puzzle sort, lacking—deliberately—all other human emotional values. . . .

So we wrote to Dashiell Hammett. His response was immediate and most enthusiastic: That is exactly what I've been thinking about and working toward. As I see it, the approach I have in mind has never been attempted. The field is unscratched and wide open. . . .

We felt obligated to stipulate our boundaries. We wanted simplicity for the sake of clarity, plausibility, and belief. We wanted action, but we held that action is meaningless unless it involves recognizable human character in three-dimensional form.[11]

Despite his claims, Shaw hardly invented the form. When he became editor of *Black Mask*, the hard-boiled detective story was already five years old. The most recent refinement of the form Shaw claimed credit for had come two years earlier with Hammett's rounding of the hard-boiled detective's character by infusing him with controlled human emotion. That innovation had come as a result of the editorial prods of Shaw's predecessor, Philip Cody.

Nonetheless, Shaw was as important as he claims to have been in the development of the hard-boiled detective story, because he was a promoter. By August 1929 he had increased circulation to 92,000 copies per issue.[12] His editorial judgment was often questionable, and he seems to have done little by way of offering helpful editorial advice to his authors; but he took an active interest in the careers of his best authors and used contacts he had established in the New York publishing world to get his elite group of *Black Mask* writers book publication and even publication in other magazines. Moreover, he raised the rates he paid for good stories. By the end of the 1920s, Shaw was paying as much as six cents a word for stories (that is $720 for a twelve-thousand-word story), though his normal rate was two cents a word.

In the December 1928 issue of *The Editor*, he described for potential contributors the kind of story *Black Mask* published:

We do not care for purely scientific detective stories which lack action, and we are prejudiced by experience against the psychological story which is not very rugged and intense in its treatment and subject matter. We avoid the old formula type of so-called detective story, as well as the gruesome, the unnatural or supernatural. We stress plausibility in all details, and we wish swift movement and action.[13]

Even so, *Black Mask* was still a pulp, and it could not compete with the slicks for the best authors. While Shaw was paying $200 to his best authors for a thirty-five-hundred-word story, *The Saturday Evening Post* was paying F. Scott Fitzgerald $4,000 for a story of the same length, and Ring Lardner was earning between $4,000 and $4,500 for his stories from such magazines as *Liberty* and *Hearst's International-Cosmopolitan*.

Shaw was, however, able to bring some measure of respectability to his authors. By the late 1920s, he could boast that President Herbert Hoover, J. P. Morgan, and Dr. A. S. W. Rosenbach, the most distinguished bibliophile of his time, ranked *Black Mask* as their favorite detective magazine, and he managed to get notices in newspaper book review columns for his monthly issues—a feat few magazines of any type were able to accomplish.[14]

In January 1927, at the same time Shaw announced in *Black Mask* that Hammett was working on another op story, Hammett secured a position as mystery novel reviewer for *The Saturday Review of Literature*, quite possibly as a result of Shaw's interest in his writing career. Between January 1927 and October 1929, Hammett reviewed more than fifty mystery novels, mystery story collections, and true crime accounts.

He was a hard critic to satisfy. His first set of reviews for the *Saturday Review*, entitled "Poor Scotland Yard!," is typical of his approach. Hammett passed on five books, as follows:

In some years of working for private detective agencies in various cities I came across only one fellow sleuth who would confess that he read detective stories. "I eat 'em up," this one said without shame. "When I'm through my day's gum-shoeing I like to relax; I like to get my mind on something that's altogether different from the daily grind; so I read detective stories."

He would have liked "False Faces" [by Sydney Horler]; it is different from any imaginable sort of day's work. . . .

Of S. S. Van Dine's *Benson Murder Case*, and Van Dine's detective Philo Vance, Hammett wrote:

This Philo Vance is in the Sherlock Holmes tradition and his conversational manner is that of a high-school girl who has been studying the foreign words and phrases in the back of her dictionary. He is a bore when he discusses art and philosophy, but when he switches to criminal psychology he is delightful. There is a theory that any one who talks enough on any subject must, if only by chance, finally say something not altogether incorrect. Vance disproves this theory; he manages always, and usually ridiculously, to be wrong. His exposition of the technique employed by a gentleman shooting another gentleman who sits six feet in front of him deserves a place in a *How to be a detective by mail* course.

Hammett thought Olga Hartley's *The Malaret Mystery* a "tiresomely slow and rambling story altogether without suspense." Hartley's method, he said, "does keep the solution concealed until the very last from those readers who have forgotten the plot, which is an old friend in not very new clothes." Hammett judged J. S. Fletcher's *Sea Fog* "in spite of its rather free use of happenstance, . . . by far the best of this group. . . . But even [Fletcher's] skill doesn't quite suffice to make the forced ending plausible." But Hammett saw "no especial reason for anyone's reading" Fletcher's book of stories, *The Mossingham Butterfly*.[15]

In his nearly three years as a reviewer for *The Saturday Review of Literature*, he recommended only a handful of books without reservation, including *The Quartz Eye* by Henry Kitchell Webster, *Perishable Goods* by Dornford Yates, *The Prisoner's Opal* by A. E. W. Mason, and *The Clever One* by Edgar Wallace. Hammett always explained why he did not like the books he criticized. He believed that a good mystery should be first of all realistic. It should have believable characters, plausibly motivated, speaking as real people speak, acting as real people act. He believed that the mystery writer should avoid the temptation to enliven his plot with superfluous action and that he should be sufficiently intelligent to interest his reader without such tricks as withholding clues, introducing irrelevant subplots,

DASHIELL HAMMETT

or relying on the unexplainable for his denouement. Hammett
objected to criminals who were too smart and to detectives or
policemen who were too dumb. If a character in a novel was shot
with a .45 caliber handgun, Hammett expected the novelist to know
exactly what the impact of the bullet would do to him. When a
detective gathered his clues, Hammett expected him to know just
how to handle them—how to trace missing persons, how to follow
suspects, how to coordinate his work with that of the authorities.
And Hammett was concerned that criminals be portrayed accurately, as neither a demented class of fallen gentry nor as masterminds making fortunes by robbing, extorting, and murdering.
Hammett's standard was his own op stories.

It is likely that his careful consideration—and usually condem-
nation—of current mystery novels caused him to consider writing a
novel of his own. He seems to have been urged by Cody to write a
longer work in the summer of 1925, and Shaw, with his press agent's
sense, renewed the pressure in the spring of 1927. He realized that
Hammett was the best of his writers; that the more successful Hammett was, the more successful *Black Mask* would be; and that it would
take a novel for Hammett to achieve real recognition.

In 1925 Hammett had tried his hand at his first novel. It was
never finished, but his copious notes on characters, outlines, and
drafts are preserved among his papers at the University of Texas.
The working title is "The Secret Emperor." The story is about a man
named Gutman who realizes he can never be president because he is
Jewish. Gutman plans to blackmail a senator whom he will get
elected president; then, he will control the presidency by proxy. The
germ for "The Secret Emperor" was Hammett's early story "The
Vicious Circle." When he abandoned the novel, at the time of Jose
Hammett's second pregnancy, he abandoned the story idea as well,
salvaging only the name Gutman for a villain in *The Maltese Falcon*.
When it was time for Hammett to write a long work for publication,
his instincts told him to make the op his main character. Readers of
Black Mask had been writing to the editor asking for more stories
about the op, and Hammett was wise enough to give his readers what
they wanted.

So, in February 1927 at the age of 32, freshened by a year-long
respite from fiction writing, with his health improving, with a firm
idea of what his readers wanted, with a healthy, playfully cynical
regard for his editor's advice, and with his talent coming to full

bloom, Hammett began his most productive period as a writer, ending in spring 1930 when he finished his fourth novel, *The Glass Key*. In those three years he wrote nearly sixty book reviews, two novelettes, and four stories in addition to four novels, of which three—*Red Harvest*, *The Maltese Falcon*, and *The Glass Key*—rank among the best detective fiction ever written by an American. By spring of 1930, with the publication of *The Maltese Falcon*, Hammett had made his reputation as a mainstream writer.

Hammett's first publications after his return to fiction writing are two related stories that were his longest works to that time, totaling about thirty-five thousand words. In "The Big Knock-Over" (*Black Mask*, February 1927) and "$106,000 Blood Money" (*Black Mask*, May 1927), there are about twenty murders (the exact number is unclear), and enough action to satisfy Shaw, who had been suggesting action, more action, until it became a joke with Hammett—there is a mutilation, an attempted suicide, a jailbreak, two stormings of criminal hideouts, and a spectacular theft.

In "The Big Knock-Over" the op tells about a double bank robbery committed by an army of 150 criminals and organized by a wizened genius named Popadopalous. After the job has been successfully completed, Popadopalous begins killing off those with power who expect a share of the take. The op, assisted by a new Continental operative named Jack Counihan, is present at Jean Larrouy's speakeasy the night the disgruntled criminals demand their money, frightened because their bosses have been killed, angry because they have been double-crossed. They state their demands to Popadopalous's representative, a "fire-topped giant' named Red O'Leary, who scornfully refuses the angry soldiers and then invites them to object. Larrouy's erupts.

The op and Counihan enter the fight on Red's side and get him to safety, hoping Red will lead them to the stolen money and the mastermind. He does, but only after Counihan gets himself knocked out for making a pass at Nancy Reagan, Red's girl. To make Red easier to handle, the op shoots him just below his right shoulder, pretending someone else fired the shot.

They go to the house of Big Flora, Popadopalous's headquarters. There, in a scene reminiscent of "The House in Turk Street," the op's cover as a friend of Red's is exposed and his life is threatened. Meanwhile, the op has been followed to Big Flora's by Bluepoint Vance, one of Popadopalous's captains who has escaped murder and wants revenge; Vance, in turn, has been followed by the police. When the police arrest Vance, he tells them about Big Flora's. Popadopalous, who seems to the op simply a frightened old man being held prisoner by Big Flora, sees one way out—to bargain for the op's help in his escape by turning over the stolen money, guaranteeing the op's freedom and the arrest of Flora. The story ends as the police storm the house and arrest Big Flora, Red, and their criminal helpers. Only then does the op find out that Popadopalous, whom he has allowed to escape along with Nancy Reagan, was the mastermind of the big knockover.

"$106,000 Blood Money" is about the hunt for Popadopalous, who has a $106,000 bounty on his head from the insurance companies, the bankers' association, and the city. The principals of the story are Tom-Tom Carey, brother of one of the thieves killed after the big knockover, who is after the bounty on Popadopalous; Nancy Reagan, Red O'Leary's girl friend who went with Popadopalous when he escaped from Big Flora's house; and Jack Counihan, the new op.

After considerable investigation, the op discovers that Popadopalous—along with Big Flora who has escaped from jail—is hiding at the home of a wealthy banker, the father of the woman who has been using the alias Nancy Reagan. He arranges to storm the house with Carey, insisting that Counihan come as well. Counihan plans to sneak into the house through a second-story window and get the drop on the criminals while Carey and the op rush the downstairs. When the plan seems to have worked, the op turns on Counihan and accuses him of a double-cross. In the ensuing gunbattle, Counihan, Carey, and Popadopalous are killed. Then the op tells the story.

Nancy Reagan, a wealthy socialite, had seen Red O'Leary at a roadhouse and found him exciting. When she began dating him, she became involved in criminal activities. Because she was the heiress to a multimillion-dollar estate, Popadopalous took a special interest in her, and, partly because she pitied him, partly because she feared he would expose her participation in a series of robberies, she let him hide out at her father's country home. Popadopalous, meanwhile, knowing he controlled her and that she was sole heir to her father's estate, hired a man to kill Nancy Reagan's father, then in Mexico. Carey learned of Popadopalous's plan in Mexico and was blackmailing the old man. Popadopalous expected to eliminate the two threats to his plan—the op and Carey—by using Jack Counihan, who had first become enamored of Nancy Reagan in her days as a socialite and had since been corrupted by her, to lead Carey and the op into a trap so that they could be killed.

Thematically, these two stories are typical of Hammett's mature fiction. There is a conspiracy of criminals, which fails because they double-cross one another. The criminals are motivated solely by greed. The mastermind loses control of his criminal pawns. There is a beautiful woman, morally corrupt, who is deadly dangerous because of her beauty and her wiliness. The story is morally complex: in order to do his job effectively the op must violate some rules, must himself commit criminal acts, as when he shoots Red. There is the further moral dilemma of what to do about a corrupted operative—if he is exposed, the agency's reputation will suffer, yet he cannot be allowed to go unpunished. The op "played the cards so we would get the benefit of the breaks" in the situation that led to Counihan's death. There is the motif of the corrupted rich—and, as is often the case in Hammett's stories, the corruption comes in the second generation to the daughter of a wealthy man. Finally there is the emotional drain, the price the op pays to do his job. The story ends with the op admitting, "I felt tired, washed out."

The real emotional toll of detective work can be seen in the op's seventy-year-old boss, the Old Man. "Fifty years of crook-hunting for the Continental had emptied him of everything except brains and a soft-spoken, gently smiling shell of politeness that was the same whether things went good or bad—and meant as little at one time as another. We who worked under him were proud of his cold-bloodedness."[16]

The cold-blooded detective, like the op and the Old Man, has become an identifying element of hard-boiled detective fiction. In his book on popular fiction, critic John G. Cawelti explained that:

... the hard-boiled detective is a traditional man of virtue in an amoral and corrupt world. His toughness protects the essence of his character, which is honorable and noble. In a world where the law is inefficient and susceptible to corruption, where the recognized social elite is too decadent and selfish to accomplish justice and protect the innocent, the private detective is forced to take over the basic moral functions of exposure, protection, judgment, and execution.[17]

The effect on an honorable man of enforcing a moral code in a corrupt society is frustration at the enormity of his task, and exhaustion—moral and physical. Like the op he is "washed out" by his work. The archetypal hard-boiled detective, who embodies that complex blend of responsibility, nobility, cynicism, and frustration, was created by Hammett.

In 1927, when Hammett was engaging in a variety of literary activities, he tried his hand at poetry. He had placed his first poem, "Caution to Travelers," in the November 1925 issue of *The Lariat*, a little magazine published in Portland, Oregon, devoted to maintaining "high pre-modern standards." The poem was an aphoristic four-line rhyme warning that things held too tightly are the easiest lost. Between March and September 1927 he placed three poems— "Yes" and "Goodbye to a Lady" in the *Stratford Magazine*, "a Periodical for Creative Readers," published in Boston, and "Curse in the Old Manner" in *The Bookman*. The poems are all short—the longest, "Goodbye to a Lady," is only twelve lines—and their common theme reflects the new sexual freedom Hammett was exercising as well as his awareness of traditional poetic conceits. In each of his poems he complained of the reluctance of women to acquiesce to his advances. In "Yes," he writes about a lady "With never a can't or no for me" . . . "Her sole defect in love is this: / She's seldom kept these promises."[18] "Goodbye to a Lady" compares a chaste woman to a blank sheet of writing paper. "Curse in the Old Manner" complains about women who "lengthily wooed, / Are not to be won till one's out of the mood."[19] It was Hammett's last poem published in a magazine. For the next three years, he focused his efforts on novels, book reviews, and an occasional short story.

Hammett's last warm-up before he began writing his first completed novel is a superb story called "The Main Death" (*Black Mask*, June 1927). The op is at his manipulative best on this case in which he is hired by an effeminate antique dealer named Gungen to find a murderer. Gungen had sent his assistant Jeffrey Main to sell a gold tiara for $20,000 cash. Main had been robbed and murdered after he returned from making the deal. Main's wife reported that two men—one of whom was small and may have been a disguised woman—broke into their apartment, struggled with her husband, and shot and robbed him. The only pieces of evidence are Main's gun—the murder weapon—his empty wallet, and a woman's handkerchief embroidered with an E and which smells of the perfume used by Gungen's young wife Enid.

The op soon finds that Gungen is less interested in recovering his money and finding Main's murderers than he is in gaining proof to support his suspicion that his wife was Main's mistress. The op dislikes Gungen and will not participate in the old man's perverse attempts to subjugate his vivacious eighteen-year-old wife. He informs Gungen he will investigate the murder, but he will not violate Mrs. Gungen's privacy. The op learns that Jeffrey Main and Enid Gungen did have an affair and were together when the money was stolen by two men, associates of her maid who threatened to reveal the affair if Main reported them. Despondent, Main went home and committed suicide. To protect her insurance claim Mrs. Main concocted the story of the two intruders and threw her husband's gun, wallet, and the handkerchief she found in his pocket out the window, where they would be found by the police.

The op's problem is to get Gungen his money back without revealing Mrs. Gungen's adultery. He breaks into the thieves' apartment and robs them of the stolen money, threatening to arrest them for robbing Main if they do not quietly leave town; they go, with Mrs. Gungen's maid. Then he goes to Gungen, returns his money, reveals Main's suicide, and tells him that Main had Enid Gungen's handkerchief when he died because he was having an affair with her maid, who had stolen the handkerchief. Mrs. Gungen, then, is free to lead her life, to satisfy her sexual impulses without additional restraints from her distasteful husband.

In "The Main Death" the op's personal sense of right and wrong is the only guide he follows. He is a law unto himself, without regard for social niceties or civil law. To the op, Gungen is a perverted little man who has trapped a woman one-third his age in marriage and who is unable to satisfy her sexual needs. It is worth freeing three thieves and lying to his client, the op decides, to protect her freedom to find suitable lovers outside of marriage.

In Hammett's fiction, there is a curiously moralistic attitude toward sex. Hammett had hinted at sexual aberrations before—"Mike, Alec or Rufus" was about a robbery committed by a transvestite; "The Scorched Face" was about an orgiastic religious cult. Sexual relationships are central to each of his novels. In all cases, aberrant sexual behavior, whether homosexuality, a woman's use of sex to control and destroy men, or a man's attempt to stifle the sexuality of a beautiful young woman, was synonymous with criminality. Healthy sexuality is absent from Hammett's work until *The Thin*

Man, his last novel, and then it is presented flippantly. More often, sexuality in Hammett's work is distorted or perverted and represents the extent to which a character has departed from a romantic ideal of man's capacity for uncorrupted love.

CHAPTER 8

There were plots and counterplots, kidnappings, murders, prisonbreakings, forgeries and burglaries, diamonds large as hats and floating forts larger than Couffignal. It sounds dizzy here, but in the book it was as real as a dime.

Dashiell Hammett in
"The Gutting of Couffignal"

In his first novel Hammett chose to treat the op as lawmaker and enforcer attempting to restore order and thus vitality to an entire town. For his setting he picked a fictional mining town in the Northwest named Personville, but called Poisonville by those who had been there. The town was based on Anaconda, Montana, a mining town Hammett knew well. Jose Hammett was raised in Anaconda and she had taken her elder daughter there in the winter of 1924-1925 while Hammett was recovering from one of his illnesses. After the war Hammett had apparently worked as a Pinkerton in and around Anaconda, probably for one of the many mining operations in the area that had labor troubles.

Southwest Montana was the center of one of the richest ore deposits in America. "Think of it," Cornelius F. Kelly, later president of Anaconda Copper Mining Company, exhorted in 1917, "a hill that has produced 7,000,000,000 pounds of copper, 4,000,000,000 ounces of silver and enough of the combined metals to redeem the debts of all the nations of the earth."[1] Anaconda was the largest mining company that developed in the area, and it led the fight against unionizing the mines from 1912 until the union effort was broken in 1920.

Such laws as there were in Montana existed to serve the interests of the fabulously wealthy mining corporations, a situation that became abundantly clear in the labor struggle there. Union troubles began in 1912 when the Western Federation of Miners (WFM), an AFL-affiliated union, attempted to eliminate the "rustling card" system under which a miner was issued a card which he had to turn over to his employer before he could work. At the termination of the employee's job, his card would be returned to him only at the company's pleasure, and without the card he could not get another job.

After two years in the area, the WFM failed to bring about reform, and the more radical, militant IWW came to town, dynamiting the WFM union hall to mark their arrival. Meanwhile, the companies were importing thugs to resist the efforts of the IWW to organize the mine workers. In the fall of 1917, six months after the United States had declared war on Germany and the resources of the Northwest ore deposits became crucial to the war effort, IWW called a strike to protest the lack of mine safety, low wages ($4.75 a day for underground work), and the rustling card system.[2] That was when Frank Little was lynched, and the companies, supported by wartime patriotic sentiment, declared their own war on labor organizers, a war that lasted from 1917 until 1920.

A series of strikes crippled the mining companies, who responded by bringing in an army of private detectives and hired gunmen, supported by federal troops when necessary, to protect their interests. By 1920 it was dangerous to be pro-union in Montana. In April 1920, for example, fifteen IWW pickets were shot in Butte, about eight miles from Anaconda. No arrests were made, and the next day the *New York Times* reported that "more men reported for work this morning than at any other time since the strike started."[3] The *Times* also reported in spring 1920 that murders were common occurrences in the area and that the IWW office in Butte was located in an abandoned church and manned by a single radical named Dunne. By then the thugs brought in to control the union forces presented their own problem. The war had ended, and the thugs took over the area.[4]

That situation attracted Hammett's interest—a town run by crooks, totally corrupt, in need of a man like the op to restore order.

Various characters and plot situations in the novel had been tested in Hammett's stories. His job now was to put them all together and to sustain for seventy thousand words the effects he had mastered in his short stories. He organized his novel into discrete sections—fifteen thousand to eighteen thousand words each, and he considered it as four long, interconnected stories.

The first episode of *Red Harvest*, "The Cleansing of Poisonville," appeared as the lead story in the November 1927 issue of *Black Mask*. Shaw provided the introduction, characteristically claiming a share of Hammett's accomplishment:

In recent years there have been too many examples where civic politics has degenerated into a business for profit. This story is the first, complete, episode in a series dealing with a city whose administrators have gone mad with power and lust of wealth. It is, also, to our minds, the ideal detective story—the new type of detective fiction which Black Mask is seeking to develop. You go along with the detective, meeting action with him, watching the development as the plot is unfolded, finding the clues as he finds them; and you have the feeling that you are living through the tense, exciting scenes rather than just reading a story. Poisonville is written by a master of his craft.[5]

The four parts of *Red Harvest* appeared monthly in *Black Mask*: "The Cleansing of Poisonville" (November 1927), "Crime Wanted—Male or Female" (December 1927), "Dynamite" (January 1928), and "The 19th Murder" (February 1928). The entire serial was called "The Cleansing of Poisonville" by Shaw, but referred to simply as "Poisonville" by Hammett; it was not titled *Red Harvest* until book publication in February 1929.

"Poisonville" was very well received by *Black Mask* readers and Hammett was encouraged to seek book publication. On February 11, 1928, he addressed a package containing the typescript for "Poisonville" to the "Editorial Department" at Alfred A. Knopf publishers on Fifth Avenue in New York, whose new Borzoi Mystery Series was considered the quality mystery line in America. In a *New Yorker* Profile the firm and its principles were characterized:

Alfred Knopf has a savant's taste for and judgment of good literature, an enormous self-confidence which makes him back these tastes to the limit, a ruthless energy which makes realization out of ideas. But his success is not due to those characteristics alone; he has two powerful allies: his father, who has greatly helped the business, and who has checked his idealism; and his wife, who had supplied the social grace and charm in which he and his father are lacking.[6]

It was Blanche Knopf, Alfred's wife, who would see Hammett's promise as a writer and who would act as editor for his first book.

With his typescript Hammett enclosed a letter offering his work, which he described as an action-detective novel, for publication. He introduced himself as a former Pinkerton operative who in recent years had been published in twenty or twenty-five magazines.[7] Hammett's novel was submitted "over the transom"; that is, there was no agent, and the submission was unsolicited. Generally a reader is assigned to read through such manuscripts, which accumulate in what is called the slush pile. Chances of publication for a manuscript in the slush pile are slight. Hammett beat enormous odds.

On March 12 Blanche Knopf wrote Hammett that she had read "Poisonville" with great interest and that if he would make some revisions, she felt the novel would have a good chance for publication. She felt, first of all, that there was too much violence, particularly in the middle of the book, and that as a result, the reader comes to doubt the story and loses interest. She quoted "one of our readers," apparently editor Harry C. Block, who subsequently did the close editorial work on Hammett's novels, with advice about how to revise the novel. The suggestions were to eliminate one character, gangster Lew Yard, altogether; to eliminate a roadhouse shoot-up; to eliminate the dynamiting of Lew Yard's house; to reorganize the criminal gangs in the novel; to eliminate the dynamiting of the police station; and to devise another method of killing Pete the Finn, a gang leader. Mrs. Knopf also called "Poisonville" a hopeless title.

Eight days after her letter was mailed, Hammett responded, with revised pages of manuscript enclosed. He refused to take Lew Yard out of the story, because, he said, most of the second half of the novel hinges on a conflict in which he is involved. He cut the dynamiting of police headquarters and the attack on the roadhouse, and he revised the dynamiting of Lew Yard's house to a simple offstage shooting. He offered to make additional revisions if she felt them necessary.

Moreover, he changed the titles of chapters XVI, XVIII, and XXI in the novel (the original titles are unknown); he eliminated two of the serial version's twenty-six murders, and he suggested new book titles. He wrote that he had thought "Poisonville" a pretty good title but that after canvassing local San Francisco book dealers who unanimously agreed with Mrs. Knopf about how bad the title "Poisonville" was, he would agree to any of the following:

> The Poisonville Murders
> The Seventeenth Murder
> Murder Plus
> The Willsson Murder
> The City of Death
> The Cleansing of Poisonville
> The Black City
> Red Harvest

Harry Block recommended the last of Hammett's suggestions for the new title and Mrs. Knopf agreed.

Hammett gave Mrs. Knopf a summary of his writing plans—he had started *The Dain Curse*, which he expected to finish by the end of April, and he was planning a detective novel to be written in a modified stream of consciousness, which would reveal all evidence to the reader as the detective learned of it and which would also reveal the detective's reaction to what he learned. He hoped to write this novel without regard for the "thou-shalts and thou-shalt-nots" of magazine publishers. He expected to finish the stream of consciousness novel by late summer, and to write another novel, which he had been planning for two years, before the end of 1928.

Finally, in his March 20 letter he explained that unlike most "moderately literate" people, he took the form of the detective story seriously. He wrote that he believed someone was going to make "literature" out of the detective story, and that he had hopes of being the first.

On April 2, 1928, Mrs. Knopf wrote Hammett that she thought his revisions were very good and she sent him a contract, which he returned on April 9. Publication was still ten months off and the revision continued, with Harry Block acting as Hammett's editor. When revisions were completed hardly a sentence in "The Cleansing of Poisonville" was unaffected. Pronouns were replaced with nouns; contractions were expanded; sentences were reordered within paragraphs; unneeded phrases were deleted. In content, however, little was changed. The serial publication is specific about dates—the action took place in 1927; yet in the novel, no dates are mentioned. There were some name changes of minor characters: a gunman in Whisper Thaler's gang was changed from Hank to Tod, and the head cashier at the First National Bank in Personville was changed from Dutton to Dritton. One of the op's hotels was changed from Hotel Windom to Hotel Crawford. But mostly Hammett's changes were intended to tighten his prose, to make it clearer and sharper.

In *Red Harvest* the op is called to Personville by Donald Willsson, the son of Elihu Willsson, the man who for forty years "had owned Personville, heart, soul, skin and guts." Elihu Willsson owned the Personville Mining Corporation, the city newspapers, and the bank. The story of his company is essentially the story of the mining companies in Butte and Anaconda, Montana, during the 1914-1920 labor disputes: he responded to labor trouble by hiring antilabor thugs, who took over the town. Donald Willsson is murdered before the op can meet with him, and the op is hired by Elihu Willsson, angry because he suspects his son was killed by one of the gangsters in town whom he can no longer control. The op is hired to find Willsson's murderer, who is arrested about one-third of the way through the novel, but, partly out of loyalty to the dead man who first hired him, the op takes on himself the much larger, more important burden of cleaning up the town.

He goes about his job in a characteristic manner. He creates dissent among the troublemakers—Noonan, the corrupt chief of police; Pete the Finn, who controlled bootlegging; Lew Yard, in control of thievery and fencing; Whisper Thaler, the gambling boss; and Elihu Willsson, the man who had opened the town up to them. When the novel ends, only Willsson among them is alive. Most of the twenty-four murders in *Red Harvest* are orchestrated by the op. There is no law to turn to and even if there were, the op reasons, "it's easier to have them killed off, easier and surer."[8]

The op's law is not always easy to know. He does not immediately bring order to Personville; he does his job by creating chaos. There is no sense in the novel of law-abiding citizens oppressed by the criminal leadership of Personville; there are no innocent victims, with the exception of Donald Willsson, who is killed out of a jealous misunderstanding by a man who does not belong to one of the four criminal gangs that control the city. The op simply sees evil in Personville, and he fights it pragmatically and resolutely. He explains his approach to two other Continental ops sent to help him in Personville.

"If it works out the way I want it to, I won't have to report all the distressing details," I said. "It's right enough for the Agency to have rules and regulations, but when you're out on a job you've got to do it the best way you can. And anybody that brings any ethics tò Poisonville is going to get them all rusty. A report is no place for the dirty details, anyway, and I don't want you birds to send any writing back to San Francisco without letting me see it first."[9]

In *Red Harvest*, more than ever before, the op has feelings and frailties. The corruption in Personville maddens him and he feels himself corrupted by the atmosphere. He becomes homicidal, and finally his motive for the cleansing of Personville is revenge and hatred. His extralegal activities, his sense that there is no law except his law, repulses decent people such as Dick Foley, the Continental op who quits the case because he disapproves of the op's behavior. When the op leaves Personville, he leaves his job uncompleted. The gangsters are dead and their mobs are wiped out, but the source of corruption in Personville, weak and greedy Elihu Willsson, remains. Willsson goes unpunished, yet he still has the power of his money, and he still lacks the character required to use his power responsibly.

A central character in *Red Harvest* is Dinah Brand, described by Chief of Police Noonan as "A soiled dove, as the fellow says, a de luxe hustler, a big-league gold digger."[10] She is tough, with a faded beauty that shows the strain of getting by in Poisonville. She is just corrupt enough to avoid being consumed by the corruption around her, and she is the op's best friend in the novel. Dinah Brand lives with a submissive lunger named Rolff, who is tall and thin, described as looking much like Hammett himself. Rolff's tuberculosis has taken his self-respect along with his strength.

The op describes Dinah Brand when he first goes to the house at 1232 Hurricane Street where she and Rolff live:

The young woman got up, kicked a couple of newspapers out of her way, and came to me with one hand out.

She was an inch or two taller than I, which made her about five feet eight. She had a broad-shouldered, full-breasted, round-hipped body and big muscular legs. The hand she gave me was soft, warm, strong. Her face was the face of a girl of twenty-five already showing signs of wear. Little lines crossed the corners of her big ripe mouth. Fainter lines were beginning to make nets around her thick-lashed eyes. They were large eyes, blue and a bit blood-shot.

Her coarse hair—brown—needed trimming and was parted crookedly. One side of her upper lip had been rouged higher than the other. Her dress was of a particularly unbecoming wine color, and it gaped here and there down one side, where she had neglected to snap the fasteners or they had popped open. There was a run down the front of her left stocking.

This was the Dinah Brand who took her pick of Poisonville's men, according to what I had been told."[11]

Dinah Brand gets along by taking advantage of situations. She explains: "It's not so much the money. It's the principle of the thing. If a girl's got something that's worth something to somebody, she's a boob if she doesn't collect."[12]

Like Hammett's other women, Dinah Brand is dangerous. As the op tells her: "You seem to have a gift for stirring up murderous notions in your boyfriends."[13] But she is less villainous than Elvira/Jeanne Delano in "The House in Turk Street" and "The Girl with the Silver Eyes" and Nancy Reagan in "The Big Knock-Over" and "$106,000 Blood Money." Dinah Brand is the best woman one could expect in Personville; she guides the op in his investigation; and his respect for her toughness is translated into something approaching real affection, even while he realizes that his feelings for her are self-destructive.

The op makes a crucial mistake in *Red Harvest*. One night in Dinah Brand's apartment he succumbs to the pressures of cleansing Personville. When he complains to her that he is "going blood-simple," getting enjoyment out of planning murders, she realizes the problem: "your nerves are shot. You've been through too much excitement in the last few days. Keep it up and you're going to have the heebie-jeebies for fair, a nervous breakdown."[14] To calm his nerves, she drinks with him and then gives him a dose of Dan Rolff's laudanum, after which the op lapses into unconsciousness. He later describes two dreams he has, one about a woman he has difficulty recognizing but whom he realizes is very important to him. That dream ends when after a long search over "half the streets in the United States" he finds her at a train station and is embarrassed as everyone stares at them kissing. The second dream has the op with an open knife in his hand hunting a man he hates. He chases "the little brown man" to a rooftop. When the op catches the man he realizes they have both gone off the roof and "we dropped giddily down toward the millions of upturned faces in the plaza, miles down."[15] He wakes up to find his hand on an ice pick in Dinah Brand's chest. She is dead.

The op believes he did not stab her, and at the end of the novel he finds the murderer, who confesses. But he was not her protector either. She was killed in his presence, and he would have been able to prevent her murder if he had been stronger—if he had not required the laudanum to calm his nerves. Her murder is the stimulus that causes the op to continue his work in Poisonville. He must clear himself of the killing and, insofar as he is able, absolve himself of his own guilt. When he finally leaves Personville, the op is a solitary figure whose work has left him demoralized.

After Hammett became active in leftist politics in the mid-1930s, it became fashionable to read *Red Harvest* as a Marxist statement on political corruption and the abuse of power by governmental officials who have no concern for their democratic responsibilities. That is an imaginative approach to Hammett's novel—or, in fact, to any of his writing—but a misguided one. Bill Quint, the IWW leader in Personville, is a hollow idealist whose arguments are unpersuasive. When he had an affair with Dinah Brand, she used information she got from him about planned IWW disruptions to play the stock market. There are no masses of politically dispossessed people in *Red Harvest*—only a detective and a group of crooks. Hammett never used his fiction as a forum for his political beliefs. Indeed, he kept whatever political convictions he had in 1929 to himself.

Red Harvest was published on February 1, 1929. The dedication was to Joseph Thompson Shaw, who had most encouraged Hammett to try writing a novel. Though it was amiably received, *Red Harvest*, which sold for $2.50, was not a best-seller. The first printing (probably of about three thousand copies) lasted for all of 1929; a second printing came in March 1930, a month after *The Maltese Falcon* was published; and a third printing in March 1931, just before publication of *The Glass Key*.[16]

Reviewers generally recognized that *Red Harvest* was a different kind of mystery. Writing for *The Bookman*, Herbert Asbury proclaimed: "It is doubtful if even Ernest Hemingway has ever written more effective dialogue than may be found within the pages of this extraordinary tale of gunmen, gin and gangsters. . . .[*Red Harvest* is] the liveliest detective story that has been published in a decade."[17] Walter R. Brooks in *Outlook and Independent* concurred: "A thriller that lives up to the blurb on the jacket is unusual enough to command respect. When, in addition, it is written by a man who plainly knows his underworld and can make it come alive for his readers, when the action is exciting and the conversation racy and amusing—well, you'll want to read it. . . .

"We recommend this one without reservation. We gave it A plus before we'd finished the first chapter."[18]

There were conservative responses as well. "F. M." in the *Boston Evening Transcript* wrote: "If the story has a purpose, it may be to show up the possible rottenness of certain city governments, but it seems more like an attempt to see how deeply the author can make his readers wade in gore and in the slime of the worst criminal life. There has been in detective stories a decided increase in the number of murders deemed necessary to complete the story. Such an appetite will certainly be glutted in 'Red Harvest.' It is crowded with characters—it had to be to supply material for the murders—the action moves dizzily and when it is all over, the reader wonders just what it was all about."[19]

By the time *Red Harvest* was published by Knopf, Hammett was well into the writing of his third novel. The reception of "Poisonville" and the book contract had given him a new outlook on the profession of authorship. Hammett enjoyed his newfound celebrity and began to develop a public image, enhanced by his sophisticated appearance. By the end of 1927 his hair, which he wore in a full pompadour, was almost entirely gray, and he had grown a mustache, which he kept, except for brief periods, until his death. Under a new provision that allowed dental work, the Veterans Administration dentists had attended to his rotten teeth, improving his appearance. To complement his lean good looks, Hammett dressed well, even overdressed. His acquaintances described him as a dandy.

The money was not big in 1927, but it was more than Hammett had ever seen. It is not known what Shaw paid Hammett for "The Cleansing of Poisonville," but he probably got as much as three or four thousand dollars, certainly no less than $1,200, and in addition to that, there was the small amount of money he received for reviewing books for *The Saturday Review of Literature* and payment for the occasional story he wrote for *Black Mask*. A very conservative estimate of Hammett's income in 1927 would be $3,500, or about twice his highest income in any year up to that time.

However, Hammett had a family to support. His daughter Mary started the first grade at the Valley High elementary school in the fall. Josephine was one year old in May. He still maintained two residences, as he did for most of the time until he moved away from his family permanently in fall 1929. Though the Hammetts lived modestly, the expense of operating two households was a drain on his income.

CHAPTER 9

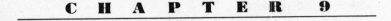

If . . . I make more than a transient connection with Fox, I'll probably . . . [stick] to the more objective filmable forms.

> Dashiell Hammett to Blanche Knopf
> April 9, 1928

Nineteen twenty-eight was a very busy year for Hammett. He rewrote *Red Harvest*, which was published early in 1929, and he wrote his second novel, published in book form as *The Dain Curse*, for serial publication in *Black Mask* beginning in November.

Early in April while he was revising *Red Harvest* for Knopf, Hammett received a request from the William Fox Studios in Hollywood for story material that could be adapted to the movies. After asking Mrs. Knopf's advice on April 6, Hammett sent them the novel and half a dozen short stories. He wrote Mrs. Knopf on April 9 that he was hopeful they would produce a movie from his work and that he would be writing objective, filmable novels in the future to make his work more attractive to filmmakers. In late June 1928, after he had finished his second novel, *The Dain Curse*, Hammett went to Hollywood to negotiate with Fox about rights to the published work he had submitted and an original screenplay he planned to write. But the studio refused to put up any money and the deal fell through. At the end of 1928 Hammett listed his occupation as writer in the San Francisco city directory for the first time; for the three previous years he had called himself an advertising man.

After each of his first three novels, Hammett wrote one op story

DASHIELL HAMMETT

for *Black Mask* and that was his only story publication until after the
next novel. When he had finished "The Cleansing of Poisonville,"
Hammett wrote "This King Business," a sixteen-thousand-word
adventure story that takes the op to the small, recently formed
fictional country of Muravia in eastern Europe. It is the only story of
Hammett's, except for "The Road Home" (December 1922) and
"Ber-Bulu" (March 1925) set outside the United States. Apart from
the time he spent in Alaska during World War II, Hammett never
traveled outside the country during his life, but he was avidly interested in foreign countries and in world history. "This King Business" is a satirical story about Lionel Grantham, a wealthy young
American from a prominent family who is conned into believing he
can become king of Muravia. Hammett makes the story seem plausible, and focuses on the procedure of a coup that will unseat the
elected leaders, repeal the constitution, and install Grantham as
King Lionel the First. The op becomes the determining force in
Muravian political affairs, as he arranges to have Grantham installed
in his nominal kingly position in order to bargain with those really in
power for the return of the $3 million Grantham has spent on the
Muravian revolution (plus a return on his investment) for King
Lionel's abdication. He is successful; he extricates Grantham from
what was a dangerous position and he leaves Muravia in better shape
than he found it—in the hands of a lazy strong man who likes things
to run smoothly so he will not be bothered with problems. The
theme of political corruption—always handled without adopting a
political stance—became a common one for Hammett in the late
1920s and early 1930s.

Hammett's chief work in 1928 was his second novel, *The Dain
Curse*, completed in June. Like *Red Harvest*, the novel seems to have
grown from a short story—this time "The Scorched Face" (May
1925)—and it is an attempt once again to portray a beautiful,
dangerous woman, but as a victim, not as a villainess.

Hammett sent one copy of his typescript to Shaw and, on June 25,
1928, one copy to Knopf. Shaw was delighted. He published the
novel in four parts: "Black Lives" (November 1928), "The Hollow
Temple" (December 1928), "Black Honeymoon" (January 1929),
and "Black Riddle" (February 1929). But at Knopf, Harry Block
wanted changes, and by the time Shaw had published the novel, it
had been rewritten for book publication in much the same way as
Red Harvest had been.

On July 10 Harry Block sent Hammett his editorial suggestions for *The Dain Curse*. Mrs. Knopf was in Europe and he did not want to delay his response until she returned. He said he was pleased with the novel and that Knopf would certainly publish it, though he felt it was not up to the standard set by *Red Harvest*. Block thought the novel was too complex, that the three sections of the novel were too independent, and that reader interest lagged between the sections. He also felt that there was too much violence and too many characters.

Hammett was not so agreeable about revisions as before. He wrote back that he was not sure he would make the revisions or that he was able. His new novel, *The Maltese Falcon*, was well along, he wrote, and he preferred to give his attention to that book because it was better than *The Dain Curse*. But Hammett was not in a strong enough position to ignore Block's suggestions. In September he wrote Block that he had considered all the suggested alterations and had been working on them throughout the summer. It was March 1929, though, the month after Shaw completed serial publication of the novel, before Hammett submitted his revised typescript to Knopf. On June 16, 1929, after all revisions were completed, Hammett wrote Block that his editorial suggestions for *The Dain Curse* had been troublesome, because the first forty pages were very heavily edited, the rest hardly edited at all. As a result of accepting Block's early changes, Hammett had to alter the end to maintain some consistency of style, and that, he complained, involved too much work.

The Dain Curse is generally considered to be Hammett's weakest novel, and he himself called it "a silly story" in a 1932 interview.[1] But while it does not rank with his best fiction, *The Dain Curse* has been underrated. Hammett was experimenting, attempting a more "literary" structure than he had ever tried before. His use of symbolism and imagery patterns, such as the descriptions of characters by animal metaphors, is somewhat awkward at times, and the story teeters uncomfortably on the edge of mysticism, a continuing interest of Hammett's. Finally, though, it is a successful novel that bears up fairly well under close scrutiny.

The Dain Curse is the last op novel, and the op appeared in only three more short stories. The characterization of the op is the strength of the novel. His nobility is emphasized once again, perhaps more dramatically than before, by his vulnerability. The op is not immune to temptation, fatigue, and fear; rather, he resists them. His personal involvement with the beautiful woman he cares for is greater than ever, and the selflessness required of him to solve his case tests the basic principles of his detective's code.

The beautiful woman in *The Dain Curse* is Gabrielle Leggett, who believes she has inherited a family curse from her mother which has caused Gabrielle to corrupt those closest to her. She has been told that when she was a child she murdered her mother as part of a cruel game devised by Alice Dain, Gabrielle's aunt. Alice Dain was in love with Gabrielle's father, whose real name is Maurice de Mayenne. He took the blame for his wife's murder to shield Gabrielle; he was subsequently convicted and sent to Devil's Island, from which he escaped and fled to San Francisco, taking the alias Edgar Leggett. Alice Dain and Gabrielle began searching for Gabrielle's father after they learned of his escape, and during the search they came to know the mad villain of the novel, the novelist Owen Fitzstephan, himself a Dain, Gabrielle's second cousin. When Alice Dain finds Leggett, she forces him to marry her.

In the course of an affair with Alice Dain, Fitzstephan has fallen in love with Gabrielle and has set out with the determination of a psychotic genius to have her. He murders first her father, then her stepmother-aunt. He causes her to come under the influence of a religious cult leader and to become addicted to morphine. When the op frees her from the influence of the cult and Gabrielle marries, Fitzstephan hires a man to murder her husband.

Gabrielle believes herself to be the cause of all the deaths in the book—eight murders occur during the present-time action—and it is due only to the op's sagacity and perseverance that she is not blamed for them finally. He exposes Fitzstephan as the criminal responsible for the murders, and he cures Gabrielle of her morphine addiction. When the book ends, Gabrielle is emotionally a whole person for the first time.

The Dain Curse is an allegory of pure evil attempting to pervert innocence. Fitzstephan's motive is not so simple as that of Hammett's other criminals. He does not want money or power or fame; he simply wants Gabrielle, not exclusively in a sexual sense—he had ample opportunity to rape her or to take sexual advantage of her in her drug-induced stupors—but to possess her body and soul. Fitzstephan half accomplishes his goal: he convinces Gabrielle that she is evil and possesses her insofar as he has made her to deny herself to any other man. In her demented state, Gabrielle interprets men's normal sexual advances toward her as proof of her corrupting influence. As a result, she has resisted all sexual advances, even those of her husband whom she loved "because he was clean and fine,"[2] and she is a virgin when the op solves the case.

The op's success in curing Gabrielle is measured by his ability to rekindle her sexuality. He accomplishes this goal in two ways: first, he cures her of morphine addiction, which caused her sexual interests to wane and made her see the advances of others as abnormal; second, he convinces her that she is not cursed and that she is safe with him—and she is. It is a sure sign of her cure when she offers herself to the op, and he is perfectly in character when he refuses her:

"I'm twice your age, sister; an old man. I'm damned if I'll make a chump of myself by telling you why I [went through all this with you], why it was neither revolting nor disgusting, why I'd do it again and be glad of the chance."

She jumped out of her chair, her eyes round and dark, her mouth trembling.

"You mean——?"

"I don't mean anything that I'll admit," I said; "and if you're going to parade around with that robe hanging open you're going to get yourself some bronchitis. You ex-hopheads have to be careful about catching cold."[3]

As is typical in Hammett's later fiction, Owen Fitzstephan is not punished by law; justice is meted out to him by his accomplices. A minor character named Tom Fink is afraid Fitzstephan will implicate him in the murders at the Temple of the Holy Grail, headquarters for a fraudulent, mystical religious cult where Gabrielle was first addicted to morphine. He fashions a bomb to silence Fitzstephan, but it is only partially successful, blowing away most of the right side of Fitzstephan's body. When Fitzstephan is tried for one of his murders, the courts are more merciful—after a successful plea of not guilty by reason of insanity, Fitzstephan spent a year in a state asylum and was discharged: "they thought he was too badly crippled ever to be dangerous again.[4]

Hammett develops Gabrielle's psychological character by a pattern of animal imagery, which became a point of contention between him and Harry Block. Block argued that Gabrielle was repulsive as Hammett described her, and it would be difficult for a reader to imagine her as beautiful or to be sympathetic toward her.

"Look at my ears—without lobes, pointed tops. People don't have ears like that. Animals do." She turned her face to me again still holding back her hair. "Look at my forehead—its smallness, its shape—animal. My teeth." She bared them—white, small, pointed. "The shape of my face." Her hands left her hair and slid down her cheeks, coming together under her oddly pointed small chin.[5]

Hammett argued in his letter of March 30, 1929, that he gave Gabrielle many of his own physical characteristics—lobeless ears, stiff-jointed thumbs, and an underdeveloped little toe—and that he wanted her to be somewhat objectionable at first so he could lure the reader slowly into sympathy with her. After stating his argument he told Block that if he still thought Gabrielle's description should be emended—if he was really sure—he should go ahead and do the job himself.[6] Block deferred to Hammett's judgment.

Hammett responded also to Block's objection that the novel was disjointed due to its having been written for serial publication. Hammett obliged on the matter of structure by "bridging the gaps" between the parts of the story, but he admitted that "the dingus is still undoubtedly rather complicated."[7] The structure of the novel is indeed complex. The histories of the Leggett family and the Dain Curse are revealed in the op's first-person narration of a series of cases he is employed to solve. He is first hired by an insurance agency to investigate the theft of diamonds stolen from the Leggett house. By the end of the first quarter of the book, he has found that Mrs. Leggett (Alice Dain), Gabrielle's aunt and now stepmother, arranged the theft and gave the diamonds to a crooked private investigator she had earlier hired to find her brother-in-law, Edgar Leggett (Gabrielle's father). He also reveals that Mrs. Leggett had arranged the murder of her sister, which she tricked four-year-old Gabrielle into committing some fifteen years earlier. In addition, she seems responsible for Leggett's "suicide," the murder of a would-be blackmailer, and finally she herself appears to commit suicide. At that point, the case seems solved for the op. He considers the case "*Discontinued*," and the first part ends.

Soon, the op is assigned to the Leggett matter again, this time hired by the lawyer administering the Leggett estate, to watch over Gabrielle. She is despondent over what she now believes is the family curse that caused her to murder her mother and that has caused the deaths in the first part of the book. She has gone to live at the Temple of the Holy Grail under the care of religious charlatans. After two more murders, the op exposes the fraudulence of the Temple, and Gabrielle leaves to marry her fiance. Thus, the second part ends.

The final part of the book—published in *Black Mask* in two

sections—begins with the op being wired by Eric Collinson, Gabrielle's husband, to come immediately because there is trouble. When the op arrives, Collinson is dead. The investigation of his death leads to the discovery that Fitzstephan, who has appeared throughout as a seemingly interested spectator, has instigated all of the criminal action of the book.

Unlike Shaw, who felt the more murders the better, Block and Mrs. Knopf objected to the violence of the novel. Hammett eliminated one murder in the book version of the novel, which he admitted was still "rather full of slaughter." According to the standards established by other hard-boiled writers in the 1930s, and certainly by comparison to *Red Harvest*, *The Dain Curse* is not excessively violent; but in 1929, Hammett's novels were considered to be suitable only for mature readers. In *Death in the Afternoon* (1932) Ernest Hemingway tells about his wife reading him *The Dain Curse* aloud and substituting "umpty-umped for the words killed, cut the throat of, blew the brains out of, spattered around the room, and so on,"[8] to keep their children from being unduly disturbed.

The novel was dedicated to Albert S. Samuels, and it was calculated to delight him, filled with in-jokes about the diamond business and Samuels's store. In an interview, just before his death, with William F. Nolan, Samuels recalled the characters' names Hammett had taken from Samuels employees: "Leggett was our switchboard operator. . . , David Riese, who also worked for us, became a doctor in the novel—and a minor character was named after our Mrs. Priestly, who was in silverware."[9]

When *The Dain Curse* was published in America on July 19, 1929, the reviewers were complimentary. It was generally agreed that the plot was intelligent and gripping, that Hammett's dialogue was splendid, and that the revelation of Fitzstephan as the mad criminal in the novel was unexpected, yet not unexplainable. Walter R. Brooks in the *Outlook and Independent* wrote: "We can think of only one story of the kind better than this second book of Mr. Hammett's, and that is his first book";[10] and Will Cuppy in the *New York Herald Tribune* "recommended" the book "for its weird characters and really astonishing speed."[11] *The Dain Curse* brought Hammett his first notice in the *New York Times*, a favorable review,[12] and reinforced his growing reputation as a mystery writer.

Mystery writer was a tag Hammett was coming more and more to resent, regardless of the adjective which preceded it. He himself, as his book reviews in *The Saturday Review of Literature* make clear, considered mystery writing as a subliterary genre. He was eager either to elevate the genre or to write outside it. He had already introduced new elements into novels—the sociopolitical realism of *Red Harvest*, the psychologically disturbed characterizations in *The Dain Curse*. But, as before when the popularity of the op in *Black Mask* dictated that Hammett write op stories, now that he was on the verge of big money, the identification of Hammett's name with detective fiction was too strong for him to abandon the genre. So he continued to write detective novels, but they depended less on plot than on character. His novels took on a richness of characterization and content that was then rare in the genre.

The immediate sales of *The Dain Curse* were better than for *Red Harvest*. Priced at $2.00, the novel quickly sold its first printing (probably of some five thousand copies, though the exact figure is unknown) and went into two more printings in August. There were no paperbacks as we know them today, and when a book had exhausted its hardcover sales it was effectively finished. There were, however, several hardcover companies, such as Grosset & Dunlap, who bought the rights to successful books and reprinted them in cheap formats to sell at about one-half the trade publication price. Grosset & Dunlap republished both *Red Harvest* (in 1931) and *The Dain Curse* (in 1930) and each title sold out multiple printings,[13] though the income to Hammett was minimal.

The Dain Curse was the first of Hammett's books printed for distribution in Great Britain as well as in the United States. When it was initially published, *Red Harvest* had some limited British circulation, but that was due to imported copies of the American printing. *The Dain Curse* was published in England by Knopf in January 1930, six months after American publication. The interest of British readers in his second novel is an indication of the popularity of Hammett's novels (though he was received at first with mild disdain by English reviewers), but he was not enriched significantly by foreign sales of his books. The printings were low and the royalties were reduced.

CHAPTER 10

Spade had no original. He is a dream man in the sense that he is what most of the private detectives I worked with would like to have been and what quite a few of them in their cockier moments thought they approached. For your private detective does not–or did not ten years ago when he was my colleague–want to be an erudite solver of riddles in the Sherlock Holmes manner; he wants to be a hard and shifty fellow, able to take care of himself in any situation, able to get the best of anybody he comes in contact with, whether criminal, innocent by-stander or client.

Dashiell Hammett
Introduction to Modern Library
publication of *The Maltese Falcon* (1934)

In his March 8, 1929, letter to Harry Block, Hammett promised to have his third novel, *The Maltese Falcon*, ready for him by the following month. He had been working on the novel for nearly a year, a long time for Hammett. Internal evidence shows that his last draft was written no earlier than December 1928, the time of the action in the book. He admitted to Block that the novel should have been ready months ago and that he thought it would be a rather satisfactory job. Hammett said it was the first fiction he had written that, whatever its faults, was the best he was capable of writing at the time he was writing it.

On June 14, 1929, Hammett mailed *The Maltese Falcon* to Block at Knopf, and on June 16 he sent Block a letter about the novel, expressing confidence in its quality and warning Block to go easy on the editing of the book. Hammett also needed money. He was contemplating leaving San Francisco and he called on Knopf for an advance against royalties, which he had not received on his previous novels, to finance his move. He suggested various plans for a quick publication. He could provide a book of connected stories—like *Red Harvest* and *The Dain Curse*, he pointed out—and he suggested "The Big Knock-Over" and "$106,000 Blood Money" as the best choice. Moreover, he claimed to have two hundred fifty thousand words of short stories about the op, of which he considered about 80 percent worthy of republication. He suggested a collection of the best of them—which he would revise for book publication—to be published under the title *The Continental Op*. In addition, he had a Frankenstein-like horror story entitled "AEAEA"; a detective story called "Two Two's Twenty Two"; "The Secret Emperor," which he described as a "political murder mystery"; a novel similar to *The Maltese Falcon* called "That Night in Singapore"; and an underworld mystery called "Dead Man's Friday." Of these works that Hammett claimed to have completed, only a fragment and notes for "The Secret Emperor," which was abandoned in 1925, and "AEAEA" are known to exist among his manuscripts, and none of these works was ever published. On July 14 Hammett wrote Block that he had reconsidered book publication for these works and had decided against it because too much rewriting would be required. Hammett had also intended to do a story about a gunman, he said, but Herbert Asbury had told him W. R. Burnett's *Little Caesar* (1932), which Hammett had not read, was a good gangster novel, and he decided to give up the idea, because he felt gangsters would be out of fashion within a year's time anyway.

Block liked *The Maltese Falcon* and he asked for only minor revisions. He felt Spade's sexual attraction to Brigid O'Shaugnessy was at times too explicitly described, and he objected to the homosexuality in the novel. Block argued that while such topics might be acceptable in an "ordinary novel," they were not appropriate for detective fiction. Hammett disagreed and finally they compromised on minor rewriting of the scenes Block found offensive.[1]

Shaw serialized the novel in five parts that ran monthly from September 1929 to January 1930, but *The Maltese Falcon* was not episodic as *Red Harvest* and *The Dain Curse* had been. Hammett made no concession to magazine publication for his third novel.

In his introduction to the 1934 Modern Library edition of *The Maltese Falcon* (the first detective novel included in that prestigious series), Hammett explained how the novel came to him: "If this book had been written with the help of an outline or notes or even a clearly

defined plot-idea in my head I might now be able to say how it came
to be written and why it took the shape it did, but all I can remember
about its invention is that somewhere I had read of the peculiar
rental agreement between Charles V and the Order of the Hospital
of Saint John of Jerusalem, that in a short story called THE WHOSIS KID I
had failed to make the most of a situation I liked, that in another
called THE GUTTING OF COUFFIGNAL I had been equally unfortunate with an
equally promising denouement, and that I thought I might have
better luck with these two failures if I combined them with the
Maltese lease in a longer story."[2] Hammett failed to mention that
Brigid O'Shaughnessy, the villainess of *The Maltese Falcon*, was the
epitome of the beautiful, dangerous woman he had been developing
in his stories since spring 1924.

For his third novel Hammett turned away from the op. He
created a new detective, a loner who operates best outside an agency
and outside the law. Spade has much in common with the Continental op—they adhere to the same detective's code; they both
believe in a personal sense of right which supersedes civil law; they
both regard crooked or incompetent policemen with disdain and
grudgingly respect the good ones; they both are experienced travelers on the back streets and in the alleyways of the city; most impor-
tantly, they both have the calloused emotions it takes to do their jobs
effectively.

In a switch from the first-person narration of all the op stories and
novels, Hammett adopted a third-person narrative voice for *The
Maltese Falcon* that gives the characterization of Spade added
strength. Sam Spade is the romantic embodiment of the private
detective's code. He would never discuss his cases, as a first-person
structure implies the narrator is doing. His survival depends on his
being an entirely private and unpredictable man. By telling Spade's
story in the omniscient third-person voice, Hammett was able to
characterize him fully while not compromising that characterization
with the implied openness of a first-person narration.

Spade has been called stupid and crooked but he is, of course,
neither. He is a man doing his job as well as he knows how, without
superior powers, but with an unusual savvy gained by experience
and an instinct for survival in a lawless city. Like the op in the stories
and the novels, Spade takes his job personally. He becomes emotionally involved, and not always for the best motives, but he never allows
his emotions to overrule his instinct for survival. Spade is not a fool
like his partner Miles Archer.

The novel is set in San Francisco during a five-day period—between Wednesday and Sunday—in December 1928. The time can be identified by a clue Hammett gives: Sam Spade meets Joel Cairo outside the Geary Street Theater and over Cairo's shoulder is a theater sign "on which George Arliss was shown costumed as Shylock." Arliss starred in *The Merchant of Venice* at the Geary Street Theater from December 3-15, 1928. Spade's meeting with Cairo, on a Thursday night, would have been on the sixth or the thirteenth of December.[3]

The action of the novel is initiated when Brigid O'Shaughnessy comes to Spade and Archer for help. She hopes to use them in a plot to rid herself of Floyd Thursby, her criminal boyfriend whom she befriended when she needed protection from others while in search of the Maltese falcon, an ornamental artifact of incalculable worth. She fabricated for Spade a tale about her sister who had run away with Thursby. Though Thursby had been located, she said, he would not tell her where her sister was. She wanted to hire Sam Spade to shadow Thursby and find her sister. The purpose of this deception (which is similar to a scheme Hammett first used in "Who Killed Bob Teal?" in 1924) was to get rid of Thursby so that when the falcon arrived in San Francisco by boat, under an arrangement which only Brigid and he knew about, she would not have to share the bird.

Thursby had worked as a bodyguard for a gambler who had been murdered and he feared reprisal. Brigid hoped that one of two things would happen when he found he was being followed: he would kill the shadow, or in the attempt he would be killed himself. If Thursby were killed, Brigid's problem was solved; if he won the gunbattle Brigid anticipated, she could finger him for murder; but if he did not react as Brigid suspected he would, she would take matters into her own hands by killing the shadow herself and implicating Thursby. Brigid was a beautiful woman and she coldly used her attractiveness to manipulate others. She asked that Spade or Archer personally shadow Thursby so that if she had to resort to her third alternative, she could use her charm to spring the trap.

Archer eagerly took the job out of dumb lust, and Brigid killed him and Thursby that night. When she had to murder Archer herself, Brigid saw that she could also get rid of Thursby for good by killing him and pointing suspicion at Spade, who would seem to have murdered Thursby out of revenge for Archer's death. It was no secret that Spade disliked his partner and was having an affair with

Archer's wife, and he was suspected of both murders. Spade's instinct for self-protection made him pursue the case. If he did not find the murderer, the district attorney would indict him; if he did not see that Archer's murderer was punished, the word would spread that Spade was weak, and he would be vulnerable, because in his world weaknesses are always exploited.

The object of Brigid's plot was to obtain a sixteenth-century bejeweled falcon given as tribute by a group of Crusaders to Charles V of Spain. She is in competition with two others, also on the falcon's trail, who matched her ruthlessness: Caspar Gutman, another of Hammett's criminal masterminds, and Joel Cairo, an affected homosexual who survived a temporary alliance with Brigid only because he was sexually immune to her attractions.

Spade is confronted by Cairo and Gutman, as well as the police and the district attorney, but the key relationship is that of Spade and Brigid. At the end of the novel Spade, who has enjoyed the temptation of Brigid's charms, is faced with a choice: he must either turn her in to the police for Thursby's and Archer's murders, or spare her and somehow attempt to beat the raps himself. She offers to go away with him, to love him. But although Brigid is sexually enticing, she is a very dangerous companion, who knows no loyalty. She has lied to Spade repeatedly about the gravest matters, and clearly he does not trust her; moreover, she is a criminal who killed his partner as easily as she would have killed him if circumstances had been different, and who then allowed Spade to be accused of murder himself. Only a fool—like Miles Archer had been—would allow Brigid to go free. If Spade ever acts foolishly in the novel, it is because he agonizes over his final decision to hand Brigid over to the police, when, in fact, he had no reasonable alternative. He was fighting emotions that he knew would be fatal to him.

After *The Dain Curse* Hammett was trying to do more with his fiction than tell a story. He was seeing his characters not only as people playing out a set of roles but as representatives of general themes and conflicts. *The Maltese Falcon* is a novel about the destructive power of greed, and in the artifact referred to in the title, Hammett found a suitable symbol for illusory wealth which also met his criterion of historical accuracy.

The history of the Hospitalers of Saint John is essentially as Hammett gave it in his novel. The Hospitalers were a religious order charged in about 1023 with providing lodging for the healthy and care for the sick pilgrims making their way to Jerusalem. They were the unimaginably wealthy inhabitants of the Isle of Rhodes from 1307 to 1523, when they were displaced by the Turks and by Suleiman the Magnificent. In 1530 they settled in Malta under the guardianship of Emperor Charles V. Grand Master Villiers de l'Isle Adam was their leader from 1521-1534.

The Emperor gave the Hospitalers four islands—not three as Gutman says when he recites the Maltese falcon's history for Spade—Malta, Tripoli, Gozo, and Comino "in order that they may perform in peace the duties of their Religion for the benefit of the Christian community, and employ their forces and arms against the perfidious enemies of the Holy Faith." Unlike the story told by Gutman, the Hospitalers were less than pleased with the gift of barren islands inhabited by barbarians, but the islands were "free and independent gifts at the price of the simple presentation of a yearly falcon on All-Saints Day."[4] What form the first annual gift of a falcon took is unclear, but probably it was a live bird. Later, be-jeweled statuettes were given.

There is no Maltese falcon in Hammett's novel—only the prom-ise, the hope of one, and only a worthless imitation of the real thing. In 1928 the falcon is without a rightful owner, and the promise of wealth it represents attracts only the dreamers consumed with greed. In the words of Gutman, "it took me seventeen years to locate that bird, but I did it. I wanted it, and I'm not a man that's easily discouraged when he wants something."[5] What he had located was a worthless replica.

The falcon was a symbol of the Hospitalers' fealty to Charles V, and by that gift they were able to live in a place that was their own. Sam Spade, too, is forced to pay a kind of tribute to the powers who control San Francisco—which he refers to three times in the novel as his city. He explains to Gutman:

At one time or another I've had to tell everybody from the Supreme Court down to go to hell, and I've got away with it. I got away with it because I never let myself forget that a day of reckoning was coming. I never forget that when the day of reckoning comes I want to be all set to march into headquarters pushing a victim in front of me, saying: "Here, you chumps, is your criminal." As long as I can do that I can put my thumb to my nose and wriggle my fingers at all the laws in the book. The first time I can't do it my name's Mud. There hasn't been a first time yet. This isn't going to be it. That's flat.
. . . This is my city and my game. I could manage to land on my feet—sure—this time, but the next time I tried to put over a fast one

they'd stop me so fast I'd swallow my teeth. Hell with that. You birds'll be in New York or Constantinople or some place else. I'm in business here.[6]

Spade's business leaves no place for dreams. Even in the role he assumes as an accomplice to Gutman, Spade chooses a sure $10,000 to a split of the profit when the falcon is located. The similar dream he is invited to entertain of Brigid's love is also rejected in order to pay his tribute to the district attorney by handing over a murderer. The price Spade pays for his place to live is the rejection of dreams.

Running throughout *The Maltese Falcon* is the motif of the unexpected and the way people deal with it. The most critically discussed part of any Hammett work is the Flitcraft parable Sam Spade tells Brigid about a man satisfied with his well-ordered life who is one day nearly killed by a falling beam. His response is to adjust his life to random possibility by leaving his well-ordered life behind him and setting up a new life—which in time becomes just as ordered as his old one—under a new name, Charles Pierce. (The nineteenth-century philosopher Charles Sanders Peirce wrote extensively about random occurrence.) Spade explains about Flitcraft: "He adjusted himself to beams falling, and then no more of them fell, and he adjusted himself to them not falling."[7] Like Flitcraft, Spade adjusted his life to circumstance.

With the publication of *The Maltese Falcon*, Hammett's reputation was made. In *The New Republic* Donald Douglas wrote: "It is not the tawdry gum-shoeing of the ten-cent magazine. It is the genuine presence of the myth. . . . No one save Mr. Hammett could have woven . . . such a silver-steely mesh."[8] Walter R. Brooks in *Outlook and Independent* wrote: "This is not only probably the best detective story we have ever read, it is an exceedingly well-written novel. There are few of Mr. Hammett's contemporaries who can write prose as clean-cut, vivid and realistic."[9] Ted Shane in *Judge* wrote: "The writing is better than Hemingway; since it conceals not softness but hardness,"[10] and Alexander Woollcott called *The Maltese Falcon* "the best detective story America has yet produced."[11] Will Cuppy in the *New York Herald Tribune* agreed: "it would not surprise us one whit if Mr. Hammett should turn out to be the Great American Mystery Writer. (The fact is, he may be that right now, and this department is merely hopping aboard the Hammett bandwagon ere it be too late—Herbert Asbury, Walter Brooks and Joseph Shaw have already discovered him.)"[12]

L. F. Nebel in the *St. Louis Post-Dispatch* took his praise of the novel a step further. "It seems a pity that this should be called a detective story. . . . Truly, it is a story about a detective, but it is so much about a detective that he becomes a character, and the sheer force of Hammett's hard, brittle writing lifts the book out of the general run of crime spasms and places it aloof and alone as a brave chronicle of a hard-boiled man, unscrupulous, conscienceless, unique."[13] Franklin P. Adams, known as F. P. A. to the readers of his highly regarded column "The Conning Tower" in the *New York World*, called *The Maltese Falcon* "the only detective tayle that I have been able to read through since the days of Sherlock Holmes."[14]

But the best measure of the respect *The Maltese Falcon* garnered for Hammett came in an article by William Curtis in staid, sophisticated *Town & Country*, the magazine for the American upper middle class. Curtis's article ran some fifteen hundred words and is effusive in its praise of Hammett's talents:

I believe I have discovered a new technique in the writing of murder-mystery stories and a new technician. . . .
. . . if you were to consider an amalgamation of Mr. Hemingway, the Mr. Burnet [*sic*] who wrote "Little Caesar" and "Iron Man," that other disciple of Hemingway, Morley Callaghan, and Ring Lardner in his prize-fighting aspect, you would have a fair idea of the style and technique of Mr. Hammett. . . .
It may surprise Mr. Hammett to be compared to the Hemingway-Burnet-Callaghan group. To my mind, however, speaking purely as one who has been following the progress of the novel for yahrs and yahrs and yahrs, I think Mr. Hammett has something quite as definite to say, quite as decided an impetus to give the course of newness in the development of the American tongue, as any man now writing. Of course, he's gone about it the wrong way to attract respectful attention from the proper sources. He's never been in Paris, has never played around with the Little Review group. He has not been picked up by any of the fog-horn columnists. He's only a writer of murder mystery stories.[15]

Red Harvest had been modestly well received, but one printing was sufficient for sales in its first year of publication. *The Dain Curse* went through three printings in the first two months of publication. In addition to publication in London by Knopf in July 1930, *The Maltese Falcon*, published at $2.00, was reprinted seven times in America during its first year and motion picture rights were sold to Warner Brothers the year after publication. By the fall of 1929, Hammett had his first taste of the big money to come and his prospects for the future looked very good. Paramount had bought movie rights to *Red Harvest*, and Hammett was widely regarded to be the best detective novelist in America as well as one of this country's most promising writers. The royalty checks from his novels were not large by today's standards, but to a writer who had for six years been supporting himself on his income as a pulp writer, they were cause for celebrating.

Moreover, Hammett's health was improving. His tuberculosis had gone into remission and he felt good. In the spring he had left his apartment at 891 Post Street for a more impressive one at 1155 Leavenworth Street. He left his family behind. Although he had not felt himself bound by the traditional marital responsibilities for some three years, this move marked his formal break with Jose Hammett. Hammett loved another woman, Nell Martin. In October 1929 Hammett moved to New York with her[16] and left Jose Hammett in San Francisco with their children. They were never legally divorced, but their marriage was over. Yet when *The Maltese Falcon* was published on Valentine's Day 1930 it carried Hammett's dedication: "To Jose."

Hammett arranged publication of four stories between August 1929 and November 1930. Three of those were op stories, and of the four, two were very bad; one, "The Diamond Wager," was so embarrassing that Hammett submitted it to *Detective Fiction Weekly*, where it was published on October 19, 1929, under a pseudonym, Samuel Dashiell.

"Fly Paper" (*Black Mask*, August 1929) and "The Farewell Murder" (*Black Mask*, February 1930) are good solid op stories. In "Fly Paper" the op is hired to find a runaway girl from a wealthy and respectable family. He learns that, like other wealthy young women in Hammett's stories, she is attracted to the underworld and becomes romantically involved with a crook, Babe McCloor. Also like Hammett's other fallen women, this one is treacherous. She kills herself in an attempt to build up an immunity to poison by taking small doses each day so that once her tolerance level is heightened she can poison the jealous McCloor without arousing his suspicions. When "Fly Paper" was syndicated by King Features in 1936, Hammett claimed the real-life model for Babe McCloor was a member of Jimmie the Riveter's mob, which had pulled a series of robberies on the Pacific Coast in the winter of 1921. When they were captured in Seattle, each member of the gang was handcuffed and taken to the police station, where McCloor's original, still handcuffed, made a dive for a deputy's gun and shot it out with police. (Hammett uses a similar incident in "The Big Knock-Over" when Bluepoint Vance dives, in handcuffs, for a policeman's gun.)[17]

In "The Farewell Murder" the op is called to investigate the harassment of a man by a former business associate. When the threatened murder takes place, the obvious suspect has just enough of an alibi to get an acquittal before a jury. The op solves the mystery by identifying the dead man's son-in-law and indirect heir as the murderer. The plan of the son-in-law and the former partner was to draw suspicion and attention away from the real murderer, and it almost worked.

"Death and Company" (*Black Mask*, November 1930) is about a man who comes to the op with a ransom note for his wife signed "Death and Company." The op discovers that the kidnapping is a ruse the man concocted after he killed his wife in the apartment of her lover, a petty crook who flees because he fears his criminal record will cause him to be blamed for the murder. Before the op can arrest his client, the dead woman's boyfriend returns to kill the husband in revenge.

When Hammett and Nell Martin went to New York in the fall of 1929 to see *The Maltese Falcon* through the press and to enjoy the full effects of its publication, they lived well. Hammett was a minor literary celebrity and he learned quickly that such a distinction was more meaningful in New York than in San Francisco. He and Nell Martin took an apartment at 155 East Thirtieth Street and he worked on his new novel, already in progress. He later said that he was ruined as a novelist when he finished *The Glass Key* in one continuous writing session of thirty hours. He kept believing he could do it again, but he could not.[18] After *The Glass Key* Hammett was ruined as a novelist, but that writing session was not to blame— the liquor, the women, the money, and the celebrity were. The hard-boiled novelist grew soft.

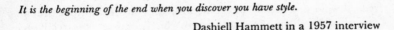

C H A P T E R 11

It is the beginning of the end when you discover you have style.

Dashiell Hammett in a 1957 interview

On February 6, 1930, Hammett wrote to his friend Herbert Asbury (the crime writer and journalist who had recently written *The Gangs of New York*, 1928, and who had reviewed Hammett's novels enthusiastically) that *The Glass Key*, which he said had been held back thus far by laziness, drunkenness, and illness, promised to be finished by the latter part of the next week.[1] It was finished on time and serialized immediately by Shaw in *Black Mask* to take advantage of publicity attendant to the publication of *The Maltese Falcon*. The serial was in four parts—"The Glass Key" (March 1930); "The Cyclone Shot" (April); "Dagger Point" (May); and "The Shattered Key" (June). Book publication did not come in America until April 24, 1931. For reasons that are unclear, *The Glass Key* was the only one of Hammett's books to be published first in England; it was published there by Knopf on January 20, 1931, to respectful but unenthusiastic reviews.

The Glass Key ranks with *The Maltese Falcon* as one of Hammett's two best novels, and it rivals *Red Harvest* and *The Maltese Falcon* for the innovations in technique it displays. *The Glass Key* is a hard-boiled version of a love triangle story in which two friends love the same woman. The characters are developed entirely through their actions during the novel. Hammett reveals almost nothing of their pasts, very little of what they look like, nothing of their actions which does

DASHIELL HAMMETT

not relate directly to the story he is telling. Though the novel is about Ned Beaumont's solution of a murder, he is not a detective and he does not act like one. Beaumont is a gambler who is a friend and the most trusted assistant of Paul Madvig, a political boss in an unnamed city near New York, modeled on Baltimore. It is an election year, and Madvig is faced with getting his slate of candidates reelected. Madvig's town is a rough one, run by a corrupt political system, but Madvig is not a villain. He is a hard, practical politician who knows how to get what he wants.

Madvig is in love with Janet Henry, daughter of a senator who needs his influence to get reelected, but she despises the political boss, whom she considers uncouth and corrupt. Early in the novel, Senator Henry's son Taylor is murdered, and suspicion falls onto Madvig, who is at first able to defy the accusations because of his political power. But as the evidence against him accumulates, Madvig's slate is threatened with defeat in the election, and he is faced with charges of first-degree murder. More important for him, Janet Henry is convinced that Madvig killed her brother, and she hates him for it.

Ned Beaumont's responsibility is to see that Madvig does well in the election and that he is not tried for Henry's murder. He goes about his job single-mindedly. He finds that Madvig was present when Taylor Henry died, but that the senator killed his son. Out of desire for Janet Henry and political savvy, Madvig is covering up the senator's crime. Ned Beaumont does not approve of his friend's plans to marry Janet Henry. He explains to her at the end of the novel: "I tried to tell him you both considered him a lower form of animal life and fair game for any kind of treatment. I tried to tell him your father was a man all his life used to winning without much trouble and that in a hole he'd either lose his head or turn wolf. Well, he was in love with you, so—."[2]

Though Ned Beaumont is disgusted at the way Senator Henry has used Janet to draw political support, in the course of his job he seems to fall in love with her, despite his friendship with Madvig. As the strength of the case against Madvig increases, it becomes clear to Beaumont that he must act to clear his friend, or else Madvig will be indicted for Taylor Henry's murder.

Against Madvig's wishes, Beaumont reveals the senator as his son's murderer and explains the circumstances of Taylor Henry's death. In a clumsy attempt at lovemaking, Madvig had tried to kiss Janet Henry, who found him repulsive. When her brother heard

117

about the incident he rushed after Madvig to defend his sister's honor; the senator, in turn, rushed after his son to protect the source of his political support in the upcoming election. In protecting Madvig, the senator hit his son who fell against a curb and was killed. After presenting his case against the senator, Beaumont leaves town, and, at her request, allows Janet Henry to come with him. The novel ends as Beaumont awkwardly informs Madvig of their departure.

The Glass Key is a novel about human relationships and about the corrupting, blinding, dehumanizing effect on people of power, particularly political power. Senator Henry murders his son and panders his daughter for political support. Paul Madvig naively believes he can win Janet Henry's love by supporting her father in his election and protecting him from the consequences of murdering his son. Janet Henry, indignant at Madvig and his politics, recklessly attempts to manipulate the political forces that oppose him so he will be tried for her brother's murder. Ned Beaumont, on the other hand, the ablest behind-the-scenes politician of all and the moral center of the book, sees clearly the limits of power, the limits of friendship, and the uncompromising nature of love.

For a novel in which political power plays so great a part, *The Glass Key* is remarkably apolitical. No liberal or conservative stance is adopted, and it is left to the reader to form an opinion about the corruption of Madvig's regime, which, considering the alternatives, is preferable to any other in sight. Hammett makes it difficult for the reader to judge right and wrong in the book. While no character is without serious fault, only Senator Henry is without redeeming qualities. Ned Beaumont, the most moral man in the book, plants evidence implicating a bookie in Taylor Henry's murder to blackmail him into paying a gambling debt; he manages an intricate system of graft and favoritism in which he can set murderers free and punish innocent men who cross him. Janet Henry, a sincere woman willing to act on her beliefs, recklessly accuses Madvig of her brother's murder without sufficient evidence. Madvig manipulates a corrupt political system, but there is a certain innocence in his willingness to risk his position for the woman he loves, in the belief that love is a commodity power can buy.

Objectivity had long been the principal factor in Hammett's artistic plan, but with *The Glass Key* he accomplished a new level of third-person narrative distance. Ned Beaumont is always referred to by his full name; his boss might be called Madvig, the senator's daughter Janet, but he is always Ned Beaumont. Hammett was betraying no sympathies for his character by treating him familiarly. The narrative comment is restricted to straight description. Characters are developed fully, but entirely by means of dialogue and action. Hammett does not analyze his characters. Each clue to Taylor Henry's murder, Janet Henry's romantic intentions, Beaumont's motives, and Madvig's political influence is revealed in dialogue rather than through narration.

The quality of the love story in *The Glass Key* is a direct result of the objective style of the novel. It is a story in which feelings are not distorted by sentimentality. Janet Henry's attraction to Beaumont is complex—she meets him in a hospital where he is recovering from a severe beating he took at the hands of Madvig's political enemies. When Madvig must leave for a meeting, she asks to stay with Beaumont so she can get away from his boss, whom she hates, and so she can ingratiate herself with Madvig's best friend to gain more information about her brother's murder. Beaumont is rude and direct, and these qualities finally convince her, after rumors of a break in the friendship between him and Madvig, that Beaumont will help her expose Madvig. When finally she learns from Beaumont that it was her father who committed the murder, she wants to go away, and asks Beaumont to take her.

Beaumont is contemptuous of "senators' daughters who are in the roto all the time."[3] He cultivates his hard, rude demeanor, particularly toward Janet Henry. But at the same time, he is careful to write gracious, grammatically correct thank-you notes for the gifts she sends him in the hospital. Beaumont hates Janet Henry's father, he says, because the senator is a pimp who offers up his daughter for his political future. He is attracted to Janet because she is willing to give up her position for what she believes in, to desert her father because she finds him corrupt. Beaumont cannot ignore her helplessness.

Neither he nor Janet Henry professes love for the other. Just before they agree to go away together, she tells him, "I don't hate you," and he admits to her, "You're all right."[4]

The last scene in the novel is in Ned Beaumont's apartment as he is packing to leave for New York. Janet Henry is with him. Madvig comes to the door and she hides in the bedroom, while Madvig and Beaumont say their farewells. Madvig acknowledges that Beaumont was right about exposing the cover-up of Taylor Henry's murder. He has given up plans to win this election and has decided instead to use the four years until the next election to build a stronger organization. He asks Ned Beaumont to help him, and he restates his intentions to make up for his foolishness in the Henry affair. Beaumont says that has nothing to do with his decision to leave, and he tells Madvig Janet Henry is going away with him:

Madvig's lips parted. He looked dumbly at Ned Beaumont and as he looked the blood went out of his face again. When his face was quite bloodless he mumbled something of which only the word "luck" could be understood, turned clumsily around, went to the door, opened it, and went out, leaving it open behind him.

Janet Henry looked at Ned Beaumont. He stared fixedly at the door.[5]

That open door relates directly to the title of the novel, taken from a dream Janet Henry told Ned Beaumont about—in two versions—as they were attempting to solve her brother's murder. In the first version, she and Beaumont were lost in a forest. They were tired and starving when they came upon a little house in which there were piles of food on a big table. They found a key under the doormat, but when they opened the door, hundreds of snakes were slithering and hissing on the floor. They relocked the door in fear. Then Ned Beaumont took Janet Henry up on the roof, leaned over and unlocked the door from above and let all the snakes out. When the snakes had left, the two of them went inside, locked the door, and ate all the food. After Beaumont had exposed her father, Janet said she had changed her dream in the telling of it from a nightmare; that in her real dream the key under the doormat had been glass and that when they first opened the door, the key shattered so they could not lock the snakes in again. The snakes came out all over them.

Freudian-symbol hunters have distorted this passage as a clue to Beaumont's impotence and to his and Janet Henry's guilt-ridden sexuality. Even with Hammett's interest in psychology, that is unlikely. The glass key is symbolic of the action in the novel, but in a more artistic way. It represents the various kinds of knowledge Ned Beaumont and other characters gain during the course of the novel. Once a door is opened and you learn what is on the other side, you must live with all that is found there, not simply the best of it, and what is found there can never be unlearned. A glass key works only once, to unlock a door. The metaphor applies to Senator Henry, who learns the extent to which he has been consumed by his lust for political power; to Paul Madvig, who is unable to undo his foolishness in attempting to cover up the senator's crime; to Janet Henry, who learns for the first time the extent of her father's corruption; and to Ned Beaumont, who ironically must break with his friend Paul Madvig to save his friend's life.

Hammet dedicated *The Glass Key* to Nell Martin; then they went separate ways. It was the second book in succession he had dedicated to a woman after he had left her.

Hammett considered *The Glass Key* his best book. In a 1932 interview he said he thought *The Maltese Falcon* was too manufactured and that *The Glass Key* was "not so bad—. . . the clews were nicely placed there, although nobody seemed to see them."[6] The initial reception was the best of any Hammett novel so far. There were five printings of *The Glass Key*, which sold for $2.50, in the first two months of publication (as opposed to seven printings in ten months for *The Maltese Falcon*) and twenty thousand copies were sold by December 1933. Critical reception matched that of *The Maltese Falcon*. The book was acclaimed as one of the best detective stories ever written by an American, second only to *The Maltese Falcon*. It was the peak of Hammett's writing career. Bruce Rae in the *New York Times* wrote, "There can be no doubt of Mr. Hammett's gifts in this special field, and there can be no question of the success of his latest book."[7] Will Cuppy in the *New York Herald Tribune* called *The Glass Key* "about twice as good as his 'The Maltese Falcon' " and concluded that the new novel was "a whiz of an opus."[8] Walter Brooks in *Outlook* wrote that Hammett "has now written the three best detective stories ever published."[9]

Hammett also continued to gain favor in the pages of the sophisticated, tastemaking slicks. In a column in *The New Yorker* "Oh, Look—Two Good Books!" Dorothy Parker exclaimed her discovery of Hammett.

It seems to me that there is entirely too little screaming about the work of Dashiell Hammett. My own shrill yaps have been ascending ever since I first found "Red Harvest," and from that day the man has been, God help him, my hero; but I talked only yesterday, I forget why, with two of our leading booksy folk, and they had not heard of that volume, nor had they got around to reading its better, "The Maltese Falcon." . . . Surely it is that Beaumont, . . . a man given perhaps a shade too much to stroking his moustache with a thumbnail, can in no way stack up against the magnificent Spade, with whom, after reading "The Maltese Falcon," I went mooning about in a daze of love such as I had not known for any character in literature since I encountered Sir Launcelot when I hit the age of nine. (Launcelot and Spade—ah well, they're pretty far apart, yet I played Elaine to both of them, and in that lies a life-story.) The new book, or, indeed, any new book, has no figure to stand near Sam Spade, but maybe all the matter is not there. For I thought that in "The Glass Key" Mr. Hammett seemed a little weary, a little short of spontaneous, a little dogged about his simplicity of style, a little determined to make startling the ordering of his brief sentences, a little concerned with having his conclusion approach the toughness of the superb last scene of "The Maltese Falcon." But all that is not to say that "The Glass Key" is not a good book and an enthralling one, and the best you have read since "The Maltese Falcon." And if you didn't read that, this is the swiftest book you've ever read in your life.[10]

Hammett was amused at and somewhat disdainful of his new-found attention. On March 7, 1931, *The New Yorker* quoted from a review of *The Glass Key* in the *Baltimore Observer* for one of its "News-breaks" (filler material consisting of unintentionally humorous quotes followed by a witty remark, usually by a member of the *New Yorker* staff): "This fellow Hammett is the same fellow that wrote 'The Dain Curse,' and there is something creeping up my back to tell me that it was punk, too, but I don't know what it is. Just something." Hammett supplied the remark: "Your undershirt?"[11]

In April 1930, his fourth novel behind him, Hammett took on another position as mystery book reviewer. His last piece for *The Saturday Review of Literature* had been written about the time he had left San Francisco for New York, in October 1929. The new position was with the *New York Evening Post*, a politically liberal daily newspaper. His reviews in the *Post* appeared twice a month under the title "Crime Wave" in the Saturday book section. He passed judgment on as many as thirteen books a column, and before he gave up his position in October 1930, Hammett had reviewed eighty-five books, an average of twelve a month. His standards had not slackened since his reviews for *The Saturday Review of Literature*, and his impatience with the mountain of poorly written books he was faced with had grown. In his June 7 column, he vented his dissatisfaction:

There is not much nourishment for adult readers in this group [of books to be reviewed]. The first part of the Crawley work [*The Valley of Creeping Men*] is acceptable melodrama, but the rest of it deals with rather aimless doings in African jungles. The other members of our list are, from beginnings to endings, carelessly manufactured improbabilities having more than their share of those blunders which earn detective stories as a whole the sneers of the captious.

A fellow who takes detective stories seriously, I am annoyed by the stupid recurrence of these same blunders in book after book. It would be silly to insist that nobody who has not been a detective should write detective stories, but it is certainly not unreasonable to ask any one who is going to write a book of any sort to make some effort at least to learn something about his subject. Most writers do. Only detective story writers seem to be free from a sense of obligation in this direction, and, curiously, the more established and prolific detective story writers seem to be the worst offenders. Nearly all writers of Western tales at least get an occasional glimpse of their chosen territory from a car-window while en route to Hollywood; writers of sea stories have been seen on the waterfront; surely detective story writers could afford to speak to policemen now and then.

Meanwhile, a couple of months' labor in this arena has convinced me that the following suggestions might be of value to somebody:

(1) There was an automatic revolver, the Webley-Fosbery, made in England some years ago. The ordinary automatic pistol, however, is not a revolver. A pistol, to be a revolver, must have something on it that revolves.

(2) The Colt's .45 automatic pistol has no chambers. The cartridges are put in a magazine.

(3) A silencer may be attached to a revolver, but the effect will be altogether negligible. I have never seen a silencer used on an automatic pistol, but am told it would cause the pistol to jam. A silencer may be used on a single-shot target pistol or on a rifle, but both would still make quite a bit of noise. "Silencer" is a rather optimistic name for this device which has generally fallen into disuse.

(4) When a bullet from a Colt's .45, or any firearm of approximately the same size and power, hits you, even if not in a fatal spot, it usually knocks you over. It is quite upsetting at any reasonable range.

(5) A shot or stab wound is simply felt as a blow or push at first. It is some little time before any burning or other painful sensation begins.

(6) When you are knocked unconscious you do not feel the blow that does it.

(7) A wound made after the death of the wounded is usually recognizable as such.

(8) Finger-prints of any value to the police are seldom found on anybody's skin.

(9)   The pupils of many drug-addicts' eyes are apparently normal.

(10)   It is impossible to see anything by the flash of an ordinary gun, though it is easy to imagine you have seen things.

(11)   Not nearly so much can be seen by moonlight as you imagine. This is especially true of colors.

(12)   All Federal snoopers are not members of the Secret Service. That branch is chiefly occupied with pursuing counterfeiters and guarding Presidents and prominent visitors to our shores.

(13)   A sheriff is a county officer who usually has no official connection with city, town or state police.

(14)   Federal prisoners convicted in Washington, D.C., are usually sent to the Atlanta prison and not to Leavenworth.

(15)   The California State prison at San Quentin is used for convicts serving first terms. Two-time losers are usually sent to Folsom.

(16)   Ventriloquists do not actually "throw" their voices and such doubtful illusions as they manage depend on their gestures. Nothing at all could be done by a ventriloquist standing behind his audience.

(17)   Even detectives who drop their final g's should not be made to say "anythin' "—an oddity that calls for vocal acrobatics.

(18)   "Youse" is the plural of "you."

(19)   A trained detective shadowing a subject does not ordinarily leap from doorway to doorway and does not hide behind trees and poles. He knows no harm is done if the subject sees him now and then.[12]

On July 3 he continued:

A few weeks ago, having no books on hand that I cared to talk much about, I listed in this column nineteen suggestions to detective story writers. Those suggestions having been received with extreme enthusiasm—to the extent of at least one publisher offering me a hundred dollars for a slightly more complete list—I, not needing that particular hundred dollars at the moment, herewith present a few more suggestions at the mere usual space rate:

(20)   The current practice in most places in the United States is to make the coroner's inquest an empty formality in which nothing much is brought out except that somebody has died.

(21)   Fingerprints are fragile affairs. Wrapping a pistol or other small object up in a handkerchief is much more likely to obliterate than to preserve any prints it may have.

(22)   When an automatic pistol is fired the empty cartridge-shell flies out the right-hand side. The empty cartridge-case remains in a revolver until ejected by hand.

(23)   A lawyer cannot impeach his own witness.

(24)   The length of time a corpse has been a corpse can be approximated by an experienced physician, but only approximated, and the longer it has been a corpse, the less accurate the approximation is likely to be.[13]

Hammett clearly enjoyed his book reviews. They gave him a chance to play out his role as America's most accomplished mystery writer and to declare publicly his superiority over other writers in the genre. But that was because Hammett's celebrity was new to him. Within the next six months, he no longer had time to review books, and he did not need a biweekly column to keep his name before the public. Hollywood moviemakers had seen the potential in his work, and at the age of 36, Hammett was ready for the big money.

In 1929 Paramount had bought the movie rights to *Red Harvest*. In February 1930 they released a totally rewritten version titled *Roadhouse Nights*, with a screenplay by Garrett Fort based as much on a Ben Hecht story as on Hammett's novel. *Roadhouse Nights* starred Helen Morgan, Charles Ruggles, Fred Kohler, Jimmy Durante, and Leo Donnelly. On June 23, 1930, Warner Brothers Pictures concluded negotiations with Knopf for motion picture rights to *The Maltese Falcon*. Jacob Wilk, manager of the Warner story department, had read the novel on the recommendation of his lawyer friend Arthur W. Weil. Wilk saw the dramatic possibilities of the book and instructed Sanford J. Greenburger, his assistant in New York, to negotiate for motion picture rights.[14] A letter of agreement was signed by a Knopf representative on June 5, 1930, and the contract followed three weeks later. The purchase price was $8,500, of which Hammett received about 80 percent.[15]

Three weeks after the Warner Brothers agreement, David O. Selznick, then executive assistant to studio chief B. P. Schulberg at Paramount, wrote his boss a memo:

To: Mr. B. P. Schulberg   July 18, 1930

We have an opportunity to secure Dashiell Hammett to do one story for us before he goes abroad in about three months.

Hammett has recently created quite a stir in literary circles by his creation of two books for Knopf, *The Maltese Falcon* and *Red Harvest*. I believe that he is another Van Dine—indeed, that he possesses more originality than Van Dine, and might very well prove to be the creator of something new and startlingly original for us.

I would recommend having him do a police story for Bancroft. . . . Hammett was a Pinkerton man for a good many years before becoming a writer. . . .

Hammett is unspoiled as to money, but on the other hand anxious not to tie himself up with a long-term contract. I was in hopes that we could get him for about $400 weekly, but he claims that this is only about half of his present earning capacity between books and magazine stories, and I am inclined to believe him inasmuch as his vogue is on the rise.

So far, I have tentatively discussed some such arrangement as the following: . . .

Four weeks at $300 weekly;

An option for eight weeks at the same salary;

And a bonus of $5000 for an original. . . .

David O. Selznick[16]

Hammett was put under contract, assigned to write an original story, and he moved to Hollywood. He took one weekend to complete his first assignment. His story consisted of seven handwritten legal-size pages titled "After School."[17] The story needed work, but after some revision it was produced as *City Streets* and released in April 1931. The final credit for the screenplay was to "Oliver H. P. Garrett from an adaptation by Max Marcin of Dashiell Hammett's original story." Rouben Mamoulian directed *City Streets*, and the cast included Gary Cooper, Sylvia Sidney, Paul Lukas, and William Boyd. It is a gangster film in which Gary Cooper as The Kid protects his tough but hapless girl friend Nan, played by Sylvia Sidney, from the dangers of the underworld life in which she becomes involved. Hammett thought the movie was too long but redeemed by Sylvia Sidney's performance.[18]

Paramount regarded Hammett as an important member of their writing staff, and he was assigned to work on scripts for the studio's stars. One of Hammett's last assignments at Paramount seems to have been on the comedy *Ladies' Man* (1931), starring William Powell, who had played Philo Vance in a very successful series of movies based on the adventures of S. S. Van Dine's mystery-solving hero. Powell was a difficult actor who made no secret of the fact that he was fed up with detective roles and feared he was being typecast to the detriment of his career. (After *Ladies' Man* Powell left Paramount for Warner Brothers, where he and Hammett were paired again briefly, before both went to MGM. There Powell played the most popular role of his career as Nick Charles in a series of six movies based on Hammett's *The Thin Man*.) At Paramount in 1930, Hammett seems also to have been assigned to *Blonde Venus* (1932), which starred Marlene Dietrich. His only screen credit at Paramount, however, was for *City Streets*, and he left the studio at the end of 1930.

C H A P T E R 1 2

In the course of the interview I gathered that Mr. Hammett has written some verse. That he thinks Robinson Jeffers the best story-teller he has ever read, and the cruellest. That he likes Hemingway, Faulkner and Hecht. He thinks Wilbur Daniel Steele is a competent magazine writer. He considers The Dain Curse *a silly story,* The Maltese Falcon *"too manufactured," and* The Glass Key *not so bad—that the clews were nicely placed there, although nobody seemed to see them. (I told him that everyone hadn't been a detective.) He had Mickey Mouse's orchestra on top of his bookcase, and on his desk were a lot of his own publicity photographs, of which he gave me the most flattering.*

Elizabeth Sanderson in *The Bookman* (1932)

Hammett was in Hollywood through the spring of 1931, and he became a part of the closed, highly stratified community of movie people. A select group in Hollywood lived a life different from that of any other in America. They were young, good-looking, ambitious, and either rich or fully confident that they would be soon. They were surrounded by enormous wealth and a level of conspicuous consumption that left the entire country envious of them. Hammett was not among the inner circle of Hollywood moviemakers. He was just a writer, and whatever reputation an author achieved outside Hollywood, when he came to work for the studios he joined a class of workers inferior to producers, directors, and actors, each group of whom commanded higher salaries than writers.

Nonetheless, the writer on contract with a major studio had prestige. He not only had a chance for a screen credit, the only credential that counted in Hollywood, but he had some access to the really important people, those who controlled the money. Hammett enjoyed Hollywood and he easily assumed the local life-style. He lived well in an apartment with his black chauffeur/helper Jones. Among his frequent visitors were other literary people who had come to Hollywood to try their hands at screenwriting: the Asburys, humorist S. J. Perelman and his wife Laura, humorist Arthur Kober and his wife Lillian Hellman, Dorothy Parker and her husband Alan Campbell.[1] Hammett also entertained a number of starlets who were eager to ingratiate themselves with him and his friends. He became a regular at the Brown Derby; he drank more heavily than ever; and he contracted his second case of gonorrhea.[2]

Hammett provided an indication of what his life in Hollywood was like in his September 6, 1930, column for the *New York Evening Post*: " 'The Secret of the Bungalow' hung unread around my apartment for two or three weeks. About all the attention it got was when I pushed it out of the way to get at more attractively titled and jacketed works. Then, with half an hour to kill before dressing, I opened it. I did not read it through at a sitting, because this was Hollywood on the evening of the Eddie Southerlands' party at the Embassy Club. . . ."[3] Hammett, or the newspaper, misspelled Sutherland's name, but he knew him well. Sutherland was a director at Paramount, of comedies primarily, and he had a reputation, in the words of actress Louise Brooks, his wife from 1926 to 1928, of "drinking and playing around and dancing all night."[4]

While life in Hollywood affected Hammett profoundly, he did not forget his old friends, though he remembered them with a flair acquired in Hollywood. In 1929 Albert Samuels had lent him $500 to move east, and now Hammett decided he would repay that loan in person. He traveled to San Francisco from Los Angeles by chauffeured limousine and took a suite of rooms at the Fairmont Hotel on Nob Hill. After he repaid Samuels, Hammett threw a party. The Fairmont was one of the most expensive hotels in the city and prohibition liquor was expensive; nonetheless, the party went on for a week. When time came for the return to Los Angeles, Hammett made an embarrassing admission to Samuels. He had run out of cash and needed a loan to get him home. Samuels was happy to oblige, even when Hammett said he needed $800 to finance the 500-mile automobile trip. He told Hammett to drop by the office for the money. When Samuels's office opened the next day, his bookkeeper was greeted by Hammett's chauffeur in full uniform, with epaulets.

The chauffeur never spoke, but handed over a note: "Give the jig the bundle. Dashiell Hammett."[5]

In January 1931, Darryl Zanuck, then an executive at Warner Brothers, hired Hammett to write an original Sam Spade story for a movie starring William Powell, who had just come to Warner Brothers from Paramount. Powell was one of Paramount's stars, and the assignment indicated the high regard Zanuck had for Hammett's talent. The pay was $15,000, to be received in three installments: $5,000 on signing the contract, which was dated January 23, 1931; $5,000 on delivery of the treatment; and $5,000 on acceptance of the story in its final form. Hammett wrote a screen story titled "On the Make" based on an idea he discussed in advance with Zanuck. Zanuck approved payment of the second $5,000 for the completed treatment, but on April 28, he rejected the final story and refused to pay the final installment.[6] (The story was later bought by Universal and released as *Mister Dynamite*.) Zanuck's rejection coincided with the book publication of *The Glass Key* in America and another break in Hammett's health. He complained of headaches and troubled breathing, which prompted him to quit drinking briefly. In addition, he was broke and fed up with Hollywood, so he left for New York, where he took an apartment at 133 East Thirty-eighth Street and began writing another novel.[7]

When Hammett returned to New York, he took a literary agent to handle his fiction. He needed money and he was dissatisfied with the sales of *The Glass Key*, for which he had gotten only $1,000 advance from Knopf. That was a respectable amount in the book trade, but paltry by Hollywood standards. Hammett's Hollywood agent for movie deals was Daniel Leonardson, but Leonardson could not handle book and magazine publications, so Hammett went to Ben Wasson, of the American Play Company. Wasson had represented William Faulkner and had gained some literary notoriety as the man who cut Faulkner's first Yoknapatawpha novel, *Flags in the Dust*, which had been turned down by several publishers, into the shortened version, retitled *Sartoris*, which Wasson placed.

Hammett and Faulkner liked one another and they had two common interests—alcohol and literature. Faulkner lived in Mississippi, and his trips to New York often turned into drinking sprees. In Hammett, he found a cordial drinking partner who could match his capacity for liquor and who was just as opinionated as Faulkner about modern writing. When Faulkner called his novel *Sanctuary* a potboiler, written only to make money, Hammett replied that was not true; a good writer does not write for money, he said. And on another occasion they reportedly had a serious disagreement over Thomas Mann's *The Magic Mountain*, which Hammett called a false book by a long-winded writer.

One afternoon in fall 1931 Hammett and Faulkner had lunch with publisher Bennett Cerf, who told the writers he was having dinner that night at the Knopfs' with Willa Cather and Serge Koussevitzky. Hammett said Knopf was his publisher and he wanted to go too. Cerf agreed to arrange an invitation for them to the black-tie dinner, and he picked them up that evening at "21" on Fifty-second Street, where Hammett and Faulkner, dressed in tweeds, had spent the entire afternoon drinking. That evening at the Knopfs' Hammett passed out on a couch and slid to the floor. Wasson, by then already Hammett's agent, was among the startled guests who helped revive him. [8]

Wasson wanted something of Hammett's to sell while the good reviews of *The Glass Key* were still fresh in editors' minds. Hammett obliged with a sixty-five-page fragment of a new novel. The clean typescript Wasson circulated in the early summer of 1931 was auctioned off in 1942 at a benefit, with a two-page handwritten note by Hammett about his partially finished novel:

In 1930 I started writing a book entitled "The Thin Man." By the time I had written these 65 pages my publisher and I agreed that it might be wise to postpone the publication of "The Glass Key"—scheduled for that fall—until the following spring. This meant that "The Thin Man" could not be published until the fall of 1931. So—leaving plenty of time—I put these 65 pages aside and went to Hollywood for a year. One thing and/or another intervening after that, I didn't return to work on the story until a couple of more years had passed—and then I found it easier, or at least generally more satisfactory, to keep only the basic idea of the plot and otherwise to start anew. Some of the incidents in this original version I later used in "After the Thin Man," a motion picture sequel, but—except for that and for the use of the characters' names Guild and Wynant—this unfinished manuscript has a clear claim to virginity." [9]

Hammett's recollection of the date of composition seems slightly off. The address on the typescript, 133 East Thirty-eighth Street, dates the surviving draft as May 1931. When he wrote his novel published as *The Thin Man* in 1933, he abandoned the false start.

The original "Thin Man" is a promising fragment of a mystery novel. It is set in San Francisco and in the mountains north of the city. The detective is John Guild, with Associated Detective Bureaus, Inc. Guild becomes involved in the case when an insurance company that employs his agency reports a claim from a San Francisco bank on an altered check—changed from $1,000 to $10,000. Guild's search for Clyde Wynant, who deposited the check, leads him into a bizarre murder case, in which Wynant, an eccentric writer similar in appearance to Hammett, is the apparent murderer. His motive seems to be that Columbia Forrest, his mistress, had announced that she was leaving him to marry Charles Freemont. Guild learns that Columbia Forrest lived under the alias Laura Porter at 1155 Leavenworth (Hammett's last San Francisco address), and that coincidentally she and Freemont had the same birthday—May 27 (the same as Hammett's).

Wynant is unlocatable, though when someone shoots at Charles Freemont in Guild's presence, the assumption is that it was Wynant, whose car is found abandoned nearby. Guild's search leads him to a Chinatown restaurant, the Manchow, owned by a suspicious character named Francis Xavier Kearny, and to a relationship with a singer at the Manchow, Freemont's sister Elsa, which echoes the romance of Sam Spade and Brigid O'Shaughnessy. The fragment ends as Guild is attempting to comfort Elsa who is distraught that her brother has not been home recently. In a too obvious manner she convinces Guild to come home with her from the Manchow to search her house for intruders. In his search he finds the body of Charles Freemont, an apparent suicide.

Hammett seems to have been setting up the type of mystery he used in the completed *Thin Man*—a missing person is implicated in a series of crimes when he is, in fact, dead. The missing man in both the fragment and the finished novel is named Clyde Wynant, and the two Wynants are similar in character. The name John Guild is used for a police detective in the completed novel, in which Nick Charles solves the crime.

Wasson began circulating the fragment to magazines in May 1931, apparently offering to sell not just first serial rights, but all rights. On May 14 Wasson reached an agreement with H. H. Bromley at *Hearst's International/Cosmopolitan* for a $1,000 option against a total purchase price of $26,000. That price is the equivalent to what Hammett's royalties would have been on book sales of about one hundred thousand copies of a hardbound book at $2. Hammett was to receive $1,000 in advance, $4,000 on receipt of the completed manuscript, and $4,000 a month until the balance of the purchase price was paid. But the deal fell through, probably because it violated Hammett's contract with Knopf, which gave them the rights to his next novel.[10]

Wasson planned another project for Hammett, this one successful. He negotiated a contract with John Day Company for an anthology Hammett would edit and write an introduction for. The advance was $100 against a royalty of 10 percent of the retail price on all copies sold. *Creeps By Night*, which was published on October 8, 1931, sold some twenty-seven hundred copies at $2.50 and earned Hammett $668.09. The anthology consisted of twenty horror stories or thrillers, including tales by William Faulkner (the first book publication of "A Rose for Emily"), Conrad Aiken, and Stephen Vincent Benét. The earnings were small for him, however, and Hammett did not take much interest in the book. In all likelihood, *Creeps By Night* was actually compiled by Wasson, with little help from Hammett.[11]

In May 1931 *The Maltese Falcon*, starring Bebe Daniels as Ruth Wonderly, the renamed movie version of Brigid O'Shaughnessy, and Ricardo Cortez as Sam Spade, was released by Warner Brothers. (It was a last-minute decision to keep Hammett's title. As late as April 1931 the movie was being referred to in trade publications as "Woman of the World.") The movie was directed by Roy del Ruth from a screenplay by Maude Fulton, Lucien Hubbard, and Brown Holmes. The production was praised, and though some liberties were taken with the character of Sam Spade, who was altered for the screen into "a man of light and whimsied humors," the *New York Times* reviewer concluded that "Roy del Ruth had done splendidly by an excellent mystery story."[12] Hammett's celebrity surged. Money came easily, women followed, and Hammett believed in taking advantage of the situation. But by the end of the year he was broke, and he had chosen one woman out of the crowd as special to him.

Hammett first met Lillian Hellman late in 1930 or early in 1931. Margaret Case Harriman later described her in *The New Yorker*:

She is five feet three inches tall, and slim, with reddish hair, a fine, aquiline nose, and a level, humorous mouth. When she is in repose or talking business, her nose and mouth give her a fleeting and curious resemblance to the familiar Gilbert Stuart portrait of George Washington. At parties, dressed in chiffon or white lace, she has the gift of creating an illusion of beauty. Her voice is flexible and interesting, and her hands, feet, and legs amply reward the candid pleasure she takes in them. She likes clothes and is so sensitive to them that the right or wrong dress has been known to produce a momentary success or disaster in her social career.[13]

Hellman was born in New Orleans to a well-to-do Jewish family, but her father, a shoe merchant, lost his business when she was five and he moved his family to New York. After high school and some college work at N.Y.U. and Columbia University, Hellman held a series of literary jobs: she was a copy editor at the legendary firm of Boni and Liveright, a book reviewer for the *New York Herald Tribune*, a play reader for various producers, and a theatrical publicist. In 1925, after an abortion, she married Arthur Kober, then a press agent and later a very successful writer of Jewish humor and humorous screenplays. When she met Hammett, Hellman and Kober had just returned from Paris, where she had published her first short stories in *The Paris Comet*, a magazine that Kober had edited.[14]

Kober was in Hollywood working as a screenwriter and he was a friend of Hammett's. Hellman was working at MGM as a script reader, though Hammett remembered some years later that she had been a secretary there.[15] In *An Unfinished Woman* (1969), Hellman wrote that they had first met in a restaurant in Hollywood "when I was twenty-four and he was thirty-six," that Hammett was winding up a five-day drinking spree, and that they sat in his car and talked all night long.[16] By March 1931, he was addressing her as "darling" in his letters and they had begun a romance that lasted for the next thirty years, though in that time there were long periods when they were apart and neither was faithful to the other, in the traditional sense, from the beginning. Hellman divorced Kober in 1932, and she lived with Hammett periodically, beginning in Hollywood in the early 1930s.

Lillian Hellman has written about Hammett in her four memoirs since his death. She has also protected his memory closely, inhibiting biographical research and fostering her private image of him, which often seems incomplete and distorted. She admits to the selectivity and unreliability of her memory of Hammett in *An Unfinished Woman*: "as I come now to write about them the memories skip about and make no pattern and I know only certain of them are to be trusted. . . . (I could have done a research job, I have on other people, but I didn't want to do one on Hammett. . . .)"[17]

The thirty-year relationship between Hammett and Hellman clearly had a profound effect on both of their lives, though the details of their life together have been clouded by her highly subjective accounts. What is known with some certainty is that Hammett loved Hellman, that he helped her realize her literary ambitions, and that the history of their life together includes his decline as a writer and his increased involvement in political causes that Hellman often espoused more vociferously than he did.

Hammett had shown some interest in the stage before he met Hellman. In his letter of June 16, 1929, to Harry Block about *The Maltese Falcon*, Hammett suggested that the novel could easily be turned into a play. He asked Block to suggest someone to do the adaptation, as Hammett did not feel he should take on the project himself. Wasson sold an option on dramatic rights in 1930 to Benjamin Glazer, who negotiated with Laurence Stallings for the adaptation, but the project was dropped.[18] Hammett told Elizabeth Sanderson during their 1932 interview that he would like to try his hand at a play,[19] and it is possible that he had in mind dramatizing a story by William Roughead called "Closed Doors; or the Great Drumsheugh Case" (in his 1930 collection of true crime stories called *Bad Companions*) about a girls' school in Edinburgh, Scotland, forced to close because it was rumored that the owners were lesbians.[20] In any event, in 1933 Hammett suggested that Lillian Hellman attempt a dramatization of that story. She did so, and Hammett read her drafts, making suggestions for revisions. Hellman worked at the time as a reader for producer Herman Shumlin, and she showed him her play when it was finished. He agreed at once to produce it. *The Children's Hour* was extraordinarily successful, running 691 performances on Broadway, and Hellman earned in excess of $125,000 from the play.[21] When *The Children's Hour* was published in 1934, by Hammett's publisher Knopf, it was dedicated "For Dashiell Hammett with thanks."

From the beginning of her career as a playwright, Hellman was meticulous in the writing of her plays. She researched her subjects thoroughly, and she rewrote and revised her work through many versions, acting on advice from a number of readers, most prominently Hammett and her producer friends Herman Shumlin and, later in her career, Kermit Bloomgarden. But she rejected their advice as often as she accepted it, as her manuscripts at the Humanities Research Center show.

Hammett seems to have advised Hellman about all of her plays, with the exception of an adaptation of Bert Blechman's *My Mother, My Father and Me* produced after his death. He showed a particular interest in *The Children's Hour*, *Days To Come* (1936), *The Little Foxes* (1939), *Watch on the Rhine* (1941), and *The Autumn Garden* (1951). But always Hellman's work was entirely her own and the irresponsible charge sometimes made that Hammett was her collaborator is false.[22] Rather, he influenced her by his strict literary standards. She wanted to please him. In a 1965 interview in *The Paris Review* she said about Hammett: "He was generous with anybody who asked for help. He felt that you didn't lie about writing and anybody who couldn't take hard words was about to be shrugged off, anyway. He was a dedicated man about writing. Tough and generous."[23]

Hammett had a special feeling for Hellman, but he did not limit his attention to her. Among his female companions when he met her was a starlet named Elise De Vianne. On a visit to Hollywood in the winter of 1931, Hammett invited Miss De Vianne to his hotel room for dinner. She claimed that after they ate he beat her then attempted to rape her, and she sued him for $35,000 in damages in the Superior Court of California. Hammett was not present at the trial on June 30, 1932; in his absence he was found guilty and Miss De Vianne was awarded $2,500.[24]

Hammett was broke at the end of 1931. He was living at the Hotel Elysee at 60 East Fifty-fourth Street in New York and trying to write so he could make some money. He agreed to a lecture tour for 1932-1933 to be organized by a man named W. Colston Leigh, but apparently that deal fell through when Hammett's financial situation improved.[25] Hammett had not had a short story published for fifteen months. The pulps did not pay enough to make publication there worth his time now, but with the reputation his novels had won him, he could now write for the better-paying slicks and get as much as $2,500 a story. With Wasson's encouragement, Hammett began writing stories again. In the next two years, he wrote seven stories for *American Magazine*, *Collier's*, and *Liberty*, and three short pieces, one each for *Harper's Bazaar*, *The Mystery League Magazine*, and *Esquire*. Hammett had lost the intensity as a writer that had made his stories of 1925 so successful. Now he was in it only for the money.

Of his last stories, the shortest ones, though they are little more than vignettes, are generally the best. "On the Way," subtitled "A Brief Cinematic Interlude Enacted under Western Skies," (*Harper's Bazaar*, March 1932) is a Hollywood story about Kipper, "a long, raw-boned man" who has done well as a screenwriter but now has no job. He is left with only a grubstake, and Gladys, his girl friend who has just landed an acting role at $250 a week for six months, with options. Her first job is in a movie called *Laughing Masks* (a title Hammett had used for a 1923 short story). "On the Way" takes place during the evening she gets the job, when Kipper decides to leave her so he will not stand in the way of her career. She is eager to have him stay so she can repay him for his support and his advice about her work. That night they go out drinking to celebrate, and when a director friend of theirs makes a pass at Gladys, Kipper steps aside, knowing that her attentions to a director will be good for her career. On the way home at the end of the evening, Gladys asks Kipper to marry her. She says she will do anything he wants to do. He says he wants to go away from her. The implications are that besides not wanting to interfere with her career, he is disgusted with Hollywood and Hollywood people.

"Night Shade" (*Mystery League Magazine*, October 1, 1933) is a fifteen-hundred-word piece about a judge's daughter who is rescued by a stranger named Jack Bye from some unspecified danger at the hands of two men one dark night. She goes with him (by way of Hellman Avenue) to a Negro bar. After they drink, he suggests she take a cab home instead of riding with him. Reluctantly, she agrees. After she leaves, the bartender tells Jack Bye: "you got to remember it don't make no difference how light your skin is or how many colleges you went to, you're still a nigger."[26]

"Albert Pastor at Home" (*Esquire*, Autumn 1933) is a one-thousand-word story about a man who goes to his hometown to visit his father, a grocer, and finds that local grocers are being victimized by a protection racket. Albert Pastor, a former heavyweight boxer who would have been champion "if they did not have rules you are supposed to fight by in the ring and if he did not have a temper which kept him forgetting they had rules you were supposed to fight by,"[27] beats up the small-time racketeers. At the end of the story, it is revealed that Pastor himself runs a protection racket in the big city.

In addition to the three short-short stories, Hammett also wrote three stories about Sam Spade, capitalizing on Spade's popularity in *The Maltese Falcon*. These are the only short stories in which Hammett used Spade as a character. They are lazy, inadequately developed pieces. "A Man Called Spade" (*American Magazine*, July 1932) is a reworking of "The Tenth Clew" with less movement and a less plausible explanation of the detective's solution to the crime. Spade is called by a client who says his life has been threatened. When Spade arrives at his client's apartment, the man is dead. The clues are profuse and enigmatic, yet without leaving the room,

Spade sifts through a superabundance of suspects and identifies the murderer who had left a trail of false clues.

"Too Many Have Lived" (*American Magazine*, October 1932) is a simple blackmail story. A poet with a shady past finds out that a man he once knew who had thrown another man from a train into a canyon has since been financially successful. The poet goes to blackmail his former acquaintance and is murdered by his mark. Spade is hired by the boyfriend of the poet's widow, first to find the missing poet, then, after the poet's body is discovered, to clear himself of the murder.

The first two Spade stories were published in *American Magazine*. The third was published in *Collier's*. "They Can Only Hang You Once" (November 19, 1932) is a rewrite of "Night Shots," which had appeared in *Black Mask* eight and a half years earlier. In this story Spade is hired to investigate two murders committed in the Binnett home where wealthy Uncle Tim is convalescing. Spade soon discovers that Uncle Tim is a penniless fraud living off his nephews who believe that he made a fortune in Australia, while he was actually serving time at Sing-Sing. When his ruse is discovered, he murders to protect his secret.

Two of these three Spade stories are rewrites of earlier stories and the plot of the other is so simplistic that no model was necessary. Sam Spade is reduced to just another wisecracking detective, and the stories are padded for length. Hammett could still write, and even these lazy efforts are sometimes impressive in their dialogue, but he was cheating the customers.

It was a different matter with "Woman in the Dark," a fifteen-thousand-word story published weekly in three parts in *Liberty* magazine beginning with the April 8, 1933, issue. Hammett spent more time on the story because he saw its possibilities beyond magazine publication. Wasson sold an option on the story to Select Pictures immediately after publication for $500 against a purchase price of $5,000. The option was traded and exercised finally by RKO Radio, who released the movie made from Hammett's story, with screenplay by Sada Cowan, in 1934.[28] "Woman in the Dark" is a mystery story without a detective. The focus is on Luise Fletcher, another of Hammett's femmes fatales. As the story begins, she is the unhappy mistress of Kane Robson, the richest man in Mile Valley. She escapes from Robson's home under cover of darkness and seeks refuge with an ex-con named Brazil, who has just finished serving time for manslaughter. Robson and his hired man Conroy find the woman with Brazil and attempt to take her away by force, but Brazil stops them after a fight with Conroy.

Brazil and Fletcher then find themselves fugitives. Conroy was seriously injured the night of his fight with Brazil, and Robson presses charges of assault against Brazil and larceny against Fletcher, whom he accuses of stealing jewelry he had given her as gifts. When the two are arrested, Robson drops charges against Fletcher on the condition that she will come back to live with him. When she is back in the Robson household she learns that Conroy's injury was the result of a fight he had with Robson after they had left Brazil's; moveover, Robson is trying to assure Brazil's imprisonment by seeing that Conroy dies from his injury.

In the climactic scene, Brazil, who had been reluctant to believe Luise Fletcher would desert him, escapes from jail and confronts her at Robson's home. While he is there, Robson is discovered attempting to smother Conroy. Brazil stops him—in front of witnesses—and clears himself of the assault charge. Luise Fletcher switches her loyalties again, and as the story ends she lays the jewelry she had allegedly stolen at Brazil's feet. The story is well constructed, the characters are convincing, and Hammett is especially successful at achieving a somber mood that pervades the story.

C H A P T E R 1 3

"The Thin Man" always bored me.

Dashiell Hammett in a 1957 interview

From the winter of 1932 to spring of 1933 there was about a six-month break in Hammett's short-story writing. He was working on his fifth novel, which would be his last. Though 1932 had not been a good year for Hammett financially, in September he was living at the Hotel Pierre, one of the most expensive hotels in New York. By the end of the month he had run up a bill he could not afford, and on September 29 he sneaked his clothes out and left without paying.[1] He managed to get a small advance from Knopf on his new novel and took up residence at a less impressive address, the Sutton Club Hotel at 330 East Fifty-sixth Street, then managed by Nathanael West, who was supporting himself as a hotel manager while he struggled to complete his second novel, *Miss Lonelyhearts*, which Hammett read in proof while he was staying at the hotel.

The Sutton Club had been built to accommodate a women's club that promised to lease it. But when the deal fell through after construction had begun, it was decided to complete the structure and run it as a hotel, even though there was no formal lobby and the building had an odd arrangement of suites. Since the paid occupancy rate was never very high, West felt at liberty to offer rooms to his literary friends at reduced rates or for free. Among his special guests were Norman Krasna, Quentin Reynolds, A. Lincoln Gillespie, Robert Coates, Edmund Wilson, James T. Farrell, Erskine Caldwell, Hellman, and Hammett, who had a suite of three small rooms known as the "Royal Suite." Here Hammett took up the serious business of completing *The Thin Man*.[2]

In *An Unfinished Woman*, Lillian Hellman writes about the change that came over Hammett while he was writing his novel. He stopped drinking and playing. He worked until he was finished. The novel was completed by May 1933, and Wasson began circulating the typescript to magazine publishers to solicit serial publication. The responses were disappointing. Most magazines refused to publish *The Thin Man* because they considered it amoral if not immoral. After two months of circulating the novel, Wasson sold it to *Redbook* for $5,000.[3] The contract permitted them to publish before book publication and to include *The Thin Man* in a give-away volume called *Six Redbook Novels*, used as a premium for new subscribers to the magazine. They were also allowed by contract to condense and bowdlerize the text, which they did with a free editorial hand. *The Thin Man* was in the December 1933 issue of *Redbook*, and on January 8, 1934, Knopf published the novel, complete and unexpurgated. Though it is Hammett's least successful book artistically, it was his most successful commercially. Though sales were brisk—about thirty-four thousand copies at $2.00 in the first year and a half of publication[4]—the novel was not a best-seller. Yet Hammett was able to live off the characters he created in *The Thin Man* for a long time with the receipts from a series of Thin Man movies in the 1930s and 1940s. His total earnings from the novel, its characters, and its spin-offs between 1933 and 1950 approached a million dollars.

Hammett's detectives seem to reflect his own attitude toward his work: before Nick Charles, they were serious, single-minded men who would never allow their social lives to intrude upon their work. They were successful not because of their brilliant analytical skills, but because they followed every clue and intelligently considered all the evidence. Nick Charles's detective skills come too easily. He retired as a private eye when he married Nora. Now he would rather party than investigate a murder, and when he reluctantly becomes involved in a criminal investigation he conducts it in an alcoholic haze.

Nick lazily solves the three murders in *The Thin Man*. He withholds clues from the police as well as the reader—a defect Hammett objected to loudly when he found it in the work of others. Unlike Hammett's previous novels in which the detective went hunting evidence, in *The Thin Man* the evidence comes to Nick Charles.

Though *The Thin Man* is the weakest of Hammett's novels, measured against any standard except his own work, it is better than average. Nick and Nora Charles are Hammett's most charming characters, and Hammett capitalized on the strength of Nick's characterization by having the story told in the first person by him. The Charles's opulent, carefree life in 1932, a year before the repeal of prohibition, and in the month when the nation was suffering its gravest economic crisis of the Great Depression, was glamorously attractive to an audience that thrived on fantasies of wealth and leisure.

Nick and Nora are the epitome of urbanity. Their relationship strained the moral structures of the time, since both Nora and Nick are openly attracted to other men and women, but their relationship is strengthened because it is not restrictive. Nora is mildly jealous of Nick, but her jealousy does not turn to anger; instead, it seems only to increase her attraction to him. Nora is intelligent, impetuous, curious, and a little scatterbrained, qualities which cause her to get involved in situations that Nick must help her get out of when he would prefer simply to drink and relax.

Hammett told Hellman he had modeled Nora after her. In a 1969 interview, Hellman explained: "Mr. Hammett had once been a detective long before he was a good writer, and I used to nag him to go back to work as a detective—chiefly so, in my mind, I could follow him around and see what would happen. He'd grow very angry at the idea. But it also gave him something to write about. . . . I think [*The Thin Man*] was about a man and a woman who liked each other very much and who drank too much. . . ."[5]

The Thin Man is set in Manhattan between Thursday, December 22, 1932, and Saturday, December 31. Nick Charles is an aging former detective, retired since 1927 when his wife's father died leaving her "a lumber mill and a narrow-gauge railroad and some other things."[6] Nick and Nora are in New York to shop and visit friends during the holidays.

While drinking in a speakeasy, Nick meets Dorothy Wynant, the sensuous daughter of an eccentric inventor named Clyde Wynant who is an acquaintance of Nick's. Dorothy informs Nick that her parents are divorced and her father has disappeared—not unusual behavior for him. Nick suggests she see her father's lawyer, Herbert Macaulay. The next day, December 23, Julia Wolf, Clyde Wynant's secretary, is found dead by Mimi Jorgensen, the inventor's ex-wife.

Suspicion for her murder falls onto Clyde Wynant, who has not been seen since October.

In the next few days, there are a series of letters from Wynant—to his lawyer, to his son, to his wife, and to his sister—all crudely written on an old typewriter. Wynant sets up meetings with his lawyer and with Nick that he does not keep, and he calls Macaulay with some frequency. By the end of the following week, when the police are all but certain that Wynant is the murderer and Nick believes he is dead, probably murdered by Macaulay because only Macaulay has actually spoken to Wynant or seen him, Mimi claims her ex-husband has come to visit with $10,000 in bonds for her and his children.

Meanwhile at Nick's suggestion, the police go to inspect Wynant's workshop. There they find a body covered with lime to speed its decomposition. The clothes are a fat man's, and a belt buckle with the initials D.W.Q. is in the grave. By this time Nick is ready to make an arrest and provide an explanation. Macaulay was defrauding Wynant in collaboration with Julia Wolf. When confronted by Wynant, he killed the thin man, burying him under the floor of his workshop wrapped in a fat man's clothes meant to deceive anyone who should discover the body. Julia Wolf, an ex-con, knew of the murder and Macaulay did not trust her, so he killed her too. With Wynant apparently hiding out and Macaulay possessing power of attorney, the lawyer needed a way to exercise that power to his advantage. He convinced greedy, duplicitous Mimi to claim her ex-husband was giving her money, and they would split the take.

Nick's solution is based on a combination of facts, guesses, and instinct. When questioned by Nora about proof for his solution to the crime he retorts:

"That's for juries, not detectives. You find the guy you think did the murder and you slam him in the can and let everybody know you think he's guilty and put his picture all over newspapers, and the District Attorney builds up the best theory he can on what information you've got and meanwhile you pick up additional details here and there, and people who recognize his picture in the paper—as well as people who'd think he was innocent if you hadn't arrested him—come in and tell you things about him and presently you've got him sitting in the electric chair. . . ."

"But that seems so loose."

"When murders are committed by mathematics," I said, "you can solve them by mathematics. Most of them aren't and this one wasn't."[7]

There is an array of characters who do not participate directly in the murder plot, the most fascinating of which was for many readers the Charles's dog Asta, who is introduced on the second page of the novel: "She's had a swell afternoon—knocked over a table of toys at Lord & Taylor's, scared a fat woman silly by licking her leg in Saks's, and's been petted by three policemen."[8] (Nathanael West's biographer Jay Martin claims Asta was named after Laura Perelman's dog; employees of Samuels Jewelry Company say Asta was the last name of the credit manager at the jewelry store that was Samuels's stiffest competition.)[9] Among the humans, there are Dorothy Wynant, who competes with her mother for Nick Charles's affection; Dorothy's brother, Gilbert, a precocious, sneaking, would-be detective who declares that "Most of us have outgrown ethics and morals and so on"; the Harrison Quinns, he a lecherous old drunk groveling after Dorothy's attentions, she a distraught wife embittered over her husband's intemperance yet unable to reject him; and Levi Oscant, a gossiping piano player modeled on Oscar Levant, whom Hammett had met at the George S. Kaufmans'. There are the thugs: Studsy Burke, owner of the Pigiron Club, a speakeasy, who "claims to've cracked the safe in the Hagerstown jail while he was doing thirty days there for disorderly conduct,"[10] and Shep Morelli, Studsy's friend, who was a friend of Julia Wolf's and nearly kills Nick Charles to prove he did not murder her.

There are faceless characters: Larry Crowley, Nora's companion when Nick is busy; Margot Immes, a friend of the Charles's; the Edges, boring party givers; Art Nunheim, a pitiful crook who attempts to blackmail Macaulay and is murdered for his efforts; Miriam, Nunheim's fiery redheaded girl friend; and Sparrow, Miriam's boyfriend who, thinking Nick killed Nunheim, attempts to avenge the murder at the Pigiron Club and is severely disciplined by Studsy Burke and Shep Morelli. And the cops: John Guild, honest, plodding, and dreaming—as Hammett did—of owning a silver-fox farm; and his sidekick, Andy, dull and somewhat belligerent. They are an intriguing gallery—rich, poor, smart, stupid, law-abiding, and crooked; but they are not brought together convincingly, because Hammett plotted his novel like a short story then padded it into a novel.

In 1970, John Brady, editor of *Writer's Digest*, wrote to Lillian Hellman asking why Hammett included a two-thousand-word quote from Maurice Duke's *Celebrated Criminal Cases in America* about Alfred G. Packer, a prospector convicted of cannibalism. Gilbert

Wynant is a curious boy with an interest in curious subjects, including cannibalism. He asks Nick if such things occur in America, and Nick reads him the entire story aloud. Mr. Brady correctly observed that the story does not seem "to contribute appreciatively to the book's outcome." Hellman replied that there was a simple answer: Hammett was using the story of Packer simply to fill pages,[11] and she seems to be right. Later, in a similar exchange, Gilbert asks Nick a series of questions about detective work; and Nick answers—straight from Hammett's June 7, 1930, review in the *New York Evening Post* in which he made suggestions to hack writers of detective fiction about realism in their work and the necessity for attention to precise detail.

The Thin Man was a daring book for the time in its treatment of sex, and much of the attention it received initially was for its risqué content. The Charles's marriage might have been described as "open" in the 1960s, but it bordered on immoral in the 1930s. Nora goes out with other men, notably Larry Crowley, and Nick does not hide his attraction to other women. The Harrison Quinns are less sophisticated: he is openly lecherous and makes a spectacle of his affair with Dorothy Wynant. When Nick brings Harrison home drunk from the Edges', Alice Quinn asks, "Where'd he pass out this time?" Nick tells her. "With that little Wynant bitch?," she wants to know. When Nick is evasive, she turns the conversation to herself: "What do people think about my staying with Harrison with him chasing everything that's hot and hollow?"

"You know I'm only staying with him for his money, don't you?"[12]

The real furor over the book was about the question Nora asked Nick after he had scuffled with Mimi at her apartment: " 'Tell me something, Nick. Tell me the truth: when you were wrestling with Mimi, didn't you have an erection?'

" 'Oh, a little.'

"She laughed and got up from the floor. 'If you aren't a disgusting old lecher,' she said."[13]

Redbook censored that passage, but Knopf decided to capitalize on it. On January 30, 1934, the publisher took an ad in the *New York Times* boldly declaring: "I don't believe the question on page 192 of Dashiell Hammett's The Thin Man has had the slightest influence upon the sale of the book. It takes more than that to make a best seller these days. Twenty thousand people don't buy a book within three weeks to read a five word question."[14] The statement was signed by Alfred Knopf, and it did not prevent the Canadian government from banning sale of the novel in Canada.

The dust jacket for *The Thin Man* carried Hammett's photo. Dressed in tweeds, wearing a hat, and carrying a cane, he appeared to be his own model for Nick Charles, a circumstance that only added to the confusion over the title. The Thin Man is the murdered Wynant, but, perhaps because of the dust jacket photo of a very thin Hammett posing as Nick Charles, many readers regarded Charles, and even Hammett, as the Thin Man, a notion reinforced by the movies based on the book. Moreover, Knopf centered its promotion of the book on its author—and his sophistication. A Knopf advertisement described Hammett:

He is an indefatigable and charming host, a connoisseur of fine liquors, and an expert ping-pong player. He likes dogs and loves music. He reads endlessly—almost everything but detective stories. His favorite book is Spengler's *The Decline of the West* and he often turns to it for bedtime reading. He likes tweeds and he owns a green suit. He smokes enormously. When in New York he may be found several nights in the week at Tony's. He writes on the typewriter and needs only one draft. He almost never rewrites anything—and hence he writes very, very slowly, pondering over the keys of his machine to decide, like Oscar Wilde, whether to put in that comma or to take it out.[15]

Hammett himself was more candid in interviews, such as this one which appeared in the *New York Evening Journal* in summer 1934, though the truth is still stretched at times:

I do take most of my characters from real life. Nick's wife in "The Thin Man" is real, for instance. Nick himself is a composite of two or three detectives. . . .

I'm a two-fisted loafer. I can loaf longer and better than anybody I know. I did not acquire this genius. I was born with it. I quit school when I was thirteen because I wanted to loaf. I sold newspapers for a while, loafed, became a stevedore, loafed, worked in a machine shop, loafed, became a stock broker, loafed, went into the advertising business, loafed, tried hoboing in earnest, loafed, became a Pinkerton detective for seven years and went into the army.

I was a sergeant during the war, but—please get this straight—not in the war. The war and my service in the army were contemporary, that's all you can say about it. . . .

Hobbies? Let's see, I drink a lot. Also play poker. That's all. I had a dog once, but he died. Summers I live down at Port Washington; Winters here in Manhattan. I'm married; two children.[16]

Generally, reviewers had kind words for *The Thin Man*. The *New York Herald Tribune* review began, "We're another if Dashiell Hammett hasn't done it again. This most unusual author, darling of brows both high and low, has come through with a new hard-boiled opus worthy to stand beside the best of his other works. . . ." The reviewer goes on, "They all seem to drink a bit too much; which prevents one from following their psychology very closely, unless there's a psychology of tipsy people. And where this department got the idea that folks in books should be sober, so that you can check up on their mentality, we don't know, unless it was from Louisa M. Alcott."[17]

T. S. Matthews in *The New Republic* tempered his praise: "Not that 'The Thin Man' is not a first-rate murder story, and one that only Dashiell Hammett could have written. But, perhaps because he has turned the trick so easily before that he is now getting a little tired of it, perhaps because we are beginning to notice that he sometimes repeats his effects, 'The Thin Man' seems a less excitingly fresh performance than, say, 'The Maltese Falcon.' It is still head-and-shoulders above any other murder story published since his last one."[18]

When the novel was published in London by Arthur Barker Ltd. in May 1934, *The Times Literary Supplement* judged the book more harshly than American reviewers: "This American detective story is told largely in dialogue, of which the object is rather to amuse with the smart phrase than to advance the movement. In fact there is little movement in it, if we deduct what goes to the getting of drinks and the making of telephone calls."[19] Hammett rather agreed with the *TLS* reviewer. In a 1957 interview, he looked back at his book: "I was never too enthusiastic about the detective stories. *The Thin Man* always bored me."[20]

PART 3

Movies, Politics, and the Army

1934-1945

C H A P T E R 1 4

Maybe there are better writers in the world but nobody ever invented a more insufferably smug pair of characters.

> Dashiell Hammett about Nick and Nora Charles
> in a letter to Lillian Hellman, December 26, 1937

About the time *The Thin Man* was published, Hammett left the Sutton Club Hotel with Lillian Hellman for Homestead, Florida. She was working on *The Children's Hour*, and he was drinking and relaxing. In *An Unfinished Woman*, Hellman writes: "We got drunk for a few weeks in Miami, then moved on to a primitive fishing camp in the Keys where we stayed through the spring and summer, fishing every day, reading every night. It was a fine year: we found out that we got along best without people, in the country."[1]

In Miami Hammett met his drinking friend, Nunnally Johnson, a New York journalist and short-story writer who had gone to Hollywood as a screenwriter in 1933 and later became a very successful producer and director. One night when they were drinking they passed by Burdine's department store. The road in front was under construction and there were piles of rubble at the roadside. Hammett stopped, picked up a rock, and announced to Johnson that he did not like Burdine's. With that, he smashed a display window then stood cheering until the police arrived to arrest him. Johnson spent the night trying to borrow money for bail.[2]

Along with Hellman, Hammett spent the last days of 1933 and a portion of 1934 in Homestead. Hellman worked on *The Children's*

Hour, and Hammett read her drafts and made suggestions. In 1935, after the play was produced, Hellman told a *New York Herald Tribune* staff writer about Hammett's advice. Her comments were reported in an interview article: "There is no Judge Potter to be found in 'The Children's Hour' at Maxine Elliott's Theater, but the judge was a vital figure in the play during its Florida phases. Dashiell Hammett brought about his elimination.

"At Miss Hellman's suggestion, Hammett read the fourth version and frowned upon the judge with a destroying frown. She was not convinced. It was a Hammett notion, too, that a scene should be written showing the irate mothers descending upon the school to remove their children after Grandmother Tilford had bruited the scandal about. She wrote it in three months of travail. Hammett read it. Said the whole idea was a mistake and he apologized for offering it."[3]

Hammett returned briefly to New York (where he stayed at the Hotel Lombard) about the time *The Thin Man* was published by Knopf on January 8, 1934, but he returned to Homestead and stayed through at least part of the summer of 1934 when the movie based on *The Thin Man* was released by MGM in June. The movie was directed by W. S. Van Dyke from a screenplay by Albert Hackett and Frances Goodrich, the husband and wife writers who provided the scripts for the first three of the six movies based on Thin Man characters between 1934 and 1947. *The Thin Man*, which starred William Powell and Myrna Loy as the Charleses, and Maureen O'Sullivan as Dorothy Wynant, was very well received. Mordaunt Hall in the *New York Times* called it "an excellent combination of comedy and excitement."[4] Though Hammett had no hand in the movie, his name was used to promote it, and when he left his southern retreat in summer 1934 to return to New York City, he was one of the most sought-after literary celebrities in America.

In January 1934 William Randolph Hearst's King Features announced a daily comic strip with continuity to be written by Hammett. The pay for a successful syndicated strip was very good—as much as $500 a week—and Hammett was glad to have the money even if the association seemed to damage his new respectability as a literary figure. King advertised the strip aggressively, and like Knopf, they chose to stress Hammett in their ads. In New York he was portrayed as a sophisticated man-about-town; in California his career as a detective was emphasized. On both the East and West coasts, the announcement of Hammett's comic strip made front-page news in the papers that elected to carry it. The strip was called "the greatest detective strip ever published" and Hammett was described as "the most popular, fastest selling, detective story writer of the twentieth century."[5] His name appeared on the strip, which was drawn by young artist Alex Raymond, for a little over a year, from January 29, 1934, to April 27, 1935; after that the strip continued, but Raymond took credit for the story.

Secret Agent X-9 originated with Hearst, who felt that he needed a comic strip to compete with *Dick Tracy*. Hearst suggested Hammett as the writer, and he authorized a generous salary to get him. For his money he got a curious strip with what comic-strip authority Ron Goulart has called a "sometimes cryptic and ad-lib quality of the continuity." Agent X-9 is a well-dressed, good-looking, nameless fighter against crime who lives in an expensive apartment and has a Filipino houseboy. It is unclear whom he is an agent for, but his job is action-filled, as in the second day of the strip when on his way to see a man in distress, X-9 is run off the road, his car turns over, he is shot at, and he walks away to continue his mission. His job is "to try to prevent one of the most horrible crimes ever planned," perpetrated by a criminal called "The Top"—the theft at sea of millions of dollars in gold bullion (recalling the *Sonoma* theft). If it is read as satire, the strip is very funny, but King Features boss Connolly was not interested in humor, just action. It was Hammett's disrespect for deadlines, though, that got him fired after fifteen months.[6]

In the spring of 1934, Hammett also turned out three five-thousand-word stories for *Collier's*. "Two Sharp Knives" (January 13, 1934) is a story about a crooked policeman who murders his girl friend's wealthy husband and tries to disguise the murder as a suicide. The story is low-keyed—not hard-boiled. The detective, small-town police chief Scott Anderson, is fatherly, with the kind of rural wisdom which is often masked as gullibility.

"His Brother's Keeper" (February 17, 1934) is a sensitive first-person fight story that proves Hammett could still write superbly well. It is his best piece of fiction since *The Glass Key*. The story is told by Kid Bolan, a dumb boxer managed by his brother Loney. Loney is in love with the wife of a ward boss, and he makes a deal to throw his brother's first main event fight so he can have the money to run away with his girl friend. Kid Bolan is never told to throw the fight—he is instructed to box his opponent, a losing tactic for a puncher like Bolan. During the fight, Loney relents after seeing the punishment his brother is taking and tells the kid to fight naturally. The Kid knocks out his opponent and Loney is murdered that night. Though Kid Bolan has all the facts of his brother's death, he is not quite smart enough to piece them together. He simply wishes he could have died instead of Loney.

"This Little Pig" (March 24, 1934) is a satirical story about the movie industry. The main character is script doctor Bugs Parish, who is sent by studio chief Max Rhinewein to the Sierras where a Western is being shot on location. Max has heard that another studio is planning to release a "sexed-up" Western and, as he explains to Bugs, "I got to be always first in the field. You know that. And we can beat 'em to release by a week or two easy."[7] When he arrives on the set, Bugs finds a set of stock Hollywood characters: Fred LePage, the director; Kitty Doran, the opportunistic starlet with whom Fred is infatuated; Ann Meadows, the actress who loves Fred and is jealous of Kitty; and Betty Lee Fenton, the temperamental star. The plot is further complicated by Bugs's love for Ann Meadows. Through a very cleverly worked set of manipulations, Bugs is able to teach everyone a lesson by simply giving them what they want. The last line, spoken by Bugs, is an apt enough comment on the story itself: "This one got out of hand for a while, but the result seems to be O.K."[8]

Nineteen thirty-four, the last year Hammett wrote fiction for publication, was financially a most successful year. In addition to his royalties from Knopf, paltry compared to the rest of his income, Hammett sold the three stories to *Collier's*—the exact price is unknown, but he certainly received over $1,500 apiece for them, and probably closer to $2,500; he had a weekly income from *Secret Agent X-9*; RKO picked up an option on "Woman in the Dark" for $5,000; MGM bought movie rights to *The Thin Man* for $21,000. The movie was so successful that MGM hired Hammett at $2,000 a week in October 1934 to write a sequel. And Hammett resold "On the Make," his screen story that had been written in 1931 for Warner Brothers and rejected, to Universal.

Universal bought "On the Make" on September 27, 1934. After several title changes apparently suggested by Hammett, including "Skeleton Sleuth," "Strictly Confidential," and "Special Investigation," the title *Mister Dynamite* was settled upon and the film was released in 1935 with a screenplay by Doris Malloy and Harry Clork.[9] Edmund Lowe played Mr. Dynamite, Jean Dixon was his secretary. Hammett apparently spent a brief time in 1934 revising

"On the Make," but it is clear that the story sold because Hammett wrote it, not because of its quality.

Gene Richmond (who became Mr. Dynamite in the movie) was the kind of detective careless readers of *The Maltese Falcon* thought Sam Spade was—he was crooked, yet competent. The story opens as Richmond is being run out of town by the police for some unspecified transgression. He immediately sets up in another town—location not disclosed—where he begins scanning the papers for ways to make money. He spots a story about a stolen Chinese artifact, calls the owner, and lies that he knows where it is. Richmond manages to get a $250 retainer and when the stolen piece is soon recovered, he turns in a phony expense report with the explanation that the police were on the same trail he was.

The first third of the story establishes Richmond's character: he is smart, and he is a thief. Time after time he fabricates expense reports, until finally, his office lavishly furnished by then, he gets his big case. Herbert Pomeroy, a wealthy, socially prominent businessman, was talked into backing a bootlegger in return for favorable prices on a shipment of liquor. When the shipment was being delivered, a man was murdered; Pomeroy is thus convinced he is guilty of murder as an accessory. Because Pomeroy is associated with gangsters, his lawyer, Kavanaugh, hires the crooked Richmond to get his client out of his predicament. Richmond wants $25,000 for the job, an exorbitant fee, and he threatens to go to the police unless his terms are met.

Meanwhile, Cheaters Neely, the bootlegger, and three of his friends decide to visit Pomeroy at his house—to eat and drink at his expense for a few days as they begin to blackmail him. After they horrify Pomeroy's beautiful daughter, Ann, Richmond is hired to deal with Neely and his friends. Richmond promises to fix everything.

Because the man killed was a narcotics agent, Richmond assumes what Pomeroy thought was a liquor shipment was actually primarily a drug shipment. To prove his theory, he hires a stool pigeon and learns his guess was correct, so Pomeroy is really in no legal trouble. But Richmond keeps that information to himself because he sees bigger money than his $25,000 fee. In the course of his stay at Pomeroy's, he falls in love with Ann Pomeroy, and she with him. So Richmond strings out the case a couple of days longer than necessary to establish his romance with her so that he can marry the Pomeroy money. Then he fingers the man who is holding the drug shipment, with very little afterthought about exposing the cover of his informant and thus causing his murder. While Richmond is away from Pomeroy's arranging the arrests of Neely's gang, Neely gets suspicious and kidnaps Ann. Richmond learns immediately of her abduction and races to Pomeroy's estate. On the way he comes upon a group of cars—the police have apprehended Ann's kidnappers. She is safe and more enamored than ever of Richmond. But her spell is broken when one of the arresting officers tells Richmond in Ann's presence how he happened to catch her kidnappers so quickly. Richmond's secretary is an ex-con who had served time as an accessory to embezzlement committed by her former boss. Her neurotic fear of going back to prison drove her to tell police that the kidnapping had occurred. Moreover, she told the authorities everything about Richmond's business, from his practice of fabricating surveillance reports and inflating expense accounts, to his involvement in the Pomeroy case. Ann is appalled that Richmond would jeopardize her safety for money and turns away from him as he explains: "I'm in the game for money. Sure, I'm always on the make."[10]

Hammett's screen story was altered considerably before it was filmed. Gene Richmond's name was changed to T. N. Thompson, also known as Mr. Dynamite. The Pomeroy character is transformed into Lewis, a casino owner who is embarrassed by two murders at his place of business. And four murders were introduced to spice up the action. "On the Make" was simply an exercise in Hollywood-style writing for Hammett. One of the remarkable features of the story was the extent to which he attempted to write what he thought the studios wanted. His script was a rough rewrite of *The Glass Key* which was composed at about the same time as Hammett first wrote "On the Make." Richmond and Ned Beaumont are cut from the same cloth, as are Ann Pomeroy and Janet Henry. The basic plot—an unscrupulous character is engaged to save the family honor and falls in love with the rich, beautiful daughter—is the same; but in the telling, the story is cheapened for the movie audience.

In late September 1934 when the success of *The Thin Man* was clear, the Culver City office of MGM requested that the New York office negotiate a contract with Hammett to write the original story for another Nick and Nora Charles movie. On October 1 Culver City was advised that Hammett was inaccessible and that in any event it would be impossible to get any work from him. On October 19 Louis B. Mayer wrote the Culver City office from New York warning against Hammett's "irregular habits." He was referring to Hammett's reputation as a drinker and his lack of respect for deadlines.[11] Nonetheless, four days later Hammett signed a contract to write original story material for ten weeks at $2,000 a week. He left New York by rail on October 24 or 25, and his salary commenced on his arrival at the studio, which was the twenty-ninth. He took a six-bedroom penthouse at the Beverly Wilshire Hotel that rented for $2,000 a month and settled into his routine, reporting to Hellman after his first day on the job that he liked the people, had a comfortable office, and missed her awfully. He was busy seeing old friends—the Herbert Asburys, the Nunnally Johnsons, the Joel Sayres (Joel Sayre was a screenwriter who specialized in movies about racketeers and gangsters, such as *Rackety Rax*, 1932, and *Hizzoner the Mayor*, 1933), and others. Two days later he reported doing "a little town roaming" with Mrs. Sayre until 5 A.M. then catching some sleep before he began working on his Thin Man sequel (apparently at home) around ten.[12]

On Monday, November 5, Hammett admitted to Hellman that he was ashamed of himself. He had been drinking heavily and had not been to the studio since the previous Tuesday, his second day on the job. It was difficult for him to get down to work because he was being treated as a celebrity. Joan Crawford and Clark Gable had come by his apartment to meet him, and he had been drinking with his friends Edward G. Robinson and Arthur Kober. Hammett reported that he was being harassed by starlets and misrepresented by the MGM publicity department. It was not until January 8, after more than two months on the job, that Hammett submitted his story—thirty-four typewritten pages long—to producer Hunt Stromberg. It was a draft that would require revision.

The opening has Nick "trying to hang up a new record for fast drinking" before he and Nora go to her Aunt Katherine's for a formal family dinner. At that staid affair, which to Nick reeked of respectability, it is learned that Robert, the husband of Selma Landis (apparently Nora's sister) did not come home the previous night, and the family is torn between protecting their honor by covering up what is assumed to be Robert's unfaithfulness to his wife and teaching him a lesson. Because he is discreet, Nick is asked to find Robert. Vaguely, he agrees.

After dinner, to "wash the taste of respectability out of his mouth," Nick asks his chauffeur to take him and Nora to the "toughest dive in San Francisco." They end up at the Li-chee, where they see Robert being hustled by a bar girl named Polly. Robert returns home the next day to a most suspicious wife and the news that he has written a $10,000 check of which he has no recollection. He goes to confront Polly with charges of what amounts to extortion and Selma follows with her hotheaded brother David. They all meet in Polly's room and threaten one another. Polly and David leave, and minutes later Robert is found shot to death. It is suggested that David, who was carrying a gun, might have shot Robert to avenge his disrespect for Selma.

Nora is naively curious about the case and begins going unaccompanied to the Li-chee looking for clues. She is humored by Polly, much to the distress of Polly's overly nervous husband Phil and the owners of the Li-chee, Dancer and Lum Kee, who do not want to tangle with Nick. Finally Nora makes her way to Dancer's apartment to hide and listen. She hears too much, is discovered, and is held captive.

Nick, meanwhile, learns Nora has been sleuthing at the Li-chee, and now that she is missing he takes an active interest in the case for the first time. He begins by having everyone connected with the case arrested. But he has no luck finding Nora and so returns home, where he finds her in bed. She had been delivered home by two Chinese who claim to have found her asleep on the waterfront. When he is assured that Nora is unharmed, Nick goes to the hall of justice where all the principals are under arrest and proceeds to unravel the mystery.

Polly, Dancer, and Phil were attempting to con Robert. They forged Selma's signature (she controlled the money in the family) on a check made out to Robert and then had him, in a drunken stupor, endorse that check, deposit it in his account, then write a check to Polly. Thus suspicion was on him for the forgery. After Selma and David visited Polly's apartment, Robert surprised Polly, Dancer, and Phil by saying he would go to the police regardless of the consequences, and Phil, scared and not too smart, panicked and killed him, mostly to protect his wife from what he thought would be a sure jail term.

When Aunt Katherine learns what really happened, she reasons that since Robert is dead, an irreversible circumstance, $10,000 is a cheap price to pay to protect the family's respectability. She decides to reimburse Selma her loss and then urge everyone to "just hush up the whole thing."

In this first draft, Hammett had not finally decided on a

murderer—David is the murderer in later drafts—but he had enough of a story to encourage MGM to offer him a new contract. Hammett's original contract had expired on March 9, 1935. He returned to New York briefly before he was recalled to MGM and, on June 19, 1935, signed an extraordinary agreement which stayed in effect, except for short periods when he was fired for drunkenness or unreliability, for the next three years. He was to serve as an assistant to Hunt Stromberg, "as general editorial aide and/or assistant and/or advising, not only in connection with preparation of stories and/or continuities, but as well in connection with actual production of photoplays. He agrees to attend conferences and assist in preparation and/or developing of ideas submitted by him or others and generally to render services as motion picture executive." The terms were $1,000 a week "when writing either alone or in collaboration with others on any particular scene or scenes, without having been assigned to write complete continuity, including dialogue of such screenplay" and $1,750 a week "when we require him to write complete continuity, including dialogue for any photoplay." The contract could be terminated with one week's notice by either party. Even though Hammett's salary was reduced, his earnings were still in the upper bracket for screenwriters at the time, and it is remarkable that with his growing reputation as not only an unreliable writer, but an uncooperative one as well, Hammett was offered such generous terms.

Nonetheless, throughout the duration of his tenure at MGM he failed to show up at meetings, failed to deliver work on time, and kept scriptwriters waiting while he pondered a story line. He was taken off the payroll at least three times for violating his contract—by simply disappearing while a movie he was involved with was being shot—but each time he was rehired, a tribute to his personal charm as much as anything.

After a series of minor assignments, Hammett was first released from his contract on August 1. He was reinstated when it was clear that his new treatment of the Thin Man sequel, now called *After The Thin Man*, was nearly finished. On September 17 Hammett gave Hunt Stromberg a 115-page typescript of a story for the movie; it was finished and polished. The story begins with a murder. Pedro Dominges, a former servant of the Landis family—Nora and Selma's family—dies of gunshot wounds at the door of the Charles's apartment. From that point the story develops as originally written except that David—originally Selma's impetuous brother—is now David

Graham, her lover who is bribing Robert to leave Selma so he can marry her. David finds Selma standing over Robert's body with a gun. Despite the suspicious circumstances, she did not kill him. Dancer, Polly, and Phil (who is later killed himself) are all implicated in Robert's murder. The climax comes at the building Pedro had managed in the apartment of a man called Anderson, directly above Polly's apartment. In Anderson's rooms, listening devices and a makeshift ladder of just the length to reach from Anderson's to Polly's window are discovered. Nick explains the mystery. Anderson is really David, a demented killer who had loved Selma before Robert married her and had come to hate them both. He was watching Polly's apartment because he expected to kill Robert there. Pedro remembered David from the days when he was a servant at the Landis's and David was engaged to Selma. When Pedro got suspicious of Anderson, he was killed. On the night David murdered Robert, Phil was following him. When Phil tried to blackmail David, he too was murdered.

When Nick makes his accusation, David grabs Nora and holds her out a window. He threatens to drop her unless he is given a five-minute head start to get away. But mysteriously, Lum Kee appears on the makeshift ladder, having climbed up from Polly's apartment and grabbed Nora by the waist. Nick grabs a gun and shoots David, who falls out the window. All agree it is for the best, because he would probably have avoided the gallows on an insanity plea. Lum Kee saves Nora to pay a debt. Nick had sent his brother up, and as he explains: "I no like my brother—I like his girl . . ." The same joke in a different context had ended the first draft.

After the Thin Man was released on December 25, 1936, with James Stewart as David, Ellissa Landi as Selma and Joseph Calleia as Dancer. W. S. Van Dyke directed and Albert Hackett and Frances Goodrich wrote the screenplay, as they had for *The Thin Man*. The movie was a hit. Frank S. Nugent in the *New York Times* wrote: "If 'After the Thin Man' is not quite the delight 'The Thin Man' was, it is, at the very least, one of the most urbane comedies of the season . . ."[13]

CHAPTER 15

I've decided to live flamboyantly.

Dashiell Hammett in a remark to Albert Hackett
and Frances Goodrich, 1937.

In the fall of 1934, Gertrude Stein came to America, full of praise for Dashiell Hammett, whom she admired for the directness of his writing style. She crossed the country from New York to Los Angeles, lecturing and, as she said, rediscovering America. When she got to Los Angeles in April 1935, wealthy socialite Lillian Ehrman arranged a dinner party of movie people at her Beverly Hills home, including Charlie Chaplin, Paulette Goddard, and Anita Loos. Stein requested that Hammett also be invited, and Ehrman dutifully sent him a telegram, which he thought at first was an April fool's joke. Hammett and Hellman attended and Stein flattered him throughout the dinner. In *Everybody's Autobiography* she claims to have engaged Hammett in a long literary discussion: "I said to Hammett there is something that is puzzling. In the nineteenth century the men when they were writing did invent all kinds and a great number of men. The women on the other hand never could invent women they always made the women be themselves seen splendidly or sadly or heroically or beautifully or despairingly or gently. . . . Now in the twentieth century it is the men who do it. The men all write about themselves, they are always themselves as strong or weak or mysterious or passionate or drunk or controlled but always themselves as the women used to do in the nineteenth century." Hammett, according to Stein, agreed. He said twentieth-century men lacked the self-confidence of men in the nineteenth century, and therefore they had to exaggerate their own qualities. Hammett said he hoped to avoid that problem in his own writing by writing about a father and son. There is no further evidence that Hammett ever considered writing about a father and son in any such significant way. That evening Alice B. Toklas signed the Ehrman guest book: "To Lillian May Ehrman who hears of a mystery in the morning and produces the mystery writer in the evening."[1]

The middle 1930s were a boom time for Hammett in Hollywood. Between 1934 and 1936, six movies were made from his original stories or adapted from his work—*The Thin Man* (MGM, 1934), *Woman in the Dark* (RKO Radio, 1934), *Mister Dynamite* (Universal, 1935), *The Glass Key* (Paramount, 1935), *Satan Met a Lady* (a remake of *The Maltese Falcon* by Warner Brothers, 1936), and *After the Thin Man* (MGM, 1936), and his income stayed at about $100,000 a year—not quite enough to keep up with his expenditures. When he was not living in a Beverly Wilshire penthouse, he lived in the Harold Lloyd mansion. He rode in limousines, usually leased, and he kept a chauffeur companion. As quickly as the money came, the money went. Hammett saw no reason to save. In a 1969 interview, Lillian Hellman told about visiting Hammett while he was living at the Beverly Wilshire, apparently in 1936. His unpaid hotel bill was $11,000, he owed the pharmacy where he bought his liquor $1,300, and he was broke. When he fell ill, his friends the Charles Bracketts paid his bills and sent him to New York to recover.[2]

Between 1933 and 1936 five lawsuits were filed against Hammett in Los Angeles Municipal Court, all for nonpayment of debts, and all were settled by default judgment. In 1933 a chauffeur sued him for $71 in unpaid fees; in 1934 a secretary filed a similar suit; in 1935 it was the car-rental agency Hill's U-Drive, and Ruth Meyers, whose complaint is unknown; and in 1936 Reliance Products of California complained that Hammett owed them money.[3] In addition, he was beginning to draw the attention of the Internal Revenue Service and the California state tax authorities, both of whom found him as careless about paying his income taxes as he was about paying his other debts.[4]

Hammett's executive duties at MGM never amounted to much. When *After the Thin Man* was released, Hammett suggested to Hunt Stromberg that Albert Halper's novel *The Foundry* had movie potential. At his suggestion, the studio bought rights to Halper's book.

Hammett was assigned to write the story, and his salary was continued at the $1,750 per week rate his contract called for when he
was writing original work. At the same time, Nathanael West was
writing his Hollywood novel, *The Day of the Locust*, and he needed
money. He hoped Hammett would get him a job working on the
Foundry script. But West, already embittered about Hollywood,
found Hammett less than accommodating. West said that Hammett

made me eat plenty [of] dirt. . . . [He] had some kind of party and I
sneaked out early and spit all the way home to get the taste of arse out
of my mouth. I couldn't drink and had a miserable time of course,
drinking wouldn't have helped and he did his best to rub it in. One of
the girls there tried to make up to me and for some reason or other
he said, "leave him alone he hasn't got a pot to piss in." Another time
when I tried to talk to him about Stromberg and a job, he made
believe he didn't understand what I was saying and called out in a
loud voice so that everyone could hear, "I haven't any money to lend
you now, but call me next week and I'll lend you some."[5]

In fact, Hammett had no jobs to give. *The Foundry* project was
soon aborted and Hammett's health was failing once again. (When
West's *The Day of the Locust* was published in 1939, Hammett had only
good words for it: "This is the Hollywood that needs telling about,"
he wrote. "In his work there are no echoes of other men's books.")[6]
Hammett stayed in Hollywood long enough to attend the "First West
Coast Black Mask Get-Together" on January 11, 1936, apparently
the only time he met Raymond Chandler, who was just beginning his
career as a writer; then he left for an extended stay on the East Coast.

In fall of 1935, Hammett had moved back and forth between New
York and Hollywood, staying at the Plaza in New York and the
Beverly Wilshire in Beverly Hills. By January 1936 drinking and
partying had once again taken their toll and Hammett was admitted
to the private pavilion of Lenox Hill Hospital at Seventy-seventh
Street and Park Avenue in New York. He had told Blanche Knopf in
March 1935 that he was going to settle down and write another novel
soon but his life in Hollywood and his work on *After The Thin Man*
prevented that. Mrs. Knopf sent Hammett some books when she
learned of his hospitalization and reminded him about his own
promised book.[7]

When Hammett was released early in February 1936, he took a
room at the Hotel Madison on East Fifty-eighth Street in New York.
He was strapped for funds and asked for an early royalty payment

from Knopf. On Valentine's Day, the Knopf accounting department obliged with a check for $478.99, for royalties from the second half of 1935 not due until May 1.[8]

Hammett stayed in Manhattan throughout the summer of 1936, ostensibly working on the novel he had contracted with Knopf to write. In the fall he leased a white clapboard farmhouse at 90 Cleveland Lane in Princeton, New Jersey, from a professor on sabbatical. He wanted to be near Hellman during the out-of-town tryouts for her second and least successful play, *Days to Come*, which opened on Broadway on December 15, 1936, and closed after only seven performances. Hammett entertained Hellman and her show-crowd friends in a manner too boisterous for his staid Princeton neighbors. They complained about his late-night parties, the noise, the traffic of people at all hours, and the women who spent the night. By early 1937 they had had enough, and they requested that Hammett leave.[9]

But his neighbors' attitudes notwithstanding, Hammett was regarded as a distinguished visitor to Princeton and he was included in the campus social events. He met Archibald MacLeish, whom he considered a stuffed shirt, and Andre Malraux—"very intense, dogmatic, acteurish"—whom he liked. When Malraux insisted at a cocktail party that Hammett was the "technical link" between Dreiser and Hemingway, Hammett countered that Malraux was a French Sean O'Flaherty. "I don't think we understood one another very well," Hammett wrote Hellman.[10] (Hammett was not warmly receptive to praise from foreigners. When Hellman told him he was admired by Andre Gide, Hammett replied, "I wish that fag would take me out of his mouth.")[11]

When he first arrived in town, Hammett was interviewed by Henry Dan Piper, a sophomore at Princeton, for the campus newspaper, *The Daily Princetonian*. Typically, he exaggerated a little, lied a little, and hinted at his true feelings:

There isn't much to tell about me.... Baltimore as a kid ... school for a coupla years ... stevedore ... newsboy ... Golly, I've seen lots of things, but I never seemed to stick long at 'em.

When the Armistice came along, all I could boast was a pair of weak lungs contracted in the Ambulance Corps. I did some private detective work for Pinkerton's, but all the time I was getting sicker, and found myself shortly in a California hospital.

Then it was a case of turning to something to keep the butcher away from the door while I tried to bluff along the baker. So I rented a second-hand typewriter and pounded out my first novel. It was just a case of lucky breaks after that.

Yes, I'm working on a book here, but it's not a mystery, and it's not about Princeton. I don't really like detective stories, anyway. I get too tangled up in the plots. This one is just about a family of a dozen children out on an island. You see, all I do in a story is just get some characters together and then let them get in each other's way. And let me tell you, twelve kids can sure get in each other's way!

The plot of his new book was, of course, Hammett's joke, though Mrs. Knopf was continuing to press him for a completion date of the novel he claimed to be working on. When he was asked about the movie he had just finished, Hammett's response was more candid:

I can't understand why people get the idea all I ever write is artificial, with tinseled- and-ginned up characters. They're just like lots of people I know neurotics and what have you. . . .

Yes, it's going to be like the others . . . They say they're going to call it "After the Thin Man." Heaven only knows why. Before Hollywood started monkeying with the plot it was something like "The Thin Man," but its own mother wouldn't recognize it now.[12]

After the interview, Piper mentioned that he could get tickets to the Yale-Princeton football game. Hammett asked Piper to get him four, and gave him a twenty-dollar bill. His black chauffeur/valet was suspicious about giving a stranger that much money, and he offered to drive Piper to the athletic office in Hammett's Cadillac limousine to assure that Hammett got his tickets.

In Princeton, Hammett read *Gil Blas* and *Don Quixote*, monitored the reception of *After the Thin Man*, and listened to offers from Hollywood. He turned down a contract with Samuel Goldwyn, and William Randolph Hearst offered him $50,000 to write a screenplay for his mistress Marion Davies. Hearst had an interest in Hammett. Although Hammett's involvement with *Secret Agent X-9* was over, King Features continued to syndicate Hammett's stories in Sunday newspaper supplements. The price he was offered for the Davies film was about 25 percent more than he normally got for a finished screen story, and Hammett was too much of an opportunist to pass up the money without exploring the deal. He realized finally, though, that he was unsuited for the motion picture industry and that if he was going to write screen stories for the money, he had better stick with Hunt Stromberg, who was lenient if not understanding.

After the success of the second Thin Man movie, William Powell, who resembled Nick Charles as much off camera as on, demanded a new contract and $200,000 per picture. MGM temporarily dropped plans for a third Nick and Nora Charles movie, but when Powell's contract was settled, the studio began immediately to prepare the third picture in the series, and Hammett agreed to come back to Hollywood to write the original story. He lived at the Beverly Wilshire where he took the suite that had been occupied by the King of Siam.[13]

In February 1937 MGM had agreed to pay Hammett $40,000 for all rights in perpetuity, excepting radio serialization, to the Thin Man characters. Negotiations for that deal were complicated by the fact that Old Gold cigarettes had shown interest in sponsoring a radio serial based on *The Thin Man* and, through the Cleveland B. Chase Company, had offered Hammett $500 per weekly episode for rights. They would require no original scripts from him. Hammett wanted to keep the rights to his characters that he could sell to Chase, and MGM finally agreed, at a significant loss of possible revenue. (The radio serial was not produced until 1941.) The studio felt that they should get some advantage in their next contract with Hammett, however.

When Hammett first moved into his suite at the Beverly Wilshire, he was broke and counting on the money from his recent MGM deal to pay his hotel bill. Nevertheless, to mark his return to Hollywood he gave a round of parties and treated visitors royally, ordering them liquor and meals from room service. As his bills mounted and the money from MGM still had not come, Hammett's friends began to worry for him. The Hacketts offered to lend him money and suggested that he be less generous with his guests. Hammett declined both the offer and the advice: "I've decided to live flamboyantly," he explained.[14]

In fact, MGM was attempting to force Hammett to sign a new contract on their terms and they were withholding payment for their purchase of all rights to the title "The Thin Man" and to the characters in the novel, claiming bookkeeping difficulties, to pressure Hammett into a deal.

They succeeded in negotiating a contract by which Hammett would write an original screen story but would not be paid a weekly salary. He was to get $5,000 for a synopsis; an additional $10,000 on acceptance of the story idea; and another $20,000 for a complete screen story. Under these provisions, the studio would not be paying

Hammett to loaf. He signed the contract on April 13, and within a year he had produced a completed story.

As Hammett was living flamboyantly in Hollywood, Jose Hammett and her two children were living frugally in Santa Monica. In early summer 1937 Jose Hammett filed for a mail-order divorce in a Nogales, Sonora, Mexico court. Neither she nor Hammett appeared in court, though they were nominally represented by court-appointed attorneys, and since neither resided in Mexico, the divorce was not legal. Jose Hammett herself argued that point with the Veterans Administration after Hammett's death. She was determined by them to have been his legal wife until his death and thus eligible for widow's benefits.

In his statement to the court, Mrs. Hammett's representative, Frederico C. Serna, misrepresented the facts somewhat:

from the beginning of [their] marriage his client and her husband . . . until a few months ago lived a more or less harmonious married life and with a happy home for some time, however, this harmony became disturbed, interrupting as a result their conjugal happiness due to the unkind treatment which, without justification, Mrs. Josephine Anna Dolan Hammett, has been the victim of from her husband . . . and not only has said Mrs. Hammett been the object on the part of her husband of such unkindness, but there have also occurred threats and grave injuries to such an extent that their living together became impossible, and in consequence, this client has decided to avail herself of the laws of the state of Sonora to obtain a divorce and thus terminate the lamentable situation in which she finds herself.[15]

The statement goes on to request that Mrs. Hammett be given custody of their two children and that she be allowed to reassume her maiden name (which she seems not to have done). The statement claims that during their marriage the Hammetts "did not acquire any community property." The divorce decree was recorded on August 31, 1937. Nine days later, in the last paragraph of a long letter to Hellman, between news of a labor board meeting and a complaint about his gambling luck, Hammett announced that he was divorced. Nonetheless, he occasionally visited Jose Hammett, sometimes for extended periods, the last being for about six months in 1950 when he was in Hollywood for the last time as a screenwriter.[16]

The day after Christmas 1937, Hammett wrote to Hellman that he had been arguing with Hunt Stromberg about the script of

Another Thin Man. He was by then tired of his characters and considered them silly. He referred sarcastically to the movie as a "charming fable of how Nick loved Nora and Nora loved Nick and everything was just one great big laugh in the midst of other people's trials and tribulations. Maybe there are better writers in the world but nobody ever invented a more insufferably smug pair of characters. They can't take that away from me even for $40,000."

Script revisions continued throughout 1938 and Hammett wrote three full drafts of the story. His obligations to the movie were apparently satisfied by July. That month MGM paid him $5,000 for a one-year option on all of his writings, though the movie was not released until November 1939. As work on the movie progressed, Hammett became increasingly uncooperative. His drinking increased; he failed to keep appointments with the Hacketts, who were writing the screenplay, and with Stromberg. Hammett communicated with his producer by telegram or through the Hacketts. On one occasion he received a telegram sent by the Hacketts from Stockholm informing him that Stromberg had cabled them from Biarritz to ask Hammett about the story.[17] Stromberg complained that Hammett was withholding the motivations of his characters, so that the Hacketts could not do their work.[18] Stromberg's production unit was becoming more and more disorganized as his addiction to morphine increased. The drug was being administered by an unscrupulous doctor to ease the pain from a back injury Stromberg had suffered. He was unpredictably moody and his once prodigious powers of organization failed him.

Meanwhile, Hammett was working on another novel. After he failed to deliver his new book in 1936, Alfred Knopf had angrily washed his hands of Hammett and released him from his contract. In 1938, Hammett went to Random House and got a $5,000 advance for a new novel. Random House was only eleven years old that year, but already Bennett Cerf and his partner Donald S. Klopfer had built one of the most respected lists in modern publishing. The mainstay of the company was The Modern Library, a high quality reprint line that had republished *The Maltese Falcon* in 1934, but Cerf was also signing the best of the young authors—Irwin Shaw, William Saroyan, Eugene O'Neill, and William Faulkner, to name a few. Cerf described the circumstances of his deal with Hammett in *At Random*: "Hammett had had an agreement with Alfred Knopf. . . . Since Alfred and I were always friends, I called him and said, 'I'm not going to poach on you, but Hammett says that he'll never talk to you again.' Alfred said, 'I want nothing more to do with him . . . Go ahead, but you'll have nothing but trouble with Hammett. He is a terrible man.' "[19]

In June 1938, Hammett wrote to a friend in Connecticut that he had "dug out the partly finished book 'My Brother Felix' & hope to get it done here this summer." In August he wrote again that he was "working on the book" and feeling good: "got myself up above the 160 mark."[20]

Hammett's novel, by then called "There Was a Young Man," was announced in *Publishers Weekly* for publication in fall 1939. But there was no book, not then, not ever. After two years, Hammett returned his advance, telling Cerf, "I'm afraid I'll never write it. I'm petering out."[21]

He was right. *Another Thin Man* was his last long piece of original writing. His screen story was 144 pages, including two versions of one eighteen-page segment. The plot was a reworking of Hammett's penultimate op story, "The Farewell Murder," published in the February 1930 *Black Mask*.

Another Thin Man begins with the Charleses, including year-old Nick, Jr., preparing to leave their New York Hotel for a visit on Long Island with Colonel MacFay, the former business partner of Nora's father, who now controls certain of the Charleses' investments. He has asked to see them about financial matters. On the way they pass the body of a black man, apparently knifed to death at the side of the road, and MacFay's overly nervous chauffeur refuses to stop. When they arrive at the old man's home, Nick and Nora learn that MacFay is being terrorized by a former employee of his and Nora's father's named Phil Church. Church went to jail for a shady business deal he was arranging which could not be traced to his bosses, and now he wants revenge. He stages murders—the body Nick saw on the way to MacFay's was Church's knife-throwing assistant Dum-Dum, playing dead—he slaughters MacFay's house pets, he generally terrorizes the Colonel; and then the mysterious Church, who seems to have learned some witchcraft while living in Cuba, lets it be known that he dreamed MacFay's throat was cut. MacFay wants Nick's help.

The day after his arrival, Nick goes to visit Church and finds him packing his bags, apparently having decided to leave the Colonel in peace. Church has just dreamed a third time of MacFay's death and that, he says, means it will happen. He leaves, along with Dum-Dum and Smitty, the wife of his former cellmate, and that night the

Colonel's throat was cut. Church and his friends were all in New York with firm alibis at the time of the murder.

After some difficulty with local police and later with Lieutenant Guild, a character from *After the Thin Man*, Nick solves the murder. MacFay's throat was cut by Lois, his adopted daughter who never lost her taste for the underside of life. She was in love with Church and wanted to share MacFay's fortune with him. Church, meanwhile, was attempting to get arrested and tried for MacFay's murder because he knew he could beat the rap and could only be tried once. There was no such insurance against hanging for Lois, who in the climactic scene murders Church out of jealousy over Smitty and the realization he is double-crossing her.

Despite a too complicated climax, the movie carried on the success of the series. Frank S. Nugent in the *New York Times* observed: "This third of the trademarked Thin Men takes its murders as jauntily as ever, confirms our impression that matrimony need not be too serious a business and provides as light an entertainment as any holiday-amusement seeker is likely to find."[22]

C H A P T E R 1 6

Democracy, like charity, should begin at home.

> Dashiell Hammett in a form letter soliciting support
> for liberal candidates in the 1938 election.

Largely, though not exclusively, through Hellman's influence,
Hammett was becoming intensely interested in politics in the late
1930s. The first indication of his new political awareness is in a letter
to Hellman from Princeton dated March 13, 1937, in which he tells
her about the acknowledgment from George S. Kaufman's wife,
Beatrice, of his "modest contribution" to the medical fund for
Americans wounded in the Spanish Civil War.

The Spanish Civil War was viewed by the American left as the first
international battle against Fascism. The cause of the Loyalists
fighting against the Fascist-backed rebels, who were receiving arms
from Italy and Germany, became a popular one among liberals in
the United States. A group of Americans known as the Abraham
Lincoln Brigade went to Spain to support the Loyalists in battle,
against the wishes of the United States government, but with the
vocal support of many left-wing political groups in America and a
number of moderates as well. The literary community was particularly supportive. Among the writers who led the effort to provide
food, clothing, and money for the Lincoln Brigade were Ernest
Hemingway, Donald Ogden Stewart, John Dos Passos, Dorothy
Parker, Lillian Hellman, and Hammett. Hammett also put up $500,
along with Hellman, Ralph Ingersoll, Archibald MacLeish, Gerald

Murphy, Dorothy Parker, and Herman Shumlin, to back *The Spanish Earth*, a movie about the Spanish War produced on location in Spain by Ernest Hemingway and Dutch Communist Joris Ivens.[1]

On July 10, 1937, Hemingway and Ivens were in Hollywood to celebrate completion of *The Spanish Earth*, and Hammett attended a party at the home of the Fredric Marches. Dorothy Parker invited some of the guests including Hammett, Hellman, F. Scott Fitzgerald, Eroll Flynn, and Hemingway to her house after they left the Marches's and Hellman remembers that Hammett got very drunk. He kept telling anyone who would listen that Hemingway had never been able to write about a woman, and that he put women in his books only to admire them. Hemingway, meanwhile, had smashed a cocktail glass into the fireplace, frightening Fitzgerald, who was always in awe of Hemingway. Hammett liked Hemingway, but he was easily annoyed by Hemingway's macho, self-important poses.[2]

Hellman also tells about a dinner at the Stork Club (apparently in 1939 though her dates are confused) with Hammett, Hemingway, Hellman, and German writer Gustave Regler. Hemingway was ranting about intellectuals trapped in France and Spain after the Spanish Civil War and the reluctance of the safe people in New York to aid them. Hammett told Hemingway he resented Hemingway's lecturing manner and his implicit indictment. When Hemingway pressed the point, suggesting that Hammett was against saving the intellectuals, Hammett responded that there were other people in the world too. Then Hemingway took a spoon from the table, placed it between his biceps and forearm and bent it, daring Hammett to try the same stunt. Hammett suggested that Hemingway go back to bullying Fitzgerald, whom he called "The best." When Hemingway still persisted in taunting Hammett to try bending the spoon, Hammett left, saying he probably could not do it now, but when he did tricks like that, it was for Pinkerton money.[3] By that time Hammett had decided he no longer needed to work for anybody's money and he spent his energies on political matters.

In the Neutrality Acts of 1937 the United States declared its unwillingness to provide munitions and supplies for the use of either of the opposing forces in Spain. Supporters of the Lincoln Brigade felt that declaration doomed the Loyalist forces to defeat. The rebels received arms from the Fascists, and the Loyalists needed similar support from democratic nations, though they were receiving aid from Russia. Hammett was among the ninety-six signers of an ap-

peal dated April 8, 1938, to the democratic countries of the world
and to President Roosevelt circulated by the American Friends of
Spanish Democracy. It read in part:

We therefore appeal to the democratic powers of the world to
have done with the non-intervention pact and the embargo act, so
that people who do not choose to accept either Nazism or Fascism
may have a fighting chance for their lives, and we appeal most
particularly to the President of the United States in the name of
decency and humanity to end this discrimination, as can be done
without the slightest prejudice to our essential neutrality.[4]

Twenty days later, he endorsed a statement in support of the
Moscow trials in Russia, at which the Stalinists tried followers of
Trotsky and other dissident Communists. The statement declared:

The measures taken by the Soviet Union to preserve and extend
its gains and its strength ... find their echoes here, where we are
staking the future of the American people on the preservation of
progressive democracy and the unification of our efforts to prevent
the fascists from strangling the rights of the people. American
liberals must not permit their outlook on these questions to be
confused, nor allow their recognition of the place of the Soviet
Union in the international fight of democracy against fascism to be
destroyed. We call upon them to support the efforts of the Soviet
Union to free itself from insidious internal dangers, principal
menace to peace and democracy.[5]

Among the 150 signers were Nelson Algren, Malcolm Cowley,
Hammett, Hellman, Langston Hughes, Dorothy Parker, Irwin
Shaw, and Richard Wright.

In Hollywood, Hammett was an active supporter of the Screen
Writers Guild. From the beginning the movie industry had been run
autocratically, with little regard for those who provided the material
for the movies. Most screenwriters worked at the whim of producers
and studio chiefs. They were often fired without cause and frequently were denied credit for their work. The Screen Writers Guild
sought to establish rules for the employment of screenwriters and
guidelines for screen credits, which constitute a screenwriter's credentials.

MGM was in the forefront of the opposition to the Screen Writers
Guild. The struggle between the writers and the studios over the
issue of writers' rights was a bitter one. The movement to have the

Guild recognized was begun in 1936. In August 1938 the National Labor Relations Board supervised an election in which the writers voted between the Screen Writers Guild and the studio-backed Screen Playwrights as their bargaining agency, and the Screen Writers Guild won by a vote of 267 to 57. But it was another three years, until June 1941, before the studios negotiated a contract with the Guild. During the five-year fight waged by the Guild for recognition, considerable antagonism developed between them and the studios. Because of his active support of the Guild, Hammett was one target of MGM's bitterness.

He busied himself in Hollywood recruiting members for the Guild, a safe enough pursuit, given his reputation and film credits. Unestablished writers, however, took a greater risk. A studio blacklist was in effect, and membership in the Guild in the late 1930s would assure a writer of being branded a troublemaker and suspected of being a Communist. Hammett suffered little distress on that account. He had always been known as a troublemaker at MGM, though for different reasons. He reported to Hellman on September 9, 1937, that the Guild had been signing up an average of twelve members a week.

Hammett's political opposition to the studios went beyond his role in the organization of the Screen Writers Guild. In 1938, for instance, Hammett circulated a 600-word personalized form letter to friends and acquaintances in the motion picture business requesting their support for liberal candidates in the local elections that year. One of Hammett's letters was addressed to F. Scott Fitzgerald, who was then under contract to MGM. Hammett began:

Dear Scott:
This is a letter about politics. I know you are interested in a general way, but 1938 is an election year in this state and before this campaign is over you and all of us in the motion picture industry are going to find ourselves caught up in it. The Republican machine was too successful in making suckers out of us in 1934 not to try it again.

He reminded Fitzgerald that when Frank Finley Merriam ran successfully for governor of California in 1934 studio employees were "blackjacked" into giving a day's pay to his campaign fund, and he outlined some of the abuses of the Merriam administration, charging that Merriam failed to oppose political corruption, created a Republican machine by adding 400 state commissions to the government, opposed organized labor, and supported "government by a few dominant corporations." Hammett invited Fitzgerald to join a "studio committee for democratic political action," which would oppose reactionary government on the local and national level. The committee would draw on "the power of the motion picture industry . . . this time to aid liberals." Among the members of the committee were Philip Dunne, Milt Gross, Miriam Hopkins, Major Kieffer, Dorothy Parker, Irving Pichel, Gale Sondergaard, Donald Ogden Stewart, and Frank Tuttle.[6]

Though the work of Hammett's studio committee must have been a minor factor, Merriam was unseated in the November 1938 election. Democrat Culbert L. Olson won the election by 10 percentage points to become the only Democratic governor of California between 1918 and 1958.

Meanwhile, Hammett's political interests broadened from local to international affairs. He spoke at Communist-sponsored anti-Nazi rallies in New York in November 1938. By December, he was heading an organization known as the Professionals Conference Against Nazi Persecutions.[7] All of these activities were considered at the time to be Communist inspired, and there is evidence supporting such allegations even if they were initially voiced in a time of reactionary frenzy and were based on insufficient information. In *An Unfinished Woman*, Lillian Hellman wrote: "the truth is that I do not know if [Hammett] was a member of the Communist party and I never asked him."[8] Nonetheless, it seems likely from the responsibilities Hammett was given for Communist activities that he joined the party in 1937 or 1938.

Hammett did not, however, espouse the violent overthrow of the United States government, nor was he a political threat to democracy. Many of the views Hammett held on domestic issues would seem middle-of-the-road today. He supported voter rights and mounted voter registration drives for blacks and other minorities; he supported labor unions; he felt that state and federal employees should not be fired from their jobs because of their political beliefs; he encouraged immigration of foreign victims of political persecution; and he opposed Fascism in what he saw as its myriad forms. Such attitudes, however, were unpopular among Hollywood studio heads, and as Hammett's political activity increased, MGM found it more difficult to tolerate his irresponsible work habits. His value to the studio was measured by the success of the Thin Man movies; but after he sold his rights to the characters and the title, the studio no longer needed him.

The $80,000 MGM paid Hammett in 1938 made him one of the highest paid Hollywood writers. In 1939, the closest year for which figures are available, only 13 of more than 800 writers made as much as $80,000.[9] But 1938 was Hammett's last big earning year in Hollywood. Though he submitted original stories over the next three years, he had little success, and his days on contract at MGM were numbered.

On December 7, 1938, Hammett submitted an eight-page draft of the story for a fourth Thin Man movie, tentatively titled "Sequel to the Thin Man." The script borders on the absurd, as if Hammett were testing Hunt Stromberg's gullibility. Macaulay, the murderous lawyer from *The Thin Man* has escaped from prison and has vowed to kill Mimi. To avoid him, Mimi and her son Gilbert move from New York to San Francisco, where Nick and Nora happen to be entertaining an "antique Uncle and Aunt" of Nora's, and call Chris (Mimi's husband), who is now living with his first wife, Georgia, for help. Thinking he can make a buck from her fear, Chris goes to Mimi, just ahead of Georgia, who vows not to give Chris up unless she is paid to do so; she, in turn, is followed by her boyfriend Morelli. Macaulay, now a transvestite, is also in San Francisco.

Chris contacts a disreputable friend, the nightclub owner Dancer, and together they make plans to extort money from Mimi. Morelli, Dancer, Georgia, and Chris approach her at Nick's house, and the result is a "battle-royal," which ends when Nick throws them all out. When they leave, Chris is followed by Dancer, who in turn is followed by the lurking Macaulay dressed in drag. Georgia, Morelli, Mimi, and Gilbert eventually congregate at Chris's hotel, and as Chris approaches the hotel, he is killed. Macaulay, who drops his wig in his haste to leave the scene, is arrested for the murder. But there are five other likely suspects.

After some misleading developments, Nick solves the case—Gilbert shot Chris; and Dancer, who witnessed the murder, was blackmailing Mimi to pay him to keep the information from the authorities. Gilbert's motive was mercenary—he felt that the money Mimi was being pressured to give Chris was actually his, as his father's heir.

On Christmas Day 1938, two and a half weeks after Hammett submitted his sequel, which the studio rejected, his contract was suspended briefly, but by early spring 1939 he was back on the payroll working on an "original" story called "Girl Hunt," an adaptation of the 1929 op story "Fly Paper." On July 14, 1939, Hammett's contract with MGM was canceled for the last time, and on August 12 "Girl Hunt" was returned to his agent, rejected.

CHAPTER 17

We will work for united action by all peoples, all religious groups and all nationalities, to defend democracy and combat anti-Semitism and Fascism.

From the "Program of Equality" (1940)
Sponsored by Hammett

Hammett must have realized that his career as a screenwriter was coming to an end and he developed an interest in working as a publisher. In 1938, while he was in New York, he participated in the early planning of *PM*, a liberal New York newspaper that the FBI suspected of Communist sympathies.[1] *PM* was published by Ralph Ingersoll, who in 1936 had developed the idea for a pictorial newsmagazine called *Life*, which he convinced Henry Luce to publish. *PM* was a similarly innovative project—a newspaper without ads that would be a showcase of liberal journalism. By 1940 when *PM* was first published, Hammett was no longer associated with the paper, though he did write a book review of James Joyce's *Finnegans Wake* for a trial issue,[2] and he claimed later that he helped Ingersoll with his editorials. But, though he maintained an interest in *PM*, he lost touch with the newspaper when he moved back to Hollywood.

On September 6, 1939, *Variety* announced a new project: a "group of scribblers headed by Dashiell Hammett . . . active in controlling intolerance have formed a publishing organization to put out periodicals, books, and pamphlets as a means of furthering their cause."[3] Called Equality Publishers, the group initially consisted of Hammett, John Achreiber, Andrew W. Loew, Albert Deutsch,

Aaron Lipper, Leo W. Schwartz, and Lucy Strunsky. Their first publication was *Equality: A Monthly Journal to Defend Democratic Rights and Combat Anti-Semitism and Racism*, which first appeared in May 1939; it ran through October/November 1940. Hammett sat on the eighteen-member Editorial Council of the magazine along with Bennett Cerf, Moss Hart, Lillian Hellman, Arthur Kober, Louis Kronenberger, Albert Maltz, Dorothy Parker, and Donald Ogden Stewart.

The "Program of Equality" was published in a promotional leaflet:

We will work for united action by all peoples, all religious groups and all nationalities, to defend democracy and combat anti-Semitism and Fascism.

We will expose Fascist tendencies and anti-Semitic organizations and activities wherever they assert themselves, and we will name names.

We will urge cooperation with all movements which are fighting honestly and unequivocally against Fascism and anti-Semitism.

We will support adequate legislation and will encourage militant action for the outlawing of discrimination. We will expose and combat social and economic discrimination wherever it appears and will defend the rights of labor as an integral part of the defense of democratic rights.

We will present up-to-the-minute news, comment and analyses by competent authorities on the status and problems of the Jews in the United States and the Americas, Germany, Poland, Rumania, Palestine and the Soviet Union.

We will present articles on Jewish history with particular emphasis on the rich, dramatic but insufficiently known contributions and traditions of the Jewish people to American culture and democracy.

We will present translations of the best of Jewish literature in all languages and will encourage the growth of a contemporary American-Jewish culture in English.

We set as our goal a united American people acting in the defense of its own democracy.

We dedicate ourselves to an uncompromising fight against the enemies of humanity. [4]

Equality Publishers seems to have folded in 1940 along with *Equality* magazine.

Hammett was busy with political matters in 1940 and 1941. Though he shuttled back and forth between Hollywood and New

York during the first half of 1940, he kept an apartment at 14 West Ninth Street in New York's Greenwich Village beginning in January. He could most effectively conduct his political activities from a New York City base.

His most active political commitment was as national chairman of the Committee on Election Rights—1940. In October he wrote a letter to the editor of *The New Republic* explaining the committee's function:

SIR: Today I would hesitate to predict the future of American democracy. Into the office of the Committee on Election Rights—1940, every day come telegrams and letters from all over the nation, telling of restrictions of the right to vote. In twenty-seven states election rights have been violated by ruling minority parties off the ballot on flimsy charges, through terror, intimidation and arrest of ordinary citizens.

In every state, these violations follow the same pattern: Newspapers whip up local hysteria, the Dies Committee sends frightening letters, local prosecutors' offices send police and detectives to intimidate petition signers and grand juries indict election workers on trumped-up charges.

The Committee on Election Rights—1940 has been formed to safeguard election rights. Part of our job is the preparation of reports on violations of election rights, copies of which may be obtained at the Committee office, Room 1209, 100 Fifth Avenue. New York City   Dashiell Hammett, Chairman[5]

The work of the Committee on Election Rights—1940 was to get the Communist Party slate on as many state ballots as possible. Hammett prepared promotional material for the Committee, organized fund-raising drives, prepared documentation of voting rights violations nationwide, and gathered support for campaigns in individual states to get the Communist Party candidates on the ballot. He pursued his work energetically, though with limited success, as anti-Communist sentiment was mounting in the United States.

One of the difficulties was to maintain a unity of spirit among the supporters of his committee. Though the Committee on Election Rights—1940 was ostensibly independent politically, the various Socialist parties that sought Hammett's support were often disappointed. An FBI undercover agent reported on a meeting of the Committee at the Hotel Astor on October 9, 1940, with Hammett presiding. During the meeting, a member of the Socialist Party protested that the Committee on Election Rights was uninterested in civil liberties of Socialists. Hammett, the FBI agent reported, "made a statement to the effect that [the Socialist] had violated the spirit and purpose of the meeting, for only anti-Democratic elements could benefit by disuniting the rally."[6]

The FBI took a special interest in Hammett's political activities because they believed him to be among the upper echelon of the Communist Party in the United States. Hammett's 278-page FBI file is a curious document that blends careful investigation, innuendo, and hearsay. His file begins with a May 5, 1934, letter from the special agent in charge of the San Francisco FBI to J. Edgar Hoover, responding to the director's request for an investigation of the comic strip *Special Agent X-9*. Hoover was confused about the title of *Secret Agent X-9* and feared that Hammett's strip might reflect unfavorably upon the FBI. A two-page report from the San Francisco office seems to have allayed his fears. Hammett's file, which covers a fifteen-year period, ends with a statement dated September 4, 1959, that his federal income tax debt is uncollectable.

The bulk of his file centers on his activities in the 1940s. There are anonymous notes warning of Hammett's active role in Communist Party affairs, newspaper clippings that mention Hammett in a political context; and the reports of special agents who investigated Hammett's activities, shadowed him—often with difficulty because he knew their game—and on at least one occasion apparently broke into Lillian Hellman's home in Pleasantville, New York, where Hammett was staying at the time. The agents' reports are plodding and often inconclusive. They frequently implicate Hammett in Communist activities on flimsy or circumstantial evidence, and they unfailingly assume guilt by association. Nevertheless, Hammett's FBI file documents his full schedule of active political interests from 1938 to 1942, when he went into the army, and from his discharge in 1945 until 1951, when he was jailed for refusing to testify before a United States District Court about his knowledge of a Communist bail bond fund.

After the correspondence concerning Hoover's inquiry into *Secret Agent X-9*, the next item in Hammett's file is an anonymous communication with the New York office of the FBI dated February 5, 1941:

Dashiell Hammett is wearing himself thin trying to prevent the Communist Party being ruled off the ballot in New York. He has been set up in business as head of the Committee on Free Elections. Coordinating their work with Hammett's committee are the National Federation for Constitutional Liberties and the New York Conference for Inalienable Rights.

Hammett is passing himself off as a political independent, but in October he deluged New York unions with telegrams urging support of Earl Browder in the November presidential elections.

This letter refers to Hammett's attempts as chairman of the Committee on Election Rights—1940 to get the Communist Party on the New York presidential ballot. Earl Browder was general secretary of the Communist Party in the United States and party candidate for president in 1936 and 1940. While the information in the letter was correct, anonymous messages were hardly necessary to establish Hammett's political activities.

Between April 1938 and December 1941 he lent his name and his public support to a wide variety of leftist causes. In addition to the petitions published in the *Daily Worker* calling for the United States to lift the embargo on Spain (April 8, 1938) and supporting the Moscow Trials (April 28, 1938), Hammett signed petitions or endorsed public letters on the following issues: protesting the establishment of the Dies Committee, the House Committee to Investigate Un-American Activities (*Daily Worker*, May 13, 1940); protesting police intimidation of signers of Communist Party nominating petitions in Philadelphia (*Daily Worker*, August 3, 1940); requesting the Brazilian president to release Luiz Carlos Prestes, a political activist jailed in Brazil (*New Masses*, December 19, 1940); protesting the treatment of Jewish refugees in Great Britain (*Daily Worker*, December 4, 1940); calling for the release of Sam Darcy, Communist Party member accused of voter registration fraud in California (*Daily Worker*, December 19, 1940); endorsing the Fourth Congress of the League of American Writers, a group of political activists called a Communist front organization by the FBI (*New Masses*, April 22, 1941); establishing the Morris U. Schappes defense fund, to appeal the firing of a College of the City of New York teacher for Communist activities (*New Masses*, November 18, 1941). In addition, Hammett was appointed president of the National Board of the League of American Writers in 1941, and in his role as spokesman for that group, he issued a statement to American writers applauding the United States' declaration of war on Germany and Japan to fight Fascism (*Daily Worker*, December 16, 1941). Besides donating his services to liberal causes, Hammett generously gave money as well. He frequently stimulated public fund-raising rallies by making a $1,000 donation, and the FBI stated that his financial support of Communist organizations was $1,000 a month.

Hammett's income as a screenwriter had been drastically reduced, but he found other ways to support himself. *The Thin Man* had been broadcast on Lux Radio Theater in 1936, *The Glass Key* on Campbell (soup) Playhouse in 1939, and *After the Thin Man* on Lux Radio Theater in 1940. Though Hammett received only a modest royalty from those broadcasts, they indicated the adaptability of his work for radio, the medium that would support him for the next ten years. In July 1941 NBC began a Thin Man serial called "The Adventures of the Thin Man." Hammett was credited with the scripts for the series because his name sold the serial, but he refused to write the scripts, he refused to approve them, to meet with the scriptwriters, or even to take calls from the head of the production unit. Yet he was paid well—$500 a week for the duration of the series. Hammett's work was well received on radio, and, between 1942 and 1945, adaptations were broadcast of "Two Sharp Knives" (twice), *The Glass Key*, *The Maltese Falcon* (twice), and *The Dain Curse*.

Also in 1941 John Huston, a new director at Warner Brothers, chose *The Maltese Falcon* as his first film to direct, an odd choice since the first two movies from the novel had not been especially successful. Huston adapted the film himself, realizing that, as Hammett had pointed out to Harry Block when the novel was first submitted to Knopf, the adaptation to a dramatic version was simple. Huston picked George Raft to play Sam Spade, but Raft declined and Humphrey Bogart was chosen. Mary Astor played Brigid O'Shaugnessy, and sixty-one-year-old Sidney Greenstreet, a stage actor who had never played a movie role, was Gutman. The film has become a classic. It established Bogart as an actor of the first rank, won an Academy Award nomination for Greenstreet, and still stands as one of Huston's most remarkable movies.[7] Moreover, the film seems to have sparked a renewed interest in Hammett's works during the early 1940s. There were a series of movies based on his works—*The Shadow of The Thin Man* in November 1942, another in the MGM Thin Man movies, but Hammett had no hand in those after *Another Thin Man* (1939); a remake of *The Glass Key* in 1942 by Paramount with screenplay by Jonathan Latimer, directed by Stuart Hesler, and starring Brian Donlevy, Veronica Lake, and Alan Ladd; and two more Thin Man movies, *The Thin Man Goes Home* in 1945 and *Song of the Thin Man* in 1947.

In 1942, just before he joined the army, Hammett wrote a screenplay for Warner Brothers, adapting Lillian Hellman's anti-Fascist play *Watch on the Rhine*. The play had run for 378 performances on Broadway in 1941, where it was viewed as an important statement about the evil of Nazism at a time when American entry into the war against Germany, Italy, and Japan was imminent. Hal Wallis produced the movie, and it was directed by Herman Shumlin, who had produced and staged the Broadway play. Hammett was credited with the screenplay, with additional scenes and dialogue by Lillian Hellman, but there was little invention involved. The movie is an extremely faithful adaptation of the play. Bette Davis, Paul Lukas, and Geraldine Fitzgerald starred in the movie about a German, Kurt Müller, who is committed to freeing his countrymen from Fascist oppression, and who has come to America to gather funds to continue his struggle. When a decadent aristocrat, Count Teck de Brancovis, learns of Müller's purpose, he threatens to expose him as an anti-Nazi unless Müller gives the count the money he has collected. Müller murders the count to silence him, and Müller's American in-laws agree to cover up the murder. The movie ends as Müller says farewell to his family before leaving for Germany, where he is likely to be killed for his beliefs. The movie was released in August 1943 to very respectful reviews. Bosley Crowther in the *New York Times* called it "a distinguished film—a film full of sense, power and beauty. . . . It is meager praise to call it one of the fine adult films of these times."[8] As Victor Navasky points out in *Naming Names*, though the *Daily Worker* was critical of the play, which opened during the Stalin-Hitler Pact, it praised the movie, which was released after Germany invaded Russia.

In addition to Hollywood's interest in Hammett now that he was no longer under contract to MGM, there was renewed activity in the republication of his novels. In 1942, *The Complete Dashiell Hammett*, a one-volume collection of all his novels, was published by Knopf, and in 1943 Pocket Books, the first of the new mass-market paperback publishers that had begun revolutionizing the publishing industry in 1939, published *The Thin Man*, *The Glass Key*, and *Red Harvest* for twenty-five cents a copy; in 1944 they published *The Maltese Falcon*; in 1945, *The Dain Curse*. The income to Hammett from paperback republication of his novels was insignificant, but these publications kept his reputation alive. Whereas a trade hardback publisher such as Knopf would print only five thousand or so copies of one of Hammett's novels at a time (and the same was true of the reprint houses such as Grosset and Dunlap, who had kept Hammett's novels in print throughout the 1930s), Pocket Books could afford to print fifty thousand or more copies at a time.

Hammett's stories were also given new life beginning in 1943 when Lawrence Spivak began collecting Hammett's shorter fiction in his Mercury Mystery and Bestseller Mystery Series. Spivak eventually published ten volumes of Hammett's stories at intervals of about one volume a year. These collections sold for twenty-five cents each and had roughly the status of pulp magazines as subliterary publications. Nonetheless, through the paperback revolution, Hammett's books reached a broader reading audience than ever before, and as a result his reputation as a writer endured and even grew, though he was finished as an active novelist.

We want to give the Adak soldier—every morning—a paper that he will like to read and that will keep him as up-to-date as possible on what's going on in his world.

Dashiell Hammett in the first
issue of *The Adakian* (1944)

Hammett was eager to support the United States' war against Fascism in World War II, a cause he felt he could best serve by joining the army. He tried at different times to enlist, but he was turned down for his age (he was 47 in 1941), for his health (his tuberculosis still flared up periodically), and finally in 1942 because he had rotten teeth. By fall of 1942, the army enlistment standards had been relaxed due to the need for manpower, and when Hammett agreed to have some of his teeth pulled, he was accepted into the army as a private at the age of forty-eight. Under any circumstances, it is difficult to understand how, with his health record and his political interests, Hammett could have been inducted into the army. Nonetheless, Hammett reported to the induction center on Whitehall Street in New York City on September 17, where he took his oath of duty. The next day he was transferred to the reception center at Camp Upton, Long Island, where he stayed for one week before he was assigned to a Signal Corps Training regiment at Fort Monmouth, New Jersey.[1]

Incredibly, the FBI was unable for nearly two years to confirm that Hammett was in the army at all. After letters to the army chief of staff indicated in spring of 1944 that no record of his having joined the army could be located (because his name was misspelled "Dashiel" on induction records) the FBI, acting on reports that Hammett had been seen in uniform, considered bringing charges against him for impersonating a United States soldier. Only in July 1944 did the FBI learn that Hammett was, indeed, serving his country officially.

Hammett was amused at the reaction of the other enlisted men toward him. He wrote to Hellman that he had occasional trouble persuading his fellow soldiers, most of whom were twenty years younger, not to call him Mr. Hammett.[2] He preferred to be called Sam, the name he had gone by when he was in the army in 1918, but he was as often called Pop. He had a desk job at Fort Monmouth, writing lesson plans and orientation class lectures for recruits. In December he wrote to Hellman that he had been trying to "revise, correct, rewrite, coordinate, de-shit and otherwise make sense of three divergent courses in what they humorously but solemnly call 'army organization.'" On May 18, 1943, he was promoted to corporal.

Fort Monmouth is about twenty miles due south of Brooklyn across Lower New York Bay, so Hammett was close to his friends and the comforts of civilian life. He called Hellman daily when she was in New York, but he preferred to spend his evenings off the post in nearby Red Bank with the other enlisted men. When he needed civilian clothes, he used his charge accounts at Brooks Brothers, Tripler, and Abercrombie & Fitch, and he occasionally asked one of his friends in New York to have whatever clothing he needed sent to him.

Hammett stayed at Fort Monmouth until June 29, 1943, when he was transferred to Company A, Twelfth Battalion at Camp Shenango in Transfer, Pennsylvania. This assignment was the first indication that the army had any knowledge of or interest in Hammett's political activities before the war. Camp Shenango was a containment center for members of the army considered to be subversive. The plan was to assign all such soldiers to the camp, where they would be held under something like house arrest for the duration of the war. It was an explosive situation, because the army made no distinction among the political philosophies it considered threatening. American Nazis were housed at Camp Shenango side by side with Communists.[3] Hammett was there for just over a week, from July 1 to July 10. Eleanor Roosevelt had learned about the camp and found the idea of imprisoning members of the armed forces on simple suspicion abhorrent. She took the matter to the president, and all troops assigned to Camp Shenango were dispersed immediately. Hammett was then sent to Fort Lawton in Fort Lewis, Washington, near Tacoma, to await permanent assignment. He waited for three weeks before he was attached to the Fourteenth Signal Service Company headquartered at Fort Randall, Alaska. His job was to provide orientation services for troops on the Aleutian Chain, and his first assignment was to the island of Adak, where he arrived on September 8.

Adak is a barren volcanic island about eight hundred miles from the Alaskan mainland. In the winter winds reach eighty miles per hour on the 289-square-mile island, and the wind-chill factor dips to forty degrees below zero. After the Japanese were routed in fall 1943, the Aleutians were peaceful, used primarily for air bases and communications centers. One of the main functions of the base on Adak was to monitor foreign shortwave broadcasts, particularly from Berlin and Moscow.

There was an unusual concentration of suspected subversives stationed on Adak, and some of the men assigned there felt the island functioned as an icy prison, where they were being held until the end of the war. There is no record, aside from his assignment to Camp Shenango, that Hammett was transferred to Adak for political reasons, though that seems likely. Hammett did not mask his political sympathies—he subscribed to the *Daily Worker* while stationed on the island and read Marx for the third time while he was there—neither did he attempt to win political converts.[4]

Because the Aleutians are such a desolate place, a major effort was made to provide orientation and entertainment for the troops. Brigadier General Harry Thompson, commander of the army forces in the area, felt it was important for the men to realize that their work in the Aleutians was important to the war effort. He wanted them to know what their function was, what was going on in the States, and how the war effort was progressing.

General Thompson was a mystery fan and he admired Hammett's work. When he learned that Hammett was under his command, he gave him a priority assignment: start a camp newspaper. His job would be to cover local and national news, and he could have whatever staff he felt he needed. Aside from the broad outlines General Thompson established, there would be no restrictions on the content of the paper. Hammett would have full editorial control, and he would refer any attempts to hinder his work directly to the general.[5]

Hammett began assembling his staff and planning the paper in December 1943. He soon found that the most difficult part of his job was getting the news. Though he could get most newspapers or magazines he wanted through military channels, it took time, so he called on Hellman and her secretary for help. He asked them to serve as a clipping service for him and to send daily packages of news stories by airmail. He wanted the "Review of the Week" section of the Sunday *New York Times*; clippings from the *Times* reflecting people's worries; statements by important people; cartoons, letters to the editor, editorials, and political columns in magazines; books; and maps. In addition to *The New Masses*, Hammett had subscriptions to army periodicals such as *Yank*, daily newspapers, and the newsmagazines—*Time*, *Life*, and *Newsweek*—though he complained to Hellman that they reported "a sort of college graduate dream-world."[6]

By Wednesday, January 19, 1944, Hammett had enough material for the first trial issue of *The Adakian*. The staff was credited in alphabetical order: "Cpls. Bernard Anastasia, Bill Glackin, Dashiell Hammett, Dick Jack, Bernard Kalb, Al Loeffler, Hal Sykes, with the help of WXLB newsroom." (At least two members of the original staff became professional newsmen: Bill Glackin is now drama critic for the *Sacramento Bee*, and Bernard Kalb is an NBC news correspondent.) WXLB was a shortwave radio station manned part of the day by Hammett's friend Robert Colodny, a veteran of the Abraham Lincoln Brigade.

The first issue contained an "Editorial Note" explaining *The Adakian*'s purpose:

Here we go with the first semi-dry-run issue of a new daily newspaper. This one is not for general distribution—we don't think it's good enough. Neither will tomorrow's be, nor the next day's. After that we've got hopes. Meanwhile we're going along on the theory that to turn out a good newspaper you've got to turn out a newspaper and then keep improving it.

And that's what we're doing. We want to give the Adak soldier—every morning—a paper that he will like to read and that will keep him as up-to-date as possible on what's going on in his world.

You who see these early issues can help us by letting us know what you find wrong with our first tottering steps. You don't have to spare our feelings: we'll have found as many things wrong with what we have done as you're likely to.

That first issue also included one of Hammett's signed columns, "It Happens to Everybody":

Ring Lardner's son John, with the Fifth Army in Italy, writes in Newsweek that he figures "one reason this army or other armies in the field get rumor-drunk or gossip-happy lies in the desert-island life they lead. Cut off from the news, they make their own. If Crusoe had had two or more companions on his island, I don't doubt there would have been rumors in circulation among them within a week that three frigates were putting out from Bristol to rescue them or that the king has confiscated their homes and turned them into bowling alleys . . . There are radios here in Italy. But no more than one soldier in 50 has access to them."

In the same news weekly Lt. (j.g.) Geer reports that liquor "is still very scarce from Guadalcanal on up the line. If you can find any, it costs from $50 to $75 a quart in the black market. There is a fair amount of beer in some points and absolutely none in others."

The British Eighth Army, after some three years battle experience in Africa, was now and then criticized by visiting British staff officers for lack of general training and never seems to have had enough equipment. Corps, and even Army, engineer organizations squabbled over who was to get the few bulldozers and dump trucks, and telephone communications were bad enough to annoy everybody.[7]   -DH-

In general form, *The Adakian* remained unchanged from its first issue to the end of Hammett's editorship about fifteen months later. It was four pages. Pages one and two were international news about the war; page three was news from the States; page four was camp news and editorials. Editorials were always short, normally less than two hundred words long. Each page had an editorial cartoon or a map, and most of the news reports were from wire services. *The Adakian* used Associated Press, Army News Service, and Camp Newspaper Service, as well as news gathered from the WXLB monitors. Publication was daily, in print runs of between three thousand and six thousand copies, for distribution on Adak only. (Due to wartime restrictions, the paper could not be mailed off the island.) The single most notable fact about *The Adakian* is its objectivity. Hammett's aim was to inform enlisted men about the news, not to influence their opinions, political or otherwise. Moreover, he was less interested in running *The Adakian* than in seeing it run smoothly. With pleasure and a certain amount of pride, he quickly turned over the editorial responsibilities for the newspaper to others.

The choice of *The Adakian* staff was Hammett's, and he mildly shocked some of his supervisors by choosing an integrated staff, the only such unit on the island. There were eight men assigned to the paper, of whom two were black. Though the army was segregated in 1943, Hammett's *Adakian* staff shared quarters. He broke the official racial barriers quietly and nonchalantly and never intimated that he did so intentionally. [8]

The Adakian staff worked nights, and Hammett was with them, typically lying on a table reading. His reading tastes ran to political philosophy, but he kept his thoughts to himself. When he did write a signed article for *The Adakian* it was to encourage men to buy war bonds, or to explain why mail going off the island had to be censored. But even that was rare. During the fifteen months Hammett edited the paper, only thirteen articles appeared under his by-line.

He would discuss politics in conversation though he never brought the topic up himself, according to members of the newspaper staff. He always kept a bottle of liquor that he was willing to share with members of his staff, and the conversation frequently turned to politics and political philosophy, especially with his friend Robert Colodny. Hammett would listen patiently and respond with stubborn, confident pragmatism. Colodny recalls a typical conversation in which he argued that the United States would win World War II because the war was a conflict between ideology and brute force, and ideology would triumph. Hammett listened patiently until Colodny finished, then he called the argument bullshit. Sure we are going to win the war, Hammett said, but not because of our ideas. We are going to win because we will drown the sons of bitches in metal.

He rejected all sentimental reasons for fighting the war, and, similarly, sentimentality for the fighting man. Hammett believed that the key to winning the war was a broad industrial base, not frenzied soldiers. He also believed, according to Colodny, that two factors made men susceptible to corruption: the first is powerlessness; the second is ignorance. The informed man has increased power over his life and is, therefore, less subject to corruption.

Hammett's job in establishing and running *The Adakian* was made easier by his celebrity status. E. E. Spitzer, a friend of Hammett's who worked with a USO group on Adak and filled in on the paper from time to time, recalls that Hammett got more telegrams than the commanding general. He had plenty of money and nowhere to spend it; even so, his disregard for his army paycheck raised eyebrows. *Yank* reported that Hammett once went seven months without hitting the pay line.[9]

While Hammett was in the army, three movies he had some association with were released, radio adaptations of three of his novels and one of his stories were broadcast, and all of his novels as well as four collections of his short stories were published in paperback format.[10] Between his celebrity status and General Thompson's support, Hammett, who was then only a corporal, was remarkably insulated from the typical pressures of the army bureaucracy.

On one occasion, a chaplain called Hammett to object to the words "God damn" in the previous day's *Adakian*. Hammett told him God was lucky to have gotten his name in at all, and that if he wished to pursue the matter he could take it up with the general.[11] Spitzer recalls a visit from a major to *The Adakian* hut, ostensibly to inspect the paper, but really to meet Hammett and get his autograph. When the major entered, he was at first ignored by a group of enlisted men. He was finally directed to Hammett, who was lying on a table reading, a position he kept throughout the major's visit. The major announced that he was there to inspect the paper. Hammett's reply was, "If you have a complaint, major, take it to the general."

Stories of Hammett's disrespect for officers as a group were circulated among enlisted men with delight. *Yank* reported a conversation Hammett had with another major. He was walking with four other enlisted men when he was stopped by the major and invited to a steak dinner, where he could look at some of the major's attempts at mystery writing. Hammett accepted, but only, he insisted, if his four companions could come as well. When the major hedged on the invitation, Hammett saluted him and walked off without another word.[12]

Despite his lack of regard for authority, on August 20, 1944, Hammett was promoted to what he called "the dizzying heights of sergeancy." He liked army life. He enjoyed his freedom, yet he felt secure in a regimented environment. His drinking slowed, though it did not stop, and his health improved. One night he began coughing uncontrollably in *The Adakian* hut, frightening the staff. But Hammett told them he had coughed up only black blood, a good sign because that meant it was old and that there had been no new bleeding.

Just after Hammett arrived on Adak, he had taken on a writing project at General Thompson's request. The general felt that a history of the war against the Japanese in the Aleutian Islands would be an important publication to supplement the work of the orientation group. He asked Hammett and Colodny to prepare an illustrated booklet that explained what had happened on the chain since the beginning of the war.

Characteristically, Hammett let Colodny take control of the project. Colodny, who had been wounded in the Spanish Civil War as a member of the Lincoln Brigade and who was widely read in political theory, saw the project as an opportunity to express his theories about geopolitics. When he finished, he had written a highly political theoretical discourse. Hammett objected that Colodny had not written for the audience. He rewrote Colodny's manuscript, depoliticizing it and aiming it at the enlisted men who read *The Adakian*. He left unrevised only the captions Colodny had written for drawings by Sergeant Harry Fletcher to illustrate battle action.[13]

The result is a readable, informative twenty-four-page booklet titled *The Battle of the Aleutians* that explains what the action was like in the Aleutians between June 1942 when the Japanese attacked U.S. airfields in Dutch Harbor, among the easternmost islands, and August 1943 when allied forces occupied Attu, one of the westernmost of the Aleutian Chain. It begins by setting the action:

When, on December 7, 1941 the Japanese first attacked the United States at Pearl Harbor we had, on all our Alaskan islands, only two small army posts and naval bases. One was on Kodiak Island. The other was at Dutch Harbor on Unalaska. In all widespread Alaska we had but six small army posts.

In June, 1942, the Japanese struck at Dutch Harbor. But this time they did not catch us napping. Two secret airfields had been hastily installed just east and west of Dutch Harbor. One was at Cold Bay, near the tip of the Alaska Peninsula. The other was on Umnak Island. The Blair Packing Co. and Saxton & Co., supposed to be canners of fish, were the disguises these secret airfields wore. On June 2, 1942, two Japanese aircraft carriers were reported less than 400 miles south of Kiska. They were moving eastward. Bad weather fought against us there. Air reconnaissance was almost impossible. Patrol planes would find the Japanese, only to lose them again in fog and storm before bombers could be brought to the spot. Bad weather always played a part in Aleutian warfare. On June 3, and again on June 4, bombers and fighters based on these carriers attacked Dutch Harbor. Bad weather fought against American and Japanese alike. All available planes of the Eleventh Air Force had been rushed to our two secret airfields. They went up to meet the Japs, who had thought our nearest airfield was on distant Kodiak. Many of the Japanese planes failed to return to their carriers. Bad weather had a lot to do with that. But that same bad weather made it impossible for our planes to destroy the Japanese carriers or their convoying warships. The enemy task force withdrew from Dutch Harbor, and occupied Kiska, some 700 miles to the west. War had come to the Aleutians—to a chain of islands where modern armies had never fought before. Modern armies had never fought before on *any* field that was like the Aleutians. We could borrow no knowledge from the past. We would have to learn as we went along, how to live and fight and win in this new land, the least known part of our America.[14]

It has been estimated that about one hundred thousand copies of *The Battle of the Aleutians* were printed in 1944 for free distribution to troops stationed on the chain.[15] (Copies are scarce today and bring about $200 on the rare book market.)

In addition to his work on *The Adakian*, Hammett traveled the length of the Aleutian Chain in 1944 with an orientation unit. They stopped at camps for three or four days at a time to lecture on the progress of the war, the role of the Aleutian soldier in the war effort, and what was going on in the States. His job was to boost morale through education. These orientation tours were organized at headquarters in Fort Richardson, near Anchorage, Alaska, and Hammett spent an increasing amount of time there in the summer and fall of 1944. Though Anchorage had a population of less than ten thousand, it was the closest to civilized life Hammett got during the twenty-five months he was in Alaska and the Aleutians. He enjoyed the bars, even with the outrageously expensive liquor, and he took a special liking to a saloon called the Carolina Moon, which he bought. When the war was over and he had no further interest in owning an Anchorage nightspot, Hammett gave the Carolina Moon to the black lady who ran it for him.

The University of Alaska campus in Anchorage attracted Hammett, partly because of its library and partly because of its concentration of females. He took a special interest in a student named Jean Potter, who was writing a book about Alaska's bush pilots. He gave her editorial advice and helped her arrange publication for *The*

Flying North, published by Macmillan in 1946. It was dedicated to Dashiell Hammett.

After an orientation tour in fall and winter 1944, Hammett returned to Adak to await his next assignment. His duties as editor of *The Adakian* had been taken over in his absence by Bill Glackin and Hammett's time was mostly free. He wrote some short pieces for the paper, including a Sunday column called "Home Sweet Home" to help get soldiers ready for the return to civilian life after the war, which was clearly about over in early 1945. He suggested that the World War II soldier would have an easier time adjusting than veterans of other wars, because with some ten million soldiers returning home most families would know firsthand the difficulties and resentments the returning veterans had to face.

In another column, Hammett wrote about a new organization, the War Workers' League of America, which advocated "equal rights for war workers." Hammett advised a cautious response:

There's hardly a day that some new organization doesn't spring up somewhere, and start advocating or opposing something or other.

Many of them are simply crackpot, others are some bright boy's idea of how to make a living; a few fill a need and survive—the rest are seldom heard of again. (March 25, 1945)

Most of all he cautioned against false hope based on unreliable information. On April Fool's Day 1945, Hammett wrote "Rumors, Rumors, Rumors":

This past week has been busy as a bird dog with rumor and fuel for rumor.

Germany's final collapse and peace in Europe have seemed no more than an hour or two away.

A non-com playing with a walkie-talkie on Iwo, a radio operator picking up orphan flashes at Hickman Field in Hawaii, an Army and Navy Register report that Eisenhower is about to relieve Marshall for duty in the Pacific—anything could pin our ears to the radio.

Back in the States people were even jumpier.

The New York Stock Market was scared into a decline on Monday.

A couple of days later the Chicago grain market had its cash-in-while-you-may nervous spell.

On the same day a murder trial in the same city was adjourned and stores shut down for the day all over the country—expecting an armistice announcement that never came.

Later there was more fuel for these hopeful if short-lived fires—the statement of an unnamed German prisoner "of high rank" that Germany no longer has an organized defense or an organized government; the British PM's warning to Cabinet and Commons members to stay where they could be reached should Germany fold during the Easter holidays.

Rumors will come thicker and thicker from now on out.

If we try to believe all of them we're going to have nothing left to believe with when peace actually comes.

That happened to a lot of people last time.

As a parting gesture of friendship to *The Adakian* staff, Hammett had decided to help the three staff cartoonists get published, since all of them wanted to pursue careers as commercial artists after the war. Through Hellman, he had tried to interest a commercial publisher in a collection of editorial cartoons from *The Adakian*, but though Viking Press showed some interest, the effort was unsuccessful. It was decided then among all members of the staff that they would publish the cartoons themselves, sharing the costs and the profits. Bernard Kalb went to Anchorage to arrange for a printer and Hammett got permission for the project from Lieutenant General A. B. Buchner, who had replaced General Thompson, though Buchner insisted on final approval of the book. The men agreed on a title—"All Wet and Dripping"—but Buchner did not like it. Over their objections, he renamed the booklet "Wind Blown and Dripping."[16] It consisted of cartoons by Bernard Anastasia, Oliver Pedigo, and Don L. Miller, and an introduction by Hammett dated fourteen days before he left Adak permanently:

These cartoons originally were scratched into waxed paper stencils for our mimeographed daily newspaper at APO 980 in the Aleutians. This is a medium to make an artist long for the good old days when a craftsman had nice cave walls and handfuls of red and yellow ocher to work with. The hundred and fifty representative cartoons reproduced here have been dressed up a little with ink-line and wash; otherwise they haven't been tampered with.

Since our newspaper first appeared, fourteen months ago, we ve run from two to four cartoons a day, depending on how much space we needed for maps, and our daily average through this period must have been at least three. That multiplies up to some twelve hundred and seventy cartoons in all. So far as I can figure out, no particular plan was followed in picking out the favored hundred and fifty for this book. Each of the three artists seems simply to have picked out the ones he happened—for one reason or another—to like. Some of my favorites are absent, but I'm too old and cagey to argue with artists unless I have to. And this lot is doubtless as truly representative as any I would select.

Military life in the Aleutians is not a whole lot like any kind of life anywhere else in the world, and life on one Aleutian island often differs a good deal from life on its neighbors. But we on the wet rock that's listed as APO 980 like to think our island is the norm, the others merely slight variants on our pattern. This, of course, is healthy provincialism which shouldn't bother anybody. In any case it's a cinch we are more like the rest of the Aleutians than we are like any other place and, if this book shows what we're like here, then it can safely be said to more or less show what we're all like up and down the Chain.

This business of showing what we're like is the heart of the whole thing. It's not so much a matter of showing outsiders what we're like—though we're not modest enough to have anything against that—what's important is showing ourselves. With the first-comers to the Aleutians it may have been different. Stepping off a landing boat in icy water and wading ashore on a new island—whether occupied by the enemy or not—was a clear-cut military operation that spoke for itself. But most of us weren't in that first wave— although millions and millions must have been in one first wave or another if you're a good listener—and our life here doesn't fit into any of the familiar martial patterns. Most war art, serious or comic, misses us.

There is in man a need to see himself, to have himself and his pursuits and environment expressed. This is the necessity that set early man to daubing his cave wall with ochered representations of the hunt, that set Anastasia, Pedigo and Miller to scratching mimeograph stencils with a stylus. No art can have an older, a more honorable, a more truly authentic basis.

This, then is our art and its people are us.

DASHIELL HAMMETT

Aleutian Islands
2 April 1945[17]

During spring 1945, Hammett was considering the resumption of his writing career. On March 4, 1945, he wrote to Hellman that he was thinking about writing a novel, though he did not yet have a clear idea for it. He was planning how he would spend his time after he got out of the army, as he was advising troops to do in his orientation lectures. He felt that he had the advantage of leisure time: to do with the rest of his life anything he wanted at whatever pace he chose. He thought he would write a novel—slowly. He told a friend on Adak that he had been mulling over a novel about a man who comes home from the war and does not like his family. The tentative title was "The Valley Sheep are Fatter." He had decided that if he stayed on Adak, he would work on the book; if he were transferred, he would put it aside. He began working with three-by-five-inch index cards, as he had twenty years earlier when he was trying to organize "The Secret Emperor," his first attempt at a novel.[18] Then on April 14 he received his orders to Fort Richardson, where he joined a training unit. Hammett finished his last five and one-half months in the army as he had begun, writing curriculum descriptions and apparently editing a publication called *Army Up North*. He gave up work on his novel for the time being. In Anchorage, there was more liquor, more women, and more freedom. Hammett took advantage of all three. By May 3, he had given up the novel altogether, writing Hellman not to worry about suggestions for titles. He would not have time to work on it with his new duties, he said.

Hammett was uncomfortable at Fort Richardson, where, he complained, he was expected to sit at a desk and write all day. He missed the contact with enlisted men which his job at Alaska Headquarters deprived him of. After less than a month at Fort Richardson, Hammett began trying to get assigned to more orientation trips along the Aleutian Chain. By mid-June he was successful. He went on a month-long tour which ended with a rest in Edmonton, Alberta, on July 9. During his trip, Hammett's promotion to master sergeant (tec 3) took effect on June 27.

As always, Hammett was reading—Wallace Stegner, Georges Simenon, Heinrich Heine, and Lenin, among others. On March 18, 1945, he wrote to Hellman that he had located a copy of Lenin's *Theoretical Principles of Marxism* (volume II in the Selected Works) which he looked forward to rereading: "I had almost reached the point where there was nothing ahead of me but Westerns and mysteries." He complained that he felt much less informed about current events at Fort Richardson than he had been on Adak, and asked that her secretary send him packages of clippings as she had when he was starting *The Adakian*. Hammett's reaction to American political developments in 1945 was moderate and level-headed. For instance, he wrote to Hellman about President Truman, who had taken office on April 12 after the death of Roosevelt, suggesting that she give him a chance before she started criticizing him: "He is not likely to become a great man, but unless there is a lot I don't know about him (that's a hell of an *unless*! there are millions of things I don't know about him) he could turn out to be an able one. . . ."

Hammett began expecting his discharge in March 1945, but he stayed at Fort Richardson until he returned to the United States on August 28. After a week at the separation center at Fort Dix, New Jersey, Hammett was honorably discharged on September 6, 1945, and his record reflected his good service. He was authorized to wear the Asiatic-Pacific Service Medal, four Overseas Bars, and a Good Conduct Medal. On December 14, 1944, he had received a Letter of Commendation for his organization of *The Adakian*. After the war, Hammett told Leonard Lyons he wanted to return to the Aleutians: "I'm the only one who ever really saw it. The footing was poor, and the GIs walked with their heads down, afraid of slipping. I looked up, and saw such mountains and lakes as no other place can match."[19]

PART 4

The Last Years
1945-1961

CHAPTER 19

Are you a Communist?
I am a Marxist.

Richard Hammett's question to his brother
and Dashiell Hammett's reply, ca. 1948

When he returned to the States, at the age of fifty-one, Hammett
took an apartment in New York at 15 East Sixty-sixth Street, and he
divided his time between there and Lillian Hellman's Hardscrabble
Farm, the 130-acre estate in Westchester County she had bought in
June 1939. His primary activities were drinking and reading, and yet
the money kept coming steadily, mostly from the three weekly radio
serials based on his characters: "The Adventures of the Thin Man,"
"The Fat Man," and "The Adventures of Sam Spade."[1] His royalty
from all three shows amounted to a total of $1,300 a week[2] and, as
before, he refused any involvement in the serials beyond accepting
his royalty check, though he did allow the networks to claim he had
written the radio scripts. In addition to the weekly serials, an adaptation of *The Glass Key* was broadcast on radio three times in 1946,
and *The Maltese Falcon* once.[3]

Hammett had come back from the Aleutians a different man than
before the war, quieter, more solitary, and less apt to enjoy large
groups. When he was first discharged, he hoped Hellman's
Hardscrabble Farm would be a refuge for him, as it had been before
the war, where he could escape from the show business people and
the hangers-on whom he despised more than ever. But there was a

steady stream of visitors at the farm, most of whom Hammett found unbearably distasteful. He frequently retired to his room for long periods to avoid the company of Hellman's weekend visitors, whom he referred to as grotesques. That category included her political friends as well as her theatrical ones. She was active in the political affairs of Henry Wallace, whom Hammett disliked. He referred to Wallace and his supporters as that "Iowa yogi and his fringe of impracticals."[4] The visitors and Hellman's objections to his steady drinking, which was more seriously endangering his health than ever before, drove Hammett from the farm and temporarily from her.

Leisure time is dangerous to an alcoholic, and it had its effect on Hammett. His drinking had about it a kind of desperation that had not been evident before. By 1947, he had all but given up attempts to regenerate his writing career, and he complained to an acquaintance that most days he saw no reason to get up in the morning. Though he enjoyed solitude, at other times Hammett craved the sense of camaraderie that alcohol gives. Just after he returned to New York, he learned that a woman who had served in the USO on Adak was living in Manhattan. He asked her out for dinner and nightclubbing. They began the evening in midtown and drank their way to Harlem. As Hammett got drunker, he became louder, ruder, and more talkative. Finally, at nearly five in the morning, his date had had enough, and she asked him to call her a cab so she could go home. When he refused, she hailed a cab herself. As she was entering the car, Hammett begged her: "Please don't leave me alone."[5]

He could be rude and unfeeling toward even his closest friends, particularly when he was drunk, yet he wanted company when he was drinking. In some cases he literally bought companionship, treating acquaintances to meals and drinks at places they normally could not have afforded, like the Stork Club, where Hammett had a reserved table.

He was indifferent toward money. If he were stopped on the street by a beggar asking for a dime, Hammett would give him a dollar. He had a theory about tipping in advance. He believed that a tip to the postman or garbage collector or building superintendent should not be a reward for past work, but a show of good faith by which the tipper would inspire better service.

In winter 1947 when Hammett set up housekeeping in a duplex apartment at 28 West Tenth Street in Greenwich Village, he needed a housekeeper and asked the building superintendent to recommend someone. He was told about a very good prospect named Rose Evans, but he was warned that she was "colored." Hammett replied that he did not care if she was navy blue, and he hired her. Rose Evans became Hammett's guardian. She worked days, Monday through Friday, for nearly six years; her devotion was so strong that when he was jailed in 1951 for refusing to testify before the United States Circuit Court, she offered her life savings to help post his bail, while many much wealthier people who called themselves Hammett's friends refused to commit personal funds to free him.

Hammett placed his full trust in Rose Evans. The first week she worked for him she was given a household budget of $100. At the end of that week, he asked her to account for what she had spent. She did, to his satisfaction, and he told her he never again wanted to know how she had spent the money he gave her.

Hammett frequently entertained women friends at night when Rose Evans left. She referred to them as the gold diggers. They spent his money, which he shared freely, and drank his liquor. It was not uncommon for him to wake up Monday morning to find his wallet empty and his apartment littered with half-empty liquor bottles—his own Scotch (Johnny Walker, both Black and Red) or the cheaper brands that had been bought by his guests with his money. Rose Evans resented the gold diggers and she tried to protect Hammett from them.

One Friday in the late 1940s, Hammett sent his secretary to his bank, the Amalgamated Bank of New York on Union Square, for some cash to see him through the weekend. He asked for $3,000. He had begun drinking before Rose Evans left, and she knew that if she left him with the money, the gold diggers would have it before the weekend was through. So she went to his wallet, got the cash, and took it home with her to Harlem. On Monday morning, when he sobered up, she gave him back the money she had saved for him.

Hammett appreciated her concern for him. On one occasion he fired a secretary (with whom he had had an affair) because she was eavesdropping on a conversation he was having with Rose Evans. He gave his housekeeper credit cards in his name to buy at her discretion what she needed to run the apartment. At Christmastime he gave her the same gift as he gave his daughters, usually a $100 bill.

During the day Hammett read for hours at a time. When the phone rang, he did not look up. He trusted Rose Evans to let him know if the call was important. If it was one of the gold diggers, she would say he was out, and as a result, she was resented by many of Hammett's acquaintances.[6]

Hammett's political activites continued after the war, but he played that role with less fervor than before, though he continued to lend his name to organizations he felt needed support. He was elected president of the Civil Rights Congress of New York at a meeting held on June 5, 1946, at the Hotel Diplomat in New York, and he devoted the largest portion of his working time to CRC activities. His association with the CRC, apparently a Communist-affiliated group, led to his refusal to testify about the organization and landed him in jail. He also worked as a teacher at the Jefferson School of Social Science, a Marxist school in lower Manhattan. In its catalogue, the Jefferson School stated that its purpose was to educate students

. . . in the spirit of democracy, peace and socialism. It teaches Marxism as the philosophy and social science of the working class. Central in this teaching is the study of the crucial developments of present-day America in the light of the history of our country—its democratic traditions, its cultural heritage, and the militant struggles of the working class and the Negro people.[7]

He taught courses in mystery writing there from 1946 to 1956 and served on the board of trustees from 1949 until 1956. In October 1946 Hammett resumed his attempts to get Communist Party candidates on state ballots, and he still freely signed petitions supporting a wide range of liberal grievances.

The FBI record of Hammett's activities in the late 1940s is a model of careless reasoning and incomplete investigation, but it indicates the extent of his influence among liberal political groups and helps to explain his political notoriety. On January 17, 1950, a single-spaced twenty-page report on Hammett was submitted to Washington by a special agent in the New York FBI office. It noted the following evidence of Hammett's subversive political activities:

1) He participated in a program on February 9, 1946, to celebrate the second anniversary of the Jefferson School of Social Science, cited as subversive by the Attorney General.

2) The *New York Journal-American* carried an article on March 10, 1946, which reported that Hammett was named one of sixteen military personnel with Communist backgrounds by the House Military Affairs Committee on July 19, 1945.

3) Hammett taught a course in mystery writing at the Jefferson School of Social Science.

4) Hammett was New York State President of the Civil Rights Congress, cited as subversive by the Attorney General. His nomination was accepted at a meeting of the CRC Organizing Committee on June 5, 1946, at the Hotel Diplomat in New York City.

5) As New York president of the Civil Rights Congress Hammett called on New York City Mayor O'Dwyer to stop police brutalities directed toward Negroes.

6) *PM* carried an article on September 13, 1946, which reported that State Department Adjutant Maurice Stember named Hammett a Communist.

7) As New York president of the Civil Rights Congress, Hammett stated that many prominent professionals supported the attempts of the CRC to get the Communist Party on the ballot in New York for the 1946 election.

8) An informant advised that Hammett planned to attend a meeting in Albany with "other Communist Party Functionaries" to map a campaign to get the Communist Party on the New York state ballot for 1946.

9) According to an advertisement in the *Daily Worker*, Hammett was to speak at the New York State American Youth for Democracy Convention of 1946, cited as subversive by the Attorney General.

10) *People's Voice* on November 9, 1946, has a picture of Hammett looking at petitions supporting the move to unseat Senator Theodore Bilbo of Mississippi.

11) A confidential informant reported that Hammett contributed $1,000 to the "Oust Bilbo Campaign" at a dinner sponsored by CRC.

12) The *Daily Worker* reported on December 31, 1946, that Hammett was a speaker and sponsor for a testimonial dinner for U. S. Representative Vito Marcantonio, elected on the American Labor Party ticket.

13) A confidential informant reported that Hammett spoke at the Tenth Anniversary Dinner of the Veterans of the Abraham Lincoln Brigade, cited as subversive by the Attorney General.

14) Hammett signed a petition which appeared in the February 28, 1947, *Daily Worker* condemning "the shameful persecution of German anti-Fascist refugee Gerhardt Eisler and calling for abolition of the Un-American House Committee."

15) A confidential informant advised on March 8, 1947, that Hammett is counted among the "Friends of Italian Democracy" by the "American Society for Cultural Relations with Italy, Inc.," of which suspected Communists were members.

16) On March 12, 1947, the *Daily Worker* reported that Hammett opposed outlawing the Communist Party.

17) A confidential informant reported that on April 21, 1947, Hammett was principal speaker at a meeting held at the University of Buffalo and sponsored by "American Youth for Democracy." "He was allegedly reported to the Communist Party Headquarters for his inability as a speaker and inability to be persuasive."

18) An Anti-Communist group within Actor's Equity Association named Hammett as a Communist and noted that in *The Red Decade* by Eugene Lyons, Hammett is named among the signers of a petition in support of the Moscow Trials.

19) On July 17, 1947, an informant turned over a pamphlet sponsored by Voice of Freedom which supported liberal commentators on the radio. Hammett endorsed the program of Voice of Freedom. Dorothy Parker, Chairman of Voice of Freedom, "had been considered as a valuable alliance of the Communist Party, and it was believed by the informant that she at one time had been a Communist."

20) In the *New York Journal-American* for July 29, 1947, Hammett was described as an active member of Contemporary Writers, which described itself as "the militant reorganization of Marxist and other anti-Fascist authors." That organization was called "notoriously Communist" by Walter S. Steele, chairman of the Security Committee of the American Coalition.

21) A confidential informant reported that on August 20, 1947, Hammett sent a telegram to the brother of German Communist Gerhardt Eisler requesting that he speak on the "Effect of Thought Police on Arts" at a CRC conference in New York City on October 11, 1947.

22) The October 1947 issue of *Soviet Russia Today* carried a letter from Hammett extolling the virtues of the magazine. Although considerable information is offered to support the allegation that *Soviet Russia Today* was a Communist publication, the report fails to note that Hammett was listed on the masthead as a member of the editorial board. It is noted that a confidential informant reported that Hammett was a member of the magazine's Advisory Committee.

23) In the October 17, 1947, *Daily Worker* Hammett was photographed studying a petition calling for the abolition of the House Un-American Activities Committee.

24) On November 7, 1947, the *Daily Worker* reported that Hammett was mourning the death of Peter V. Cacchione, Communist Party Councilman from Brooklyn.

25) The *Daily Worker* for November 19, 1947, reported that

Hammett would speak at the "Town Meeting for Freedom" held in New York under the auspices of the Washington Heights Committee of the Joint Anti-Fascist Refugee Committee.

26) A confidential informant reported that Hammett was a sponsor of the National Conference of the Civil Rights Congress in 1947.

27) A confidential informant advised on December 8, 1947, that Hammett was a sponsor of the "Action Conference on Indonesia" "which denounced the United States State Department policy and outlined its own program for relations with Indonesia."

28) On January 9, 1948, the *Daily Worker* reported that Hammett lauded the decision of the New York State Commissioner of Education that Communist Party membership is not grounds for dismissing a City College teacher.

29) Hammett was among signers of an advertisement in the *New York Times* on February 2, 1948, calling for Communist Simon W. Gerson to be given the council seat made vacant by the death of Peter V. Cacchione.

30) A confidential informant advised on March 15, 1948, that Hammett was on a committee called the National Reception Committee for Madam Irene Joliot-Curie under the auspices of the Joint Anti-Fascist Refugee Committee.

31) On March 26, 1948, Hammett signed an appeal to President Truman urging executive clemency for Leon Josephson, sentenced to one year in prison for contempt of the House Un-American Activities Committee.

32) The April 10, 1948, *New Leader* reported that Hammett "served on the Advisory Board of the Communist Party front 'Film Audiences for Democracy.'"

33) *PM* reported on April 28, 1948, that Hammett was among sixty-five prominent Americans who signed a petition questioning the legality of tactics employed by the House Un-American Activities Committee.

34) On May 5, 1948, a confidential informant advised that "Dashiell Hammett, Hardscrabble Farms, Pleasantville, New York, is a contact of the Communist Party."

35) The May 25, 1948, *Daily Worker* reported that Hammett would sponsor a demonstration against the Mundt bill, which would outlaw activities "to establish, or looking toward the establishment of a totalitarian dictatorship in the United States to be under foreign control."

36) A confidential informant advised on June 9, 1948, that Hammett was one of the sponsors of the "National Conference on American policy in Greece" held on June 5-6, 1948, at the Capitol Hotel in New York City to "express their indignation and to protest

the meddling of the United States Government in the internal affairs of Greece."

37) On June 17, 1948, a confidential source informed the FBI that Hammett was a sponsor of the Eastern Planning Conference for a Council for the Advancement of the Americas. According to the FBI, "The conference was the result of a well planned program started by the Communist Party in the United States jointly with the 'Inter-American Committee of the CIO' and the head of the 'Latin American Confederation of Labor.' " A confidential informant advised that one of the conference organizers, whose name has been censored, was a member of the Communist Party and another informant advised that "most of the current work in preparation for the movement is being done in Communist Party headquarters."

38) A confidential informant advised on December 13, 1948, that a letter from the American Committee for the Protection of the Foreign Born listed Hammett as a sponsor. That organization had been declared subversive by the Attorney General. Hammett also was said by an informant to have been a sponsor of the Fifteenth Anniversary of the National Conference of the American Committee for the Protection of the Foreign Born held at the Congress Hotel in Chicago on December 11-12, 1948.

39) A confidential informant "of unknown reliability, familiar with general Communist activities" advised on December 21, 1948, that Hammett contributed $1,000 a month to the Communist Party.

40) It was reported in the *Daily Worker* on February 8, 1949, that Hammett was among signers of a telegram to President Truman urging him to accept Stalin's bid "to discuss the problems that are now blocking the path toward real peace according to the 'National Council of Arts, Sciences and Professions.' "

41) A confidential informant made available an open letter from Hammett, who was chairman, and the executive secretary of the New York Civil Rights Congress. The letter, dated February 26, 1949, "pointed out that both the Federal and state jury systems in many areas of the country have been designated and operated to assure the conviction of accused workers, negroes, and other members of exploited minority groups. . . . The letter urged the immediate and wholehearted support of the entire labor movement to back up the Communist attack on the discriminatory jury system."

42) A confidential informant advised on March 28, 1949, that Hammett was one of approximately 565 sponsors for the "Cultural and Scientific Conference for World Peace" held at the Waldorf-Astoria Hotel in New York City.

43) It was reported on May 18, 1949, in *Compass*, the liberal

newspaper that succeeded *PM*, that the Americanism Division of the American Legion had compiled "a list of 128 prominent writers, lecturers, musicians, actors, playwrights, artists, and educators ... whose past activities make them unsuitable or unappropriate for Legion sponsorship." Hammett was on the list.

44) On June 27, 1949, the *Daily Worker* stated that Hammett had been elected to a Continuation Committee of the New York Civil Rights Congress to lay plans for the freeing of twelve Communist leaders and to work against the forces for fascism.

45) The *Daily Worker* reported on August 2, 1949, that Hammett sent a telegram to the Attorney General asking him to stop persecuting noncitizens.

46) A confidential informant advised on August 15, 1949, that Hammett was a U.S. sponsor for the American Continental Congress for Peace held in Mexico City September 5-10, 1949. Another confidential informant advised that that Congress "came into existence on the initiative of the National Jewish Commission of the Communist Part, U.S.A."

47) A confidential informant advised that Hammett was a sponsor of the West Side Citizens Committee to End Discrimination on the City Owned Docks, a committee initiated by the Communist Waterfront Section "to capitalize on dissention in the International Longshoreman's Association."

48) On August 25, 1949, a confidential informant advised that Hammett had been elected to the board of trustees of the Jefferson School of Social Science.

49) On November 4, 1949, the *Daily Mirror* reported that three officers of the CRC entered the office of a U.S. Commissioner with $260,000 in Treasury bonds to post bail bond for eleven alleged subversives. When U.S. Attorney Irving Saypol refused to endorse the bonds without knowledge of their ownership, Robert W. Dunn, Treasurer of the CRC bail fund, presented the requested documents "showing that the bonds had been solicited from owners who had been given receipts and had signed statements granting use of the bonds for the purpose of bailing out their leaders." Saypol and defense attorneys drew up an affidavit to that effect, which was signed by the five trustees of the CRC bail bond fund, including Dashiell Hammett.

50) On December 14, 1949, the *New York Journal-American* reported that Hammett had been affiliated with thirty-five groups besides the CRC "named as Communists fronts by Congressional or State Committees."

51) It is stated in the report that Hammett maintained a residence

at 28 West Tenth Street, but that he lived at Hellman's farm in Pleasantville, New York, during part of the past several summers and at her apartment on the fashionable Upper East Side of Manhattan at 63 East Eighty-second Street during August and September.

52) It is also noted that Hammett traveled the thirty some miles from New York City to the Pleasantville farm by New York taxi and that when Hammett traveled in New York City, often he "never goes to a specific address, but always leaves his taxi in the vicinity of 69th Street and Park Avenue, or Fifth Avenue around 84th Street."

Throughout the late 1940s Hammett continued to teach courses in mystery writing at the Jefferson School of Social Science, described in the school catalogue as "A practical workshop in the writing of novels and short stories. Both for those who have experience in fiction writing and for beginners. Problems of class content, structure, and characterization are analyzed in terms of concrete work submitted by students."[8] There was a ten dollar per semester fee for the course. His classes, which met on Thursday evenings from 6:45 to 8:15, were well attended, and Hammett was very faithful himself about attendance. His method was to ask students to read their work for the class and he would comment, usually vaguely. He tried to stimulate peer evaluation of students' work and considered his role to be discussion leader. He also lectured on "the history of the mystery story, the relationship between the detective story and the general novel and the possibility of the detective story as a progressive medium in literature."[9] One student, Samm Sinclair Baker, recalls a class to which Hammett had brought Frederic Dannay, half of the Ellery Queen writing team, as a guest. After Baker read his story, a burlesque of advertising, Hammett's only comment was "Brrr, that story is so tough it scares me." Dannay had more precise criticism: "take out every other wisecrack." Baker followed the advice and sold the revised version to *Detective Story Magazine*.[10]

In 1948 Hammett was distracted by a lawsuit that he considered particularly annoying, because he was faced with the loss of a significant part of his income and forced into a lengthy, time-consuming legal battle. On May 28 Warner Brothers sued the broadcaster, sponsor, producer, and director of the radio series "The Adventures of Sam Spade" in U.S. District Court in California for copyright infringement and unfair competition, charging that the radio program had appropriated "among other things scenes, language, story, dialogue, plot, characters, and other materials" of *The Maltese Falcon*, to which Warner Brothers had bought all broadcast rights in 1930. Though Hammett was not named in the original suit, he filed a complaint in U.S. District Court in New York on June 9, 1948, seeking to have his right to the name Sam Spade affirmed. On January 13, 1949, that suit was decided in favor of Warner Brothers and on January 17, Hammett's appeal was denied.

Meanwhile, due to Hammett's insistence on his direct involvement, an amended complaint was filed by Warner Brothers in their California suit on June 18, 1948, naming Hammett as a party to what amounted to the plagiarism of his own work. On December 28, 1951, the California suit was decided in Hammett's favor. Warner Brothers appealed to the U.S. Court of Appeals, but on November 9, 1954, that court upheld the District Court decision, which awarded Hammett recovery of his costs in defending his case.[11] By that time it had been three years since "The Adventures of Sam Spade" was forced off the air because of its association with Hammett, who had by then been publicly branded a political subversive.

CHAPTER 20

Going to prison was like going home.

Dashiell Hammett in a 1957 interview

From fall 1948 to spring 1951 Hammett's daughter Mary lived in New York (with her father briefly before she got her own apartment), and her presence underscored to Hammett the needs of his family, whom he had largely neglected since 1929. He had stayed on friendly terms with his sister Reba, and visited with her periodically, but he had been entirely out of touch with his father and brother for nearly twenty years, and he had not even seen his wife and daughter Josephine since the early 1940s. With encouragement from Mary and from Rose Evans, Hammett began to rethink his familial responsibilities. He renewed contact with his father, who was living alone in a hotel in Berkeley Springs, Virginia, and was ill, apparently with diabetes that had cost him a leg. Annie Hammett had died earlier, and Richard Hammett was now in his mid-eighties. Hammett visited his father and brought him an artificial limb, which the old man exhibited with pride though he did not wear it. It was the last time they saw one another; Richard Hammett died on March 13, 1948, in Berkeley Springs.[1] When Rose Evans asked Hammett if he would attend the funeral, he said, I paid for it; let someone else do the crying. But he later regretted not having gone.

While he was in the army, Hammett had received the first communication from his brother Richard since he had left Maryland in

1920. He learned that his brother worked for Standard Oil and after the war was transferred to the Manhattan office. The Hammett brothers met about once a month for dinner during the late 1940s. The atmosphere was always strained. Richard Hammett was politically conservative and he was embarrassed by the adverse publicity his brother had brought the Hammett name. One evening, Richard Hammett had to know: Are you a Communist, he asked. I am a Marxist, was Hammett's reply.[2]

When he went to Hollywood in 1950, Hammett spent six months with Jose Hammett, and visited frequently with his twenty-four-year-old daughter Josephine, whose company he especially enjoyed. He bought his wife the house in western Los Angeles where she and her daughter Mary still live. He never saw Jose Hammett for an extended period again. He was in Los Angeles for the last times in April and May 1951, when he spent one week on each of two trips with Josephine and his new grandchild Ann. He brought Ann back to New York with him for two weeks in April, and he doted on her. They spent most of their visit at Hellman's farm, where Hammett enjoyed being alone with his granddaughter.[3]

Late in 1948 or early in 1949, Hammett's health broke again. He was very ill, and Rose Evans told him he would have to go to the hospital. He refused and asked her not to tell Hellman he was sick, because he would be all right. Mrs. Evans felt she had a responsibility, though, to see to his well-being, and she called Hellman to come immediately. When Hellman saw how sick Hammett was, she had him admitted to Lenox Hill Hospital, where he was told by doctors that if he continued drinking he would soon die. He quit drinking. After his recovery, Hammett took better care of his health than he had before, and he began working again. He became closer to Hellman than he had been since he left the army.

Hammett had always been interested in the theater through Hellman, and in 1949 he served as a consultant to his friend Kermit Bloomgarden, who had produced Hellman's *Another Part of the Forest* in 1946. Bloomgarden was then staging her adaptation of Emmanuel Roblés's *Montserrat*, which opened to mixed reviews in October 1949 and closed after sixty-five Broadway performances. (He produced *The Autumn Garden* in 1951, revivals of *The Children's Hour* in 1952 and *Toys in the Attic* in 1960, and *My Mother, My Father, and Me* in 1963.) Hammett advised Bloomgarden on revising and staging plays he was producing, notably *Purple Dust* by Sean O Casey, and he invested in the production of Arthur Miller's *Death of a Salesman* produced by Bloomgarden in 1949, for which he received one half of one percent interest in the play.

Meanwhile, in 1949 Hammett hired a secretary, a devoted young lady named Muriel Alexander, and he resolved to start writing again. He bought a Royal Standard typewriter for her to use, and a dictaphone and an IBM Executive typewriter for himself. He especially liked the appearance of typed copy from the IBM. He told her he was going to write a novel that was not a mystery, and in January 1950 he wrote her from Hollywood that he was working on a novel called "The Hunting Boy." Nonetheless, his typewriter remained virtually unused. He dictated notes for an article on living in the United States but the article was not finished and the notes are unpromising. His office was on the ground floor of his apartment on Tenth Street. Frequently, he would ask Alexander to come downstairs to sit with him, in his living room/bedroom which overlooked a small garden. There was a fireplace in that room, faced by his winged-back chair on one side and an armchair on the other. He sat in one chair, she in the other, silent, for hours at a time. In the winter the apartment was always kept cold because, Hammett said, it reminded him of the Aleutians.

Alexander's duties consisted of helping Hammett answer his mail, keeping track of his finances, buying his apparel at Abercrombie & Fitch and Brooks Brothers, and purchasing gifts for his friends. On her own she undertook an inventory of his published works and recorded copyright information. She also fetched him books from the public library and local used-book dealers.[4] He was interested in general science and zoology at the time. Periodically, when the books began to clutter the apartment, Hammett held what he called book burnings. He would throw some books into the fireplace and give others away to make room for new volumes.

While Hammett doubted his ability, his services as a writer were still in demand. There were offers to reprint his stories; offers that he rejected from Reliance Pictures for him to write a movie for William Powell, and from Twentieth Century-Fox to write a screenplay about Pershing. Jose Ferrer expressed interest in rights to Hammett's story "Night Shade," but did not pursue the matter. He was asked by the *Los Angeles Mirror* to write continuity for a comic strip about Sam Spade, and he refused. Miscellaneous inquiries came frequently, such as requests from J. Walter Thompson for a product endorsement, and from Agatha Christie's publisher for a blurb about her new novel, both of which he declined comment on.

Hammett's last formal job came in 1950, when director William Wyler was working on "Detective Story" for Paramount, and he convinced the studio to hire Hammett as a writer on the project. When he went to Hollywood in January 1950, he had an enjoyable time visiting old friends and taking his daughter Josephine to the races at Santa Anita. He even liked the prospect of the work at first, interesting himself in Wyler's production of *Sister Carrie,* which he apparently worked on briefly, and discussing the possibility of doing a film with Alfred Hitchcock. But when it came to the writing, Hammett failed. He wrote to Hellman early in February that he thought he could get rolling if only he could keep himself in the room with the typewriter.[5] But he was wrong. He missed New York and he missed Hellman.

Hammett's major activity was reading. On February 22, 1950, he wrote to Alexander that he had been reading a lot of current novels, among them *A Search for the King* by Gore Vidal, *Pebble in the Sky* by Isaac Asimov, *The Town and the City* by Jack Kerouac, *The Devil's Own Dear Son* by James Branch Cabell, *Weep for My Brother* by Clifford Dowdy, *Special Friendships* by Roger Peyrefitte, translated by Felix Giovanni, and *All Hallow's Eve* by Charles Williams. In addition, he wanted her to order some books for him: *Strategy in Poker, Business, and War* by John Dennis MacDonald, *Ideas and Men* by Clarence Crane Brinton, *Studies in Revolution* by Edward Hallet Carr, *Mathematical Snapshots* by Hugo Steinhaus. In an interview just before he left Hollywood, Hammett said his favorite mystery writer was Georges Simenon: "He is more intelligent. There is something of the Edgar Allan Poe about him." He called hard-boiled writing "a menace" and he claimed to be writing a novel called "December 1." (There is a two-page fragment among Hammett's papers at the Humanities Research Center with that title.) When asked if he were "up to something" in Hollywood, he replied, "Absolutely not."[6]

He was not being coy. After six months he left Hollywood without having produced enough on any project to earn himself a film credit. He had taken a large advance (apparently of $10,000, though the amount is uncertain), but he had not earned it and the money had to be returned to Paramount.

When Hammett left Hollywood, he returned to Hellman and immersed himself in her current work *The Autumn Garden.* The play is set in a summer guest house in southern Louisiana at the end of the 1949 vacation season. The action centers around the visit of meddling artist Nick Denery and his wife Nina (a sort of tragic version of Nick and Nora Charles) to the house that is owned by his former girl friend whom he jilted to marry wealthy Nina. Nick is a once-brilliant artist who has not been able to finish a portrait for twelve years (about the same length of time since Hammett's last completed work, the story for *Another Thin Man* that he finished in 1938). The moral opposite to Nick is a withdrawn, aloof alcoholic named Edward Crossman, who prefers to drink by himself rather than become involved in the melodramatic problems of the other characters in the play.

Hammett read the play in draft form and told Hellman, as she recalls in *An Unfinished Woman*, that it was "worse than bad—it's half good." She tore it up, she claims, set the torn typescript outside his door in a briefcase, and wrote it over, a process that took seven months. (In Hellman's papers at the Humanities Research Center is a revised typescript for *The Autumn Garden* which she had labeled first draft. It is not torn.) He was pleased with the rewrite; he called it "the best play anybody's written in a long time."[7] But he felt one speech in particular needed revision. When Hellman demurred, he revised it himself. (According to the evidence of her working drafts, Hammett did not write the speech, as Hellman claims. He only reworked it somewhat.) The speech comes at the end of the play and is spoken by a man who feels he has not lived up to his potential because, out of sentimentality, he has failed to leave his silly wife:

So at any given moment you're only the sum of your life up to then. There are no big moments you can reach unless you've a pile of smaller moments to stand on. That big hour of decision, the turning point in your life, the someday you've counted on when you'd suddenly wipe out your past mistakes, do the work you'd never done, think the way you'd never thought, have what you'd never had—it just doesn't come suddenly. You've trained yourself for it while you waited—or you've let it all run past you and frittered yourself away. *(Shakes his head)* I've frittered myself away, Crossman.[8]

At first Hammett took an active part in the production of the play. He attended the out-of-town rehearsals and worked with Bloomgarden, who produced it. But he felt that, like the characters it portrayed, the life went out of the play when too many compromises were made.[9] Before opening night on March 7, 1951, at the Coronet Theater in New York, he washed his hands of the show business people he blamed for ruining *The Autumn Garden*. After mixed reviews, it had 101 performances on Broadway. When the play was published in 1951, the dedication was "For Dash."

With the increasing nationwide apprehension about the threat of Communist subversion in the late 1940s Hammett's political stance became more costly, and ultimately because he refused to waver he lost his money and his freedom. In 1946, the Civil Rights Congress instituted a bail fund to be used at the discretion of three trustees to gain the release of defendants arrested for political reasons. The three trustees were Hammett, who was chairman of the group, Robert W. Dunn, and Frederick Vanderbilt Field, millionaire Communist supporter. On September 26, 1949, two additional trustees were named. They were Dr. W. Alpheus Hunton, a black political theoretician who along with Field had been active in the Council on African Affairs and was a trustee of the Jefferson School of Social Science, and Abner Green, who had organized the American Committee for the Protection of the Foreign Born.

The CRC bail fund, which consisted of contributions and loans from friends of the group, amounted to $762,000 on December 31, 1950. Responsible bookkeeping methods and audits were used to keep the accounts of the fund, but the names of contributors were considered by CRC to be privileged information, and the trustees steadfastly refused to name their benefactors. Minutes of CRC bail fund meetings were kept and they were initialed by all the trustees, including Dashiell Hammett.[10]

The bail fund came to national attention on November 4, 1949, when the CRC posted bail of $260,000 in negotiable government bonds to free eleven men appealing their convictions under the Smith Act for criminal conspiracy to teach and advocate the overthrow of the United States government by force and violence. On July 2, 1951, after all appeals had been exhausted, four of the eleven Communist leaders failed to surrender to federal authorities to begin serving their sentences. The four who failed to appear were Robert G. Thompson, New York State Chairman of the Communist Party; Gilbert Green, Illinois Chairman; Gus Hall, Ohio Chairman; and Henry Winston, Organization Secretary. At that time the U.S. District Court, Southern District of New York, issued subpoenas for the trustees of the CRC bail fund in an attempt to learn the whereabouts of the fugitives and declared a forfeiture of the $80,000 bail posted for those four. It was noted that the CRC bail fund had earlier posted $23,500 bail for Gerhardt Eisler, also convicted under the Smith Act, who left the country during the trial of the eleven.

The position of the court was that it had the right to inquire of the trustees for the bail fund about the locations of the fugitives and about the bail fund itself in a effort to gain information that might lead to the arrest of the four Communist leaders. The position of the trustees of the fund, represented by attorneys Mary M. Kaufman and Victor Rabinowitz, was that the court did not have the jurisdiction to make inquiries about the CRC bail fund; that questions about the CRC bail fund were irrelevant to the inquiry as to the whereabouts of the fugitives; and that the trustees had the right to Fifth Amendment protection when questioned about their CRC activities. All of the trustees at some point in their testimonies claimed their rights to remain silent under the Fifth Amendment, but none so often nor so consistently as Dashiell Hammett. His testimony on July 9, 1951, before United States District Court Judge Sylvester Ryan demonstrates the extent of the government's knowledge about the CRC bail fund and Hammett's resolve not to violate his trust as chairman of the fund's trustees. Close friends of Hammett's have maintained that he very possibly had no knowledge of the whereabouts of the four fugitives or of donors to the bail fund, though CRC documents subpoenaed by the court seem to indicate that Hammett's position was not merely honorary, that he actually had a major role in formulating the policy of the bail fund committee.

When Hammett began his testimony (reprinted in full in an appendix to this book), there was little doubt about the consequences of refusing to cooperate with the court. Frederick Field had testified before him, frequently taking refuge in the Fifth Amendment, and he had been sentenced to six months for contempt of court. Hammett was known to be chairman of the bail fund committee and the court felt he had a greater responsibility to divulge information than the other trustees. Moreover, Hammett was questioned by United States District Attorney Irving Saypol, who had been described by *Time* as "the nation's number one legal hunter of top Communists" and who had four months earlier successfully directed the government's case against Julius and Ethel Rosenberg.

Hammett took the stand at 2:30 on Monday afternoon. The government case that he had some information about the four Communist fugitives was formidable. They had the CRC bail fund charter, signed by Hammett. They had minutes of bail fund meetings initialed by Hammett. And they had audits of the bail fund accounts, also initialed by Hammett. What the government lacked was the names of contributors to the fund, the people who might be sympathetic enough to harbor the fugitives.

Hammett's questioning was carefully supervised by Judge Ryan, who seemed anxious to avoid any procedural error by Saypol that would nullify a contempt citation. Hammett stubbornly refused any cooperation with the court. He testified that his name was Samuel Dashiell Hammett, but that is about all. He took the Fifth Amendment when asked any question about the CRC or the bail fund committee, and he refused to identify his signature or his initials on any of the CRC documents the court had subpoenaed.

When Hammett's testimony was concluded, he was immediately found guilty of contempt of court by Judge Ryan and placed in the custody of a federal marshall until 7:30 P.M., when the court reconvened and sentenced him. That evening when Judge Ryan asked Hammett if he had anything to say before being sentenced, Hammett replied, "Not a thing." He was committed at once to the custody of the Attorney General to begin serving a term in prison for six months or until he purged himself of contempt. Hammett was taken directly to the Federal House of Detention on West Street in New York to begin serving his term.

Three days later, on Thursday, July 12, Judge Learned Hand of the United States Court of Appeals for the Second Circuit ordered bail of $10,000 for Hammett, pending a decision on Hammett's attorneys' application for bail, pending, in turn, appeal of his conviction. On two occasions Muriel Alexander went to the Federal Courthouse with $10,000 hoping to post his bond. However, in a precedent-setting action, the Court had ruled that money from the CRC would no longer be acceptable for bail bonds. When Alexander was asked the source of the money she carried, CRC lawyer Mary Kaufman objected and withdrew the offer. On the following Tuesday, July 17, Judge Hand, in response to a petition by federal attorney Irving Saypol, revoked his order, and bail was not again available to Hammett throughout the appeals process that did not end until after he had completed his sentence.

While Hammett was at the West Street detention center, he worked in the library. He had difficulty explaining to other inmates why he was in jail. Murder, robbery, rape they could understand, but not contempt of court for refusing to testify when the charge could have been avoided with a modicum of cooperation.

Muriel Alexander visited Hammett regularly while he was at West Street. She read him the mail that had come to his apartment and relayed messages from Lillian Hellman, who did not visit Hammett in jail. There was a prearranged agreement between Hammett and Hellman that because of her political involvements, her association with him during his ordeal would only complicate the situation. Shortly after his imprisonment, she left on a trip to Europe. Hammett was eager to have news of his family and asked Alexander to hold up photos of his grandchildren to the glass that separated prisoners from visitors.

On September 28, Hammett was moved to the Federal Correctional Institute near Ashland, Kentucky, where, as prisoner #8416AK, he stayed until his release. While he was in prison, he was allowed to write only to relatives and his incoming mail was censored.[11] Hammett wrote his daughter Josephine from Ashland that his job was mopping and that he rather enjoyed it.[12] Lillian Hellman claims one of Hammett's chores in prison was to clean toilets and he resolved to do that better than anyone else. Hammett was released from federal prison on December 9, 1951, ten days before his second appeal to the United States District Court to overthrow his conviction was denied. He had served twenty-two weeks—155 days—of his twenty-six-week sentence, having received a reduction in his time for good behavior. The real price of his imprisonment was not measured by time, however, but by the effect of his incarceration on his health. When Hammett left prison his health was gone, and he was never a well man again.

When he got back to New York, Hammett was met by Hellman. He told her he wanted to go home to his apartment on Tenth Street. He found Rose Evans there. She had continued to keep his apartment while he was in jail, and he had a present for her—his pennies. He had always saved his pennies for her, and he had continued to do so while he was in jail. He was not bitter about his incarceration, he let her know. It had just happened and he had accepted it.

Hellman had visited Hammett's apartment just before his release and she asked Evans to hide the liquor because she was afraid Hammett would start drinking again. Rose Evans refused; Hammett would find his apartment as he had left it, she insisted. When Hammett came home, his housekeeper asked him one favor: please do not drink for at least three or four days, she asked, so it would not appear that the liquor in the apartment had been too great a temptation for him. He agreed, though he warned her that one day he just might go on a real bender. But the days for benders had already passed.

Soon after, Hammett was forced to give up the apartment because he could no longer pay for it. Hellman wanted to hire Rose Evans, but Hammett asked her not to take the job because he feared she would not be treated with the respect and affection which he had always felt for her.[13]

C H A P T E R 21

. . . to remind myself I was once a writer.

> Dashiell Hammett's response to an interviewer
> who asked why he kept three typewriters
> in his Katonah, New York, cottage (1957)

When Hammett was released from prison, at the age of fifty-seven,
he found himself in financial straits for the first time in more than
twenty years. His radio shows were canceled; his books were out of
print; and all his income was attached by the Internal Revenue
Service in lieu of payment of more than $100,000 in back income
taxes dating from 1943, when his affairs in the States were neglected
while he was in the army. By 1954, the total amount of his liability for
tax years through 1950 was assessed at $111,008.60. By January
1957, when a civil suit against Hammett for nonpayment of taxes
was settled by default after he failed to respond to a summons served
on him on December 13, 1956, his tax liability was set at
$140,795.96.[1] While his tax debt was accumulating, Hammett was
stubborn about payment. He said he would rather give his money
away than to have it taken from him by the government.

During 1952, Hammett was sick and unable to work. Hellman was
called to testify before the House Un-American Activities Committee in May of that year. She broke with the strategy of those such as
the Hollywood Ten and Hammett who maintained that the committee and its Senate and judicial counterparts had no right to
conduct any inquiry into their political beliefs and that therefore the
proper response was to invoke either the First or the Fifth Amend-

ment to any questions about their own politics or those of acquaintances. Depending on the questioning body, such stances were often held to be criminally contemptuous, and the social and professional consequences of the blacklist sure to be felt by "unfriendly" witnesses were even more damaging. Hellman informed chairman John S. Wood in advance of her appearance before his committee that she would testify about herself, but not about others. She was not held in contempt of Congress, but her legal expenses were high and she sold Hardscrabble Farm in Pleasantville. Though she and Hammett had always shared their money, now times were hard, especially for him.[2]

Tremendous pressure had been placed on the radio networks and the movie industry to purge themselves of Communist associations, and Hammett was unable to turn to his steadiest source of income since he had quit writing fiction. In fact, it is remarkable that he was able to see profits from radio adaptations of his work as late as mid-1951, when NBC canceled "The Adventures of Sam Spade" and to work in Hollywood as late as mid-1950. Between May 1, 1952, and April 30, 1957, royalties from reprints and foreign publications of Hammett's works amounted to $4,635.87, over $1,000 of which was due to a mass-market paperback publication of *Red Harvest* in 1956. But that money was attached by the Internal Revenue Service.[3]

He was still harassed by investigators of Communism in the United States. On March 26, 1953, Senator Joseph McCarthy called Hammett to testify before his Permanent Subcommittee Investigation of the Senate Committee on Government Operations. McCarthy was at that time investigating the purchase of books written by Communists for State Department libraries overseas.

Hammett's testimony was similar to that which had sent him to prison twenty months earlier, though now he was slightly more willing to discuss his political views. He was questioned first by Roy Cohn, chief counsel to the committee, and who had earlier served as Irving Saypol's assistant in the Rosenberg case, then by committee chairman McCarthy.

Mr. Cohn. The next witness is Mr. Dashiell Hammett.

The Chairman. Mr. Hammett, will you raise your right hand? In this matter now in hearing before the committee, do you solemnly swear to tell the truth, the whole truth, and nothing but the truth, so help you God?

Mr. Hammett. I do.

Mr. Cohn. Could we have your full name, please, sir?

Mr. Hammett. Samuel Dashiell Hammett.

Mr. Cohn. Samuel Dashiell Hammett. Is that right?

Mr. Hammett. That is right.

Mr. Cohn. And what is your occupation?

Mr. Hammett. Writer.

Mr. Cohn. You are a writer. Is that correct?

Mr. Hammett. That is right.

Mr. Cohn. And you are the author of a number of rather well-known detective stories. Is that correct?

Mr. Hammett. That is right.

Mr. Cohn. In addition to that, you have written, I think, in your earlier period, on some social issues. Is that correct?

Mr. Hammett. Well, I have written short stories that may have—you know, it is impossible to write anything without taking some sort of stand on social issues.

Mr. Cohn. You say it is impossible to write anything without taking some sort of stand on a social issue. Now, are you the author of a short story known as Nightshade?

Mr. Hammett. I am.

Mr. Cohn. I might state, Mr. Chairman, that some 300 of Mr. Hammett's books are in use in the Information Sevice today located in, I believe, some 73 information centers; I am sorry, 300 copies, 18 books.

You haven't written 300 books; is that right?

Mr. Hammett. That is a lot of books.

Mr. Cohn. There are 18 books in use, including some collections of short stories and other things, and there are some 300 copies of those located in some 73 information centers.

Now Mr. Hammett, when did you write your first published book?

Mr. Hammett. The first book was Red Harvest. It was published in 1929. I think I wrote it in 1927, either 1927 or 1928.

Mr. Cohn. At the time you wrote that book, were you a member of the Communist Party?

Mr. Hammett. I decline to answer, on the grounds that an answer might tend to incriminate me, relying on my rights under the fifth amendment to the Constitution of the United States.

Mr. Cohn. When did you write your last published book?

Mr. Hammett. Well, I can't really answer that. Because some collections of short stories have been published. I imagine it was some time in the thirties, or perhaps the forties.

Mr. Cohn. In the thirties or forties. At the time you wrote your last published book were you a member of the Communist Party?

Mr. Hammett. I decline to answer on the grounds that an answer might tend to incriminate me.

Mr. Cohn. If I were to ask you, with reference to these books, whether you were a member of the Communist Party at the time you wrote the books, what would your answer be?

Mr. Hammett. Same answer. I would decline to answer on the grounds that an answer might tend to incriminate me.

Mr. Cohn. Mr. Hammett, are you a member of the Communist Party today?

Mr. Hammett. I decline to answer on the grounds that an answer might tend to incriminate me.

The Chairman. Mr. Hammett, let me ask you this. Forgetting about yourself for the time being, it is a safe assumption that any member of the Communist Party, under Communist discipline, would propagandize the Communist cause, normally, regardless of whether he was writing fiction books or books on politics?

Mr. Hammett. I can't answer that, because I honestly don't know.

The Chairman. Well, now, you have told us that you will not tell us whether you are a member of the Communist Party today or not, on the ground that if you told us the answer might incriminate you. That is normally taken by this committee and the country as a whole to mean that you are a member of the party, because if you were not you would simply say, "No," and it would not incriminate you. You see, the only reason that you have the right to refuse to answer is if you feel a truthful answer would incriminate you. An answer that you were not a Communist, if you were not a Communist, could not incriminate you. Therefore, you should know considerable about the Communist movement, I assume.

Mr. Hammett. Was that a question, sir?

The Chairman. That is just a comment upon your statement.

Mr. Counsel, do you have anything further?

Mr. Cohn. Oh, yes.

Now, Mr. Hammett, from these various books you have written, have you received royalty payments?

Mr. Hammett. I have.

Mr. Cohn. And I would assume that if the State Department purchased 300 books, or whatever it was, you would receive some royalties?

Mr. Hammett. I should imagine so.

Mr. Cohn. Could you tell us, without violating some secret of the trade, just what your royalties are, by percentage?

Mr. Hammett. Well, it is not a case of violating a secret of the trade. I would have to look up contracts. And they vary, as a matter of fact. On the books published by Alfred Knopf, $2 or $2.50 books, or whatever they were, I think it starts at 15 percent. On the short-story collections, most of which were reprints, the royalties are lower than that.

The Chairman. Did any of the money which you received from the State Department find its way into the coffers of the Communist Party?

Mr. Hammett. I decline to answer, on the grounds that an answer might tend to incriminate me.

The Chairman. Let me put the question another way. Did you contribute any royalties received as a result of the purchase of these books by the State Department to the Communist Party?

Mr. Hammett. I decline to answer, on the grounds that an answer might tend to incriminate me.

The Chairman. You have the right to decline.

Mr. Cohn. Now, is it a fair statement to make that you have received substantial sums of money from the royalties on all of the books you have written?

Mr. Hammett. Yes; that is a fair statement.

Mr. Cohn. And you decline to tell us whether any of those moneys went to the Communist Party?

Mr. Hammett. That is right.

Mr. Cohn. Now, Mr. Hammett, is it a fact that you have frequently allowed the use of your name as sponsor and member of governing bodies of Communist-front organizations?

Mr. Hammett. I decline to answer, on the ground that an answer might tend to incriminate me.

Mr. Cohn. Mr. Hammett, is it a fact that you recently served a term in prison for contempt of court?

Mr. Hammett. Yes.

Mr. Cohn. And from what did that arise?

Mr. Hammett. From declining to answer whether or not I was a trustee of the bail bond fund of the Civil Rights Congress.

The Chairman. May I ask the photographers not to use any flash pictures while the witness is testifying?

Mr. Cohn. Now, you said it was for refusal to answer. The fact is: You were a trustee of the bail fund of the Civil Rights Congress. Is that right?

Mr. Hammett. That was the question that I went to jail for not answering; yes.

Mr. Cohn. Well, let me ask you: Were you a trustee of the bail bond fund of the Civil Rights Congress?

Mr. Hammett. I decline to answer on the grounds that an answer might tend to incriminate me.

Mr. Cohn. And is it a fact that the Government's allegation was that you were one of the sureties on the bond of four fugitive Communist leaders, that when they disappeared and ran away you were called in to see if you could aid the court in discovering where they were, and that a number of questions were put to you concerning their whereabouts, your activities as a surety, as a trustee of the group that had put up the money for the bail bond, and that you refused to answer?

Mr. Hammett. I don't remember. I don't know whether I was asked anything about their whereabouts.

Mr. Cohn. Well, I will now ask you: Do you know the whereabouts of any of the fugitive Communist leaders?

Mr. Hammett. No; Gus Hall, I read, is in jail.

Mr. Cohn. You know Gus Hall has been captured. How about the other three?

Mr. Hammett. I don't know.

Mr. Cohn. You say you don't know?

Mr. Hammett. I don't know.

The Chairman. You say you do not know where they are at this moment. Did you know where they were at any time while the Government was searching for them?

Mr. Hammett. No.

The Chairman. You did not. Do I understand that you arranged the bail bond for the fugitives?

Mr. Hammett. I decline to answer, on the grounds that an answer might tend to incriminate me.

Mr. Cohn. Did you contribute any of the money that went toward the bail, which made it possible for these Communist leaders to go free on bail, and later to abscond?

Mr. Hammett. I decline to answer, on the grounds that an answer might tend to incriminate me.

The Chairman. Have you ever engaged in espionage against the United States?

Mr. Hammett. No.

The Chairman. Have you ever engaged in sabotage?

Mr. Hammett. No, sir.

The Chairman. Do you believe that the Communist system is better than the system in use in this country?

Mr. Hammett. I can't answer that question, because I really don't know what it means: is the Communist system better than the system used in this country?

The Chairman. Do you believe that communism as practiced in Russia today is superior to our form of government?

Mr. Hammett. Well, regardless of what I thought of communism in Russia today, it is doubtful if, you know, any one sort of thing—one is better for one country, and one is better for the other country. I don't think Russian communism is better for the United States, any more than I would think that some kind of imperialism were better for the United States.

The Chairman. You seem to distinguish between Russian communism and American communism. While I cannot see any distinction, I will assume there is for the purpose of the questioning. Would you think that American communism would be a good system to adopt in this country?

Mr. Hammett. I will have to decline to answer that, on the grounds that an answer might tend to incriminate me. Because, I mean, that can't be answered "yes" or "no."

The Chairman. You could not answer that "yes" or "no," whether you think communism is superior to our form of government?

Mr. Hammett. You see, I don't understand. Theoretical communism is no form of government. You know, there is no government. And I actually don't know, and I couldn't, without—even in the end, I doubt if I could give a definite answer.

The Chairman. Would you favor the adoption of communism in this country?

Mr. Hammett. You mean now?

The Chairman. Yes.

Mr. Hammett. No.

The Chairman. You would not?

Mr. Hammett. For one thing, it would seem to me impractical, if most people didn't want it.

The Chairman. Did you favor the Communist system when you were writing these books?

Mr. Hammett. I decline to answer, on the grounds that an answer might tend to incriminate me.

The Chairman. Senator McClellan, did you have a question?

Senator McClellan. You are declining to answer many questions, taking refuge in the privileges of the fifth amendment of the Constitution, because you are afraid you might incriminate yourself if you answer the questions. Are you sincere and honest in making that statement under oath?

Mr. Hammett. Very sincere, sir. I really am quite afraid that answers will incriminate me, or will tend to incriminate me.

Senator McClellan. Since you say you are afraid: Do you not feel that your refusal to answer is a voluntary act of self-incrimination before the bar of public opinion? Are you not voluntarily, now, by taking refuge in the fifth amendment to the Constitution, committing an act of voluntary self-incrimination before the bar of public opinion, and do you not know that?

Mr. Hammett. I do not think that is so, sir, and if it is so, unfortunately, or fortunately for me in those circumstances, the bar of public opinion did not send me to jail for 6 months.

Senator McClellan. Violation of a law sent you to jail; being caught; is that what you mean? Public opinion, as against being caught? Is that what you are trying to tell us?

Mr. Hammett. No, sir.

Senator McClellan. I did not want to misunderstand you. I thought maybe public opinion or at least judicial opinion had something to do with your going to jail. That was not a voluntary act, was it?

Mr. Hammett. Going to jail?

Senator McClellan. Yes.

Mr. Hammett. No, sir.

Senator McClellan. Well, public opinion must have had something to do with it, or judicial opinion at least.

I do not want to misjudge anyone. I do not think the public wants to. We want to give you every opportunity to be fair to the committee, to be fair to yourself, to be true to your country, if you care anything for this country. And I would like to ask you this question: Would this committee and the public in general be in error if they judged from your answers, or rather your lack of answers, to important questions, and from your demeanor on the witness stand here, that you are now a Communist, that you have been a Communist, and that you still follow and subscribe to the Communist philosophy? Would we be in error if we judged you that way from your actions?

Mr. Hammett. I decline to answer that question, because the answer might tend to incriminate me.

Senator McClellan. Then we are free to judge according to our observations and conclusions based on your refusal to answer and your demeanor on the stand.

Mr. Hammett. Is that a question, sir?

Senator McClellan. Well, if you want to answer it, it is a question. Do you want to take refuge under the Constitution again?

Mr. Hammett. Yes, sir.

Senator McClellan. All right. That is all.

The Chairman. For your information, in case you do not know it, Mr. Budenz, the former editor of the Communist Daily Worker, gave you as one of those used by the Communist Party to further the Communist cause, and gave your name as a Communist under

Communist Party discipline, recognized by him as such. If you care to comment on that, you may.

Mr. Hammett. No, sir. I have no comment to make.

The Chairman. I have no further questions.

Mr. Cohn. I would like to ask: Is Mr. Budenz being truthful when he told us that you were a Communist?

Mr. Hammett. I decline to answer, on the grounds that an answer might tend to incriminate me.

Mr. Cohn. When he told us that you were under Communist discipline?

Mr. Hammett. I decline to answer, on the same grounds.

The Chairman. May I ask one further question: Mr. Hammett, if you were spending, as we are, over a hundred million dollars a year on an information program allegedly for the purpose of fighting communism, and if you were in charge of that program to fight communism, would you purchase the works of some 75 Communist authors and distribute their works throughout the world, placing our official stamp of approval upon those works?

Or would you rather not answer that question?

Mr. Hammett. Well, I think—of course, I don't know—if I were fighting communism, I don't think I would do it by giving people any books at all.

The Chairman. From an author, that sounds unusual.

Thank you very much. You are excused.[4]

Hammett's books were removed from the State Department libraries briefly until President Eisenhower said he felt they posed no subversive threat, and then the books were replaced on the shelves.

The last of Hammett's attempts at his sixth novel was published in a collection of his stories, *The Big Knockover* (1966), edited by Lillian Hellman. The novel fragment abandoned in 1952 or 1953 is called "Tulip," after the nickname for one of the main characters, an ex-soldier who had been stationed in the Aleutians during World War II. Tulip is visiting Pop, his acquaintance from the army. The fragment is clearly autobiographical—Pop was Hammett's nickname in the army during the Second World War. Pop, a writer, had just gotten out of jail where he served a short sentence for political reasons. He is a lunger who reminisces about the Public Health Service Hospital in Tacoma where he stayed after World War I. And he is trying to write another novel. There is little action in "Tulip" but a lot of speculating about how one ought to spend his time, about what constitutes literature. Pop says: "if you're careful enough in not committing yourself you can persuade different readers to see all sorts of different meanings in what you've written, since in the end almost anything can be symbolic of anything else, and I've read a lot of stuff of that sort and liked it, but it's not my way of writing and there's no use pretending it is." He echoes Freud when he says a writer writes for "fame, fortune and personal satisfaction. . . . that is—and should be—your goal. Anything less is kind of piddling."[5]

Hammett gave up on "Tulip" after 12,500 words. The fragment ends with what is, by all evidence, the last prose he ever wrote:

But representations seemed to me—at least they seem now, and I suppose I must have had some inkling of the same opinion then, devices of the old and tired, or older and more tired—to ease up, like conscious symbolism, or graven images. If you are tired you ought to rest, I think, and not try to fool yourself and your customers with colored bubbles.[6]

From early in 1952, Hammett lived about twenty miles north of Manhattan at the Katonah, New York, estate of Dr. Samuel Rosen, a friend sympathetic to his political convictions. Dr. Rosen let him live rent-free in the four-room gatekeeper's cottage. Hammett visited Lillian Hellman, as he had off and on for the past twenty-five years, and his health deteriorated steadily.

On February 23, 1955, Hammett was called to testify before the New York State Joint Legislative Committee investigating charitable and philanthropic agencies and organizations. There he testified that as far as he knew he was still chairman of the Civil Rights Congress and that as far as he knew the CRC had no Communist members; but even if Communists had belonged to CRC it wouldn't have mattered: "Communism to me is not a dirty word. When you are working for the advance of mankind it never occurs to you whether a guy is a Communist." As always Hammett refused to answer whether he himself had belonged to the Communist Party.[7]

Hellman had bought a house on Martha's Vineyard and she provided Hammett an apartment when he visited. In August 1955 he had a heart attack there, another illness to add to his lung and liver diseases. He claimed total disability from that date.[8]

Through the middle fifties, Hammett maintained his political interests. He continued to teach at the Jefferson School and to serve on the board of trustees until 1956. He noticed that the enrollment of his classes had swollen, a circumstance he attributed to increased attendance by FBI agents monitoring for political statements. He was affiliated with the National Council of the Arts, Sciences, and Professions in 1955 and endorsed that group's resolution condemning armed aggression in Guatemala. He helped organize and was a sponsor of the Watchdog Committee for Legislation in the National Interest in 1956.

In 1957 Hammett gave two interviews, each in its own way reflecting the despair he had fallen into. The first was in March 1957 with the FBI, which was requested to investigate his ability to pay the $140,795.96 tax judgment against him. Hammett claimed that he lived alone, rent free, in a cottage owned by friends. He had, he said, no bank accounts, safe deposit vaults or boxes. He was unemployed and essentially without income. He had not received royalties from his work for several years, and his income for the past year had been about thirty dollars, that from a share he owned of Arthur Miller's *Death of a Salesman*, bought eight years earlier. He owned no stocks or bonds, had no insurance policies, and was not engaged in any business. He had started a book called "Tulip" "some years ago, but he had done nothing for the past couple of years." "Tulip" was his only work-in-progress. He owned no car, and his personal property consisted only of the majority of his furniture.

In addition to his debt to the federal government, Hammett claimed to owe $300 to Burrelle's Press Clipping Service in White Plains, New York; $1,000 to Bernard Reis Associates, his accountant; and $15,000 or $16,000 to New York State in back taxes. Finally, "He explained that he had no reason to anticipate any change in his financial position."

The record showed further that Hammett continued in 1957 to make modest purchases at two of his favorite stores in New York, Abercrombie & Fitch and Brooks Brothers. He charged his purchases and paid the bills promptly by money order. Burrelle's Press Clipping Service was less fortunate. On May 7, 1956, a judgment was entered against Hammett for $316.95 and he was ordered to pay five dollars a week. No payment was made.

The second interview with Hammett in 1957 was conducted by journalist James Cooper for the *Washington Daily News*. Hammett described himself as "a two-fisted loafer" and said he kept three typewriters in his cottage "chiefly to remind myself I was once a writer." Hammett said, "I am concentrating on my health. I am learning to be a hypochondriac. I stopped writing because I found I was repeating myself. It is the beginning of the end when you discover you have style.

"But the thing that ruined me was the writing of the last third of 'The Glass Key' in one sitting of 30 hours.

". . . Ever since then I have told myself: 'I could do it again if I had to.' " When asked why he hadn't written in jail, Hammett replied, "I was never bored enough. I found the crooks had not changed since I was a Pinkerton man. Going to prison was like going home."[9]

Hammett spent the last four years of his life as a recluse. He refused to see old friends; he refused to go out. At age sixty-two in 1957 he looked ten years older, and he was a sick man. The simple act of breathing was exhausting, and he could sit up for only short periods.

On April 29, 1959, he applied for compensation from the Veteran's Administration. He expected to earn $200 to $300 dollars in 1959, he said. One month later, he was granted a pension of $131.10 per month. His claim was based on respiratory illness: "My present complaint is a great shortness of breath with not enough oxygen getting through to my muscles so that I'm practically bedridden most of the time. Dr. Charles E. Kossmann, of the Lenox Hill Hospital, has been treating me for that. . . ."

Hammett died on January 10, 1961, at 7 P.M. in private room 823 at Lenox Hill Hospital. The primary cause of death was a cancerous tumor in the right lung, complicated by emphysema and pneumonia, in addition to disease of his heart, liver, kidneys, spleen, and prostate gland. The doctors had known about Hammett's cancer, though he apparently was not aware of it. His funeral was held at Frank E. Campbell's Funeral Home on Madison Avenue. It cost $931.90 of which $532.53 was paid by the Veteran's Administration and $399.37 by his estate.[10] Among those attending the service were Quentin Reynolds, Bennett Cerf, Dorothy Parker, Kermit Bloomgarden, Patricia Neal, Leonard Bernstein, Arthur Kober, Lionel Trilling, Muriel Alexander, and Rose Evans. His eulogy was delivered by Lillian Hellman, who called Hammett "a man of simple honor and great bravery."[11]

On January 13 Hammett was buried at Arlington National Cemetery in accordance with his wishes. The burial service was attended by Lillian Hellman; Reba Hammett, Dashiell's sister; Agnes Mattingly, Hammett's first cousin, and her husband Charles; and Jane Yowaiski, Hammett's second cousin.[12]

The FBI continued its interest in Hammett after his death. An interoffice memo dated January 17, 1961, notes that news reports indicated Hammett was buried in Arlington National Cemetery, and the FBI verified that fact by calling the cemetery. The memo concludes that the attention of the press might be called "to the incongruous situation which exists wherein one who has been a member of an organization which believes in the overthrow of our government by force and violence receives a hero's burial among those who gave their lives to support this government."[13] But the era of McCarthyism was over, and Hammett's grave remained undisturbed.

E P I L O G U E

Hammett's will was made on July 1, 1952, six months after his release from jail. It is a very simple, two-page document. He divided his estate into four parts: one part to go to his daughter Mary, two parts to his daughter Josephine, and one part to his friend Lillian Hellman. Hellman was named as executrix and Josephine Hammett Marshall was named as alternate executrix. To most of the parties involved, the probate of Hammett's will seemed a meaningless exercise, since he had assets of less than $10,000 and liens against his estate of over $220,000, including nearly $180,000 in federal and state tax judgments, $40,000 claimed by Lillian Hellman as "advances to decedent during his lifetime," and about $1,000 claimed by Hellman as advances against the estate during Hammett's last illness. Hellman estimated the value of Hammett's copyrights at $1,000 for the purposes of probating his estate. Under law, all of Hammett's copyrights renewed before his death (that is, for those works published before 1933) belonged to his estate, but copyrights for those works published after 1933 were the property of his wife and children, who alone had the right to renew copyrights. On April 5, 1963, Hellman, with the help of her friend Arthur W. A. Cowan, began moves to settle the insolvency of the Hammett estate by negotiating a tax settlement with the IRS and by purchasing Hammett's copyrights in full from the family.[1]

The reason stated for this move was cited in her petition to Surrogate's Court, County of New York: "Since the deceased's death, certain suggestions have been made to deponent that she write a book about the deceased or his works, and deponent would consider such a proposition if the opportunity presents itself and a reasonable offer is made. In view of this possibility, deponent believes it may be of some interest or benefit to her to obtain all rights and interests which the deceased and/or his Estate may have or be entitled to with respect to or arising from deceased's literary works, copyrights, etc., free and clear of all claims and especially, all claims and liens of the United States Government. Deponent is, therefore, willing to offer the Estate the sum of $2,000., for all such rights subject to this Court's approval of such sale, which sum together with the moneys now in possession of Alfred A. Knopf [$7,941.23], less the funeral expenses [$446.77], administration expenses [$2,000], the hospital bill [$490.78] and doctor's bill [$217.50] would be turned over to the United States Government in payment of all its claims against the Estate."[2]

In other words, she was offering the government a net amount of $6,786.18 to settle a debt of $163,286.46 plus interest, and the government would have paid Hammett's creditors from funds they had already attached. The government declined. In a compromise the court ordered that a public sale of the Hammett copyrights should be held by Hellman as executrix, and that the minimum bid should be $5,000. If there were no acceptable bid, the copyrights would be distributed among the government agencies with claims against the estate. On November 18, 1963, a sale was held in the offices of Hellman's attorneys O'Dwyer & Bernstein in New York, and the copyrights were sold to Hellman and Cowan for the minimum bid. The sale was approved by surrogate court on January 4, 1964, and a final accounting was made. It was agreed that royalties earned by Hammett's works, then held in escrow by Knopf, should go directly to the United States government since they had had a lien against any such earnings for some twelve years, and the government should also receive the estate's one-half of one percent interest in *Death of a Salesman*, valued at $100. After deduction of attorney's fee of $2,000, Hammett's last doctor's fee and hospital bill, and a portion of his funeral expenses, the sale of his copyrights netted some two thousand dollars. Hellman and Cowan owned Hammett's copyrights (Cowan's interest was left to her at his death), and his family was left no legal claim to his works.

Since his death, Hammett's fiction has been constantly in print. In 1961, Permabooks published mass-market paperback editions of *Red Harvest*, *The Dain Curse*, *The Maltese Falcon*, and *The Glass Key*. In

1966, Hellman edited a collection of nine op stories and "Tulip," called *The Big Knockover*. The same year Dell published paperback editions of *The Maltese Falcon*, *The Glass Key*, and *The Thin Man*, followed in 1968 by *Red Harvest* and *The Dain Curse*. In 1972, Vintage, a paperback imprint of Knopf, published all five novels and Hellman's collection, *The Big Knockover*, and has kept them steadily in print since. In May 1978, *Publishers Weekly* reported that *The Dain Curse*, perhaps Hammett's least popular novel, had sold over seventy thousand copies since 1972, or an average of some twelve thousand copies a year. Random House published a second collection of Hammett's op stories, *The Continental Op*, edited by Steven Marcus, in 1974, and it was republished under the Vintage imprint in 1975.[3] On May 22-24, 1978, CBS televised an adaptation of *The Dain Curse* in three two-hour segments, reportedly paying $250,000 for television rights.

Appreciation of Hammett's works has not been limited to American readers. When his literary reputation was being overshadowed by his political activities in the United States during the 1950s, he was just being discovered on a large scale by foreign readers. His novels and short stories were published in sixty-eight separate translations in various languages between 1948 and 1961, and between 1961 and 1975, 115 additional translations were published. Hammett is now widely regarded internationally as one of the finest mystery writers of all time, whose literary accomplishment is just what he had written Blanche Knopf in 1928 he had hoped it would be—to elevate the American mystery novel to the level of fine literature.

A P P E N D I X

WORKS

Novels:

Red Harvest (New York & London: Knopf, 1929).

The Dain Curse (New York & London: Knopf, 1929).

The Maltese Falcon (New York & London: Knopf, 1930).

The Glass Key (New York & London: Knopf, 1931).

The Thin Man (New York: Knopf, 1934; London: Barker, 1934).

Story Collections:

$106,000 Blood Money (New York: Spivak, 1943). Includes "The Big Knockover" and "$106,000 Blood Money."

The Adventures of Sam Spade & Other Stories (New York: Spivak, 1944). Includes "Too Many Have Lived," "They Can Only Hang You Once," "A Man Called Spade," "The Assistant Murderer," "Nightshade," "The Judge Laughed Last," and "His Brother's Keeper."

The Continental Op (New York: Spivak, 1945). Includes "Fly Paper," "Death on Pine Street," "Zigzags of Treachery," and "The Farewell Murder."

The Return of the Continental Op (New York: Spivak, 1945). Includes "The Whosis Kid," "The Gutting of Couffignal," "Death and Company," "One Hour," and "The Tenth Clue."

Hammett Homicides, edited by Ellery Queen (New York: Spivak, 1946). Includes "The Main Death," "Two Sharp Knives," and "Ruffian's Wife."

Dead Yellow Women, edited by Ellery Queen (New York: Spivak, 1946). Includes "Dead Yellow Women," "The Golden Horseshoe," "House Dick," "Who Killed Bob Teal?," "The Green Elephant," and "The Hairy One."

Nightmare Town, edited by Ellery Queen (New York: Spivak, 1948). Includes "Nightmare Town," "The Scorched Face," "Albert Pastor at Home," and "Corkscrew."

The Creeping Siamese (New York: Spivak, 1950). Includes "The Creeping Siamese," "The Man Who Killed Dan Odams," "The Nails in Mr. Cayterer," "The Joke on Eloise Morey," "Tom, Dick or Harry," and "This King Business."

Woman in the Dark, edited by Ellery Queen (New York: Spivak, 1951). Includes "Arson Plus," "Slippery Fingers," "The Black Hat That Wasn't There," "Woman in the Dark," "Afraid of a Gun," "Holiday," and "The Man Who Stood in the Way."

A Man Named Thin (New York: Spivak, 1962). Includes "A Man Named Thin," "Wages of Crime," "The Gatewood Caper," "The Barber and His Wife," "Itchy the Debonair," "The Second-Story Angel," "In the Morgue," and "When Luck's Running Good."

(All of the Spivak collections were prepared for publication by Ellery Queen, who was not always credited as editor.)

The Big Knockover, edited by Lillian Hellman (New York: Random House, 1966). Includes "The Gutting of Couffignal," "Fly Paper," "The Scorched Face," "This King Business," "The Gatewood Caper," "Dead Yellow Women," "Corkscrew," "Tulip," and "The Big Knockover."

The Continental Op, edited by Steven Marcus (New York: Random House, 1974). Includes "The Tenth Clew," "The Golden Horseshoe," "The House in Turk Street," "The Girl with the Silver Eyes," "The Whosis Kid," "The Main Death," and "The Farewell Murder."

Other Books:

Creeps by Night (New York: John Day, 1931)—an anthology edited with an introduction by Hammett.

Secret Agent X-9, Books One and Two (Philadelphia: David McKay, 1934)—a two volume collection of Hammett's comic strip.

The Battle of the Aleutians, by Hammett and Robert Colodny (Adak, Alaska: Intelligence Section, Field Force Headquarters, Adak, 1944).

Magazine Publications:

"The Parthian Shot." *The Smart Set* (October 1922). Anecdote.

"The Great Lovers." *The Smart Set* (November 1922). Article.

"Immortality." *10 Story Book* (November 1922). Story.

"The Barber and His Wife." *Brief Stories* (December 1922). Story.

"The Road Home." *The Black Mask* (December 1922). Story.

"The Master Mind." *The Smart Set* (January 1923). Article.

"The Sardonic Star of Tom Doody." *Brief Stories* (February 1923). Story.

"From the Memoirs of a Private Detective." *The Smart Set* (March 1923). Article.

"The Vicious Circle." *The Black Mask* (June 15, 1923). Story.

"The Joke on Eloise Morey." *Brief Stories* (June 1923). Story.

"Holiday." *The New Pearsons* (July 1923). Story.

"The Crusader." *The Smart Set* (August 1923). Story.

"Arson Plus." *The Black Mask* (October 1, 1923). Story.

"The Dimple." *Saucy Stories* (October 15, 1923). Story.

"Crooked Souls." *The Black Mask* (October 15, 1923). Story.

"Slippery Fingers." *The Black Mask* (October 15, 1923). Story.

"The Green Elephant." *The Smart Set* (October 1923). Story.

"It." *The Black Mask* (November 1, 1923). Story.

"The Second-Story Angel." *The Black Mask* (November 15, 1923). Story.

"Laughing Masks." *Action Stories* (November 1923). Story.

"Bodies Piled Up." *The Black Mask* (December 1, 1923). Story.

"Itchy." *Brief Stories* (January 1924). Story.

"The Tenth Clew." *The Black Mask* (January 1, 1924). Story.

"The Man Who Killed Dan Odams." *The Black Mask* (January 15, 1924). Story.

"Night Shots." *The Black Mask* (February 1, 1924). Story.

"The New Racket." *The Black Mask* (February 15, 1924). Story.

"Esther Entertains." *Brief Stories* (February 1924). Story.

"Afraid of a Gun." *The Black Mask* (March 1, 1924). Story.

"Zigzags of Treachery." *The Black Mask* (March 1, 1924). Story.

"One Hour." *The Black Mask* (April 1, 1924). Story.

"The House in Turk Street." *The Black Mask* (April 15, 1924). Story.

"The Girl with the Silver Eyes." *The Black Mask* (June 1924). Story.

"In Defence of the Sex Story." *The Writer's Digest* (June 1924). Article.

"Our Own Short Story Course." *The Black Mask* (August 1924). Letter.

"Women, Politics and Murder." *The Black Mask* (September 1924). Story.

"Mr. Hergesheimer's Scenario." *The Forum* (November 1924). Book review.

"Who Killed Bob Teal?" *True Detective Stories* (November 1924). Story.

"The Golden Horseshoe." *The Black Mask* (November 1924).
Story.

"Nightmare Town." *Argosy All-Story Weekly* (December 27, 1924).
Story.

"Mike, Alec or Rufus." *The Black Mask* (January 1925). Story.

"The Whosis Kid." *The Black Mask* (March 1925). Story.

"Ber-Bulu." *Sunset Magazine* (March 1925). Story.

"Vamping Samson." *The Editor* (May 9, 1925). Article.

"The Scorched Face." *The Black Mask* (May 1925). Story.

"Genius Made Easy." *The Forum* (August 1925). Book review.

"Corkscrew." *The Black Mask* (September 1925). Story.

"Ruffian's Wife." *Sunset Magazine* (October 1925). Story.

"Caution to Travelers." *The Lariat* (November 1925). Poem.

"Dead Yellow Women." *The Black Mask* (November 1925). Story.

"The Gutting of Couffignal." *The Black Mask* (December 1925).
Story.

"The Nails in Mr. Cayterer." *The Black Mask* (January 1926).
Story.

"The Assistant Murderer." *The Black Mask* (February 1926).
Story.

"The Creeping Siamese." *The Black Mask* (March 1926). Story.

"The Advertisement IS Literature." *Western Advertising* (October
1926). Article.

"The Cabell Epitome." *The Forum* (January 1927). Book review.

"Poor Scotland Yard!" *The Saturday Review of Literature* (January
15, 1927). Book review.

"The Advertising Man Writes a Love Letter." *Judge* (February 26,
1927). Parody.

"The Big Knock-Over." *Black Mask* (February 1927). Story.

"Yes." *Stratford Magazine* (March 1927). Poem.

"$106,000 Blood Money." *Black Mask* (May 1927). Story.

"Goodbye to a Lady." *Stratford Magazine* (June 1927). Poem.

"The Main Death." *Black Mask* (June 1927). Story.

"Curse in the Old Manner." *The Bookman* (September 1927).
Poem.

"The Cleansing of Poisonville." *Black Mask* (November 1927).
Serialization of *Red Harvest*.

"Advertising Art Isn't ART—It's Literature." *Western Advertising*
(December 1927). Article.

"Crime Wanted—Male or Female." *Black Mask* (December 1927).
Serialization of *Red Harvest*.

"Have You Tried Meiosis?" *Western Advertising* (January 1928).
Article.

"This King Business." *Mystery Stories* (January 1928). Story.

"Dynamite." *Black Mask* (January 1928). Serialization of *Red Harvest.*

"The Literature of Advertising—1927." *Western Advertising* (February 1928). Article.

"The 19th Murder." *Black Mask* (February 1928). Serialization of *Red Harvest.*

"The Editor Knows His Audience." *Western Advertising* (March 1928). Article.

"Black Lives." *Black Mask* (November 1928). Serialization of *The Dain Curse.*

"The Hollow Temple." *Black Mask* (December 1928). Serialization of *The Dain Curse.*

"Black Honeymoon." *Black Mask* (January 1929). Serialization of *The Dain Curse.*

"Black Riddle." *Black Mask* (February 1929). Serialization of *The Dain Curse.*

"Fly Paper." *Black Mask* (August 1929). Story.

"The Maltese Falcon." *Black Mask* (September 1929, October 1929, November 1929, December 1929, January 1930). Serialization of the novel.

"The Diamond Wager." *Detective Fiction Weekly* (October 19, 1929). Story.

"The Farewell Murder." *Black Mask* (February 1930). Story.

"The Glass Key." *Black Mask* (March 1930). Serialization of *The Glass Key.*

"The Cyclone Shot." *Black Mask* (April 1930). Serialization of *The Glass Key.*

"Dagger Point." *Black Mask* (May 1930). Serialization of *The Glass Key.*

"The Shattered Key." *Black Mask* (June 1930). Serialization of *The Glass Key.*

"Behind the Black Mask." *Black Mask* (June 1930). Letter.

"Death and Company." *Black Mask* (November 1930). Story.

"On the Way." *Harper's Bazaar* (March 1932). Story.

"A Man Called Spade." *American Magazine* (July 1932). Story.

"Too Many Have Lived." *American Magazine* (October 1932). Story.

"They Can Only Hang You Once." *Collier's* (November 1932). Story.

"Woman in the Dark." *Liberty* (April 8, 1933, April 15, 1933, April 22, 1933). Story.

"Night Shade." *Mystery League Magazine* (October 1, 1933). Story.

"Albert Pastor at Home." *Esquire* (Autumn 1933). Story.

"The Thin Man." *Redbook* (December 1933). Bowdlerized version of the novel.

"Two Sharp Knives." *Collier's* (January 13, 1934). Story.

"His Brother's Keeper." *Collier's* (February 17, 1934). Story.

"This Little Pig." *Collier's* (March 24, 1934). Story.

"Committee on Election Rights." *The New Republic* (October 21, 1940). Letter.

"A Communication to All American Writers." *New Masses* (December 16, 1941). Public letter.

"The Thin Man and the Flack." *Click* (December 1941). Photo story.

"Help Them Now." *New Masses* (May 19, 1942). Public letter.

Letter advertisement. *Soviet Russia Today* (October 1947).

"A Man Named Thin." *Ellery Queen's Mystery Magazine* (March 1961). Story.

"Secret Agent X-9." *Captain George Presents* (1971?). Entire double issue devoted to reprint of Hammett's comic strip. Includes all of *Secret Agent X-9* Book One and a portion of Book Two.

"The Thin Man." *City Magazine* (November 4, 1975). Fragment of unfinished novel.

Hammett also reviewed mystery fiction and true crime books for *The Saturday Review of Literature*. His reviews appear in the following issues: March 19, 1927; April 16, 1927; May 21, 1927; June 11, 1927; December 10, 1927; February 11, 1928; April 21, 1928; October 13, 1928; October 20, 1928; October 27, 1928; December 1, 1928; December 8, 1928; December 22, 1928; December 29, 1928; January 5, 1929; January 12, 1929; January 26, 1929; February 9, 1929; April 27, 1929; May 4, 1929; September 7, 1929; September 21, 1929; October 5, 1929; and October 12, 1929.

The Following Stories Are Unlocated:

"The Man Who Loved Ugly Women." *Experience* (probably before May 1925).

"Another Perfect Crime." *Experience* (probably before May 1925).

"A Tale of Two Women." *Saturday Home Magazine* (n.d.).

"A First Aide to Murder." *Saturday Home Magazine* (n.d.).

Newspaper Publications:

Hammett was book reviewer for the *New York Evening Post* from April 5, 1930, to October 11, 1930. His reviews appeared in the Saturday book review section.

Hammett's comic strip *Secret Agent X-9* was syndicated by King Features Syndicate. The strip began on January 29, 1934, and ran daily except Sunday until April 27, 1935, with credit to Hammett for continuity.

Movies for which Hammett provided original material:

City Streets, Paramount, 1931. Screenplay by Oliver H. P. Garrett from adaptation by Max Marcin. Original story by Hammett.

Mister Dynamite, Universal, 1935. Screenplay by Doris Malloy and Harry Clork. Original story by Hammett.

Satan Met a Lady, Warner Brothers, 1936. Screenplay by Brown Holmes. Partially based on original story by Hammett.

After the Thin Man, Metro-Goldwyn-Mayer, 1939. Screenplay by Frances Goodrich and Albert Hackett. Original story by Hammett.

Another Thin Man, Metro-Goldwyn-Mayer, 1939. Screenplay by Albert Hackett and Frances Goodrich. Original story by Hammett.

Watch on the Rhine, Warner Brothers, 1943. Screenplay by Hammett.

Hammett's full testimony before United States Second District Court Judge Sylvester Ryan, July 9, 1951, in New York City.

AFTERNOON SESSION
2.30 o'clock P.M.

The Court: All right, now, Mr. Hammett, will you take the stand.

SAMUEL DASHIELL HAMMETT, called as a witness, being duly sworn, testified as follows:

The Court: Did you want to say something, Mr. Rabinowitz?

Mr. Rabinowitz: Your Honor, I wanted to note first that Mrs. Kaufman and I will both appear for Mr. Hammett.

And then I wanted to make a preliminary motion to quash the subpoena here on the ground that the subpoena bears the caption "United States v. Hall." There is no index number on the subpoena. I am unable to trace the action, and so far as I know there is no action pending in this court entitled U.S. v. Hall.

The Court: The witness is present in court. The Court will now proceed to examine him irrespective of the validity of any subpoena served upon him.

The motion is denied.

Mr. Saypol, you may proceed.

By Mr. Saypol.

Q. Mr. Hammett—

The Court: Before you begin, Mr. Hammett, so that you might understand your position here, you are called here as a witness by the Court. If, during the course of your examination you feel that it is necessary to consult with counsel before answering any question, simply ask the Court for an opportunity to do so and the opportunity will be granted to you.

Do you understand?

The Witness: Yes.

Q. Mr. Hammett, are you one of the five trustees of the bail fund of the Congress of Civil Rights? A. I decline to answer that question on the ground that the answer might tend to incriminate me. I am exercising my rights under the Fifth Amendment of the Constitution.

The Court: Mr. Saypol, I think the name of the fund was not correctly given by you in your question. I therefore suggest that you ask the question again.

Mr. Saypol: All right.

Q. Mr. Hammett, I show you this—

The Court: No. Ask the question again so that we may get an answer to it.

Q. Are you one of the five trustees—

The Court: No. One of the trustees. Are you one of the trustees of the—

Q. —bail fund of the Civil Rights Congress of New York? A. I decline to answer. Do I have to repeat my reasons for declining to answer?

The Court: Yes.

A. (continuing) I decline to answer on the ground that the answer may tend to incriminate me, and I am relying on my rights under the Fifth Amendment to the Constitution of the United States.

The Court: I direct you to answer the question.

The Witness: I decline to answer the question, your Honor, for the same reasons.

The Court: For the same reasons that you have given?

The Witness: Yes.

Q. I show you Exhibit 6 in evidence, the minute book of the bail fund of the Civil Rights Congress of New York, and I direct your attention particularly to a minute dated November 14, 1949, which reads as follows:

"The trustees agreed to post bail up to $1,000 each for a 30-day period for the 16 members of the Federation of Greek Maritime Unions now held on Ellis Island.

"It was reported that on November 3, 1949 bail in the aggregate amount of $260,000 had been posted in the case of the 11 Communist leaders convicted under the Smith Act. This action was taken in pursuance of the authorization given by the trustees at their meeting on July 22, 1948."

Signed "Frederick V. Field."

I ask you, have you seen this minute book before? A. I decline to answer—

The Court: Showing the witness Exhibit No. 6; is that right?

Mr. Saypol: Yes, your Honor.

A. (continuing) I decline to answer the question on ground that the answer may tend to incriminate me.

Q. Have you examined this—

The Court: Excuse me, Mr. Saypol.

Q. Have you examined this—

The Court: Excuse me, Mr. Saypol.

(To witness) I direct you to answer the question.

A. I decline to answer the question on the same grounds.

The Court: All right.

Q. Before you declined, did you examine this document that I handed you? A. May I consult counsel?

The Court: Yes, surely.

(Witness consults with counsel.)

Mr. Rabinowitz: May I ask to have the question read?

The Court: Yes.

(Queston read.)

(Witness consulted with counsel.)

Mr. Saypol: May the record show that the witness consulted with his counsel and returns to the witness stand now?

The Witness: May I hear that question?

(Last question read as follows: "Before you declined did you examine this document that I handed you?")

Q. Government's Exhibit 6? A. Yes, now.

Q. Did you examine now the minutes that I referred to dated November 14, 1949? A. Yes.

Q. And after examining it do you decline to answer the question directed to you by the Court that you answer? A. I do.

Q. Referring to this minute dated November 14, 1949, which I have read, do you see in the left hand margin a group of initials, four to be exact? A. I do.

Q. Do you recognize those? A. I decline to answer that—now I would like before I decline to ask, do I recognize them as initials? I would say Yes.

By the Court.

Q. Do you recognize the handwriting of the individual? A. I decline to answer that on the ground that the answer may tend to incriminate me.

Q. I direct you to answer that. A. I decline, your Honor, for the reasons given.

By Mr. Saypol.

Q. Without telling me whether the first initials are those of yourself or somebody else, do they appear to you to be the initials D.H.? A. They do appear.

Q. Are they your initials? A. I decline to answer that question.

By the Court.

Q. Are they your handwriting? A. I decline to answer that question for the reasons given.

Q. That is, you feel that the answer may tend to incriminate you? A. Yes.

Q. I direct you to answer the question. A. I respectfully decline, for the reasons given.

Q. Let me ask you one question, Mr. Hammett—is that the name? A. It is.

Q. Have you in any way conspired, aided or abetted or arranged or assisted in the arrangements for the nonappearance of Robert G. Thompson, Gilbert Green, Gus Hall and Henry Winston, or any of them in this cause since the issuance of process against them? A. I decline to answer on the ground that the answer may tend to incriminate me.

Q. I direct you to answer. A. I decline to answer for the reasons already given.

Q. Do you know Robert G. Thompson? A. I decline to answer on the ground the answer may tend to incriminate me.

Q. I direct you to answer. A. I decline to answer for the reasons given.

Q. Have you seen Robert G. Thompson since Thursday, July 5th? A. I decline to answer on the ground the answer may tend to incriminate me.

Q. I direct you to answer. A. I decline to answer for the same reason.

Q. Do you know Gilbert Green? A. I decline to answer on the ground that the answer might tend to incriminate me.

Q. I direct you to answer. A. I decline to answer for the reasons given.

Q. Have you seen Gilbert Green since Thursday, July 5th? A. I decline to answer on the ground the answer may tend to incriminate me.

Q. Do you know Gus Hall? A. I decline to answer on the ground that the answer may tend to incriminate me.

Q. I direct you to answer. A. I decline to answer for the reasons given.

Q. Have you seen Gus Hall since Thursday, July 5th? A. I decline to answer for the reason that the answer may tend to incriminate me.

Q. I direct you to answer. A. I decline to answer for the reasons given.

Q. Do you known Henry Winston? A. I decline to answer for the reasons, on the ground—

Q. Take your time. A. (continuing) —that an answer may tend to incriminate me.

Q. I direct you to answer. A. I decline to answer for the reasons given.

Q. Have you seen Henry Winston since Thursday, July 5th? A. I decline to answer on the ground the answer may tend to incriminate me.

Q. I direct you to answer. A. I decline to answer.

The Court: Go ahead, Mr. Saypol.

By Mr. Saypol.

Q. When since last Monday, July 2nd, were you in New York last? New York City, I mean? A. The question was when since—

Q. When since Monday, July 2nd, have you been in New York City last. (Witness left the stand to consult with counsel and thereafter returned to the stand.)

Mr. Saypol: May the record show that the witness has returned to the witness box after consulting with both his counsel.

Q. Now then will you respond?

(Last question read by the reporter.)

A. I was in New York City from about 11 o'clock Thursday morning until around 4 o'clock Friday afternoon and from, oh, about 1 o'clock yesterday to the present time.

Q. You mean from Thursday, July 5th, until, when you say yesterday, you mean Sunday, July 8th? A. Yes.

Q. When before Thursday, July 5th, were you in New York City last? A. My best memory would be—oh, I had not been in New York City for, I think, one day short of two weeks. Two weeks. Friday, two weeks previous. One day. About 13 days.

Q. I direct your attention once again to this Exhibit 6. Will you please examine this minute, the minutes of the bail fund of the Civil Rights Congress of New York, dated May 18, 1949, reading as follows:

"The trustees surveyed the various acts of the bail fund from its first meeting to date. The auditor's report of the bail fund of the Civil Rights Congress of New York as of December 31, 1948, prepared by Bernard Ades, certified public accountant, was noted and filed. The trustees approved the payment of $340 to Mr. Ades for the preparation of this report on January 27, 1948, and for all other accounting services previously rendered to the bail fund. The trustees also approved the payment of $50 as rent for its safe deposit box at the Amalgamated Bank."

Signed "George Marshall, Secretary,
Bail Fund of the Civil Rights
Congress of New York."

Mr. Marshall was Mr. Field's predecessor, was he not? A. I decline to answer on the grounds that the answer might tend to incriminate me.

The Court: I direct you to answer.

The Witness: I decline to answer for the reason stated.

Q. That answer was given after you followed the reading of this paper with me; is that so? A. It is.

Q. I direct your attention to the lefthand margin, the left side margin of this resolution of this minute of May 18, 1949, and you see there, do you not, the pen written initials, the first of which appear to be "D. H."? A. I do.

Q. Are those your initials? A. I decline to answer the question on the ground that the answer might tend to incriminate me.

The Court: I direct you to answer.

The Witness: I decline to answer the question for the reasons given.

Q. Did you affix those initials? A. I decline to answer.

Q. Did you affix the initials "D. H."? A. I decline to answer the question for the reasons given.

The Court: I direct you to answer.

The Witness: I decline to answer.

By the Court.

Q. Do you know the present whereabouts of Robert G. Thompson, Gilbert Green, Gus Hall and Henry Winston, or either of them? A. I decline to answer on the ground that the answer might tend to incriminate me.

Q. I direct you to answer. A. I decline to answer for the reasons given.

Q. Mr. Hammett, a bond was given in this court, four bonds were given in this court by the bail fund of the Civil Rights Congress of New York, to secure the appearance or to assure the appearance of these four individuals whose names I have just given you. The testimony before the Court is that you functioned as one of the trustees of that fund, that you have functioned as one of the officers and trustees of that fund for some time past. When these men were released on bail, they were released in the custody of the bondsmen, and since the bondsmen are members of an unincorporated association, in effect it means that they were released in the custody of those who operated and managed the affairs of this bail fund, and that they were released in the custody of the trustees, and the testimony before the Court indicates that you were one of the trustees, and by your refusal to answer you are not only violating the trust imposed in you, that you voluntarily assumed when you acted as a trustee for this fund, but you are thwarting the processes of this court. I feel that your claim of immunity has neither legal basis nor factual foundation. It is the intention of the Court, if you persist in your refusal to answer these questions which have been put to you, particularly those questions concerning the present whereabouts of these four men who were released under bail given by the bail fund of the Civil Rights Congress of New York, to deal with you just as drastically as the law permits. I trust that you will not make that necessary. A. (No response.)

The Court: Next question.

By Mr. Saypol.

Q. Mr. Hammett, I direct your attention to this paper in Exhibit 6 which reads as follows:

"Minutes bail fund Civil Rights Congress of New York September 26, 1949.

"The trustees decided that it would be desirable to have two additional trustees, making a total of five.

"The trustees thereupon elected W. Alpheus Hunton and Abner Green as additional trustees of the bail fund of the Civil Rights Congress of New York."

Signed "Frederick V. Field, Secretary."

I direct your attention to the lefthand side of that paper where appear some written initials. I ask you if it appears to you that the first of those initials are "D. H."? A. It does.

Q. Did you write those initials? A. I decline to answer that question on the ground that the answer might tend to incriminate me.

The Court: I direct you to answer.

The Witness: I decline to answer for the reasons given.

By the Court.

Q. Do you know whether the bail fund of the Civil Rights Congress of New York had a bank account? A. I decline to answer the question on the ground that the answer might tend to incriminate me.

Q. I direct you to answer. A. I decline to answer for the reasons given.

Q. Do you know whether the bail fund of the Civil Rights Congress of New York had a safe deposit box? A. I decline to answer the question on the ground that the answer might tend to incriminate me.

Q. I direct you to answer. A. I decline to answer for the reasons given.

Q. Do you know whether the bail fund of the Civil Rights Congress of New York had a checkbook? A. I decline to answer the question on the ground that the answer might tend to incriminate me.

Q. Do you know where such a checkbook of the bail fund of the Civil Rights Congress of New York is now located? A. I decline to answer because the answer might tend to incriminate me.

Q. I direct you to answer both of those questions. A. I decline to answer for the reasons given.

Q. Do you know whether the bail fund of the Civil Rights Congress of New York had a receipt book or a book which kept a record of the receipts? A. I decline to answer the question on the ground that the answer might tend to incriminate me.

Q. I direct you to answer. A. I decline to answer for the reasons given.

Q. Do you know where the receipt book or the book showing the receipts of the bail fund of the Civil Rights Congress of New York is now located, or who has its possession? A. I decline to answer on the ground that the answer might tend to incriminate me.

Q. I direct you to answer. A. I decline to answer for the reasons given.

Mr. Saypol: Shall I go ahead, your Honor?

The Court: Yes, you may.

By Mr. Saypol.

Q. I show you Exhibit 6, Mr. Hammett, a paper which reads as follows, and will you read it along with me:

"Minutes of the bail fund of the Civil Rights Congress of New York, October 3, 1949.

"It was reported that W. Alpheus Hunton and Abner Green have accepted their election as trustees of the bail fund of the Civil Rights Congress of New York.

"It is further reported that they, together with the previous trustees, Dashiell Hammett, Robert W. Dunn and Frederick V. Field, signed the deed of trust the 26th day of September, 1949.

"A copy of the new deed of trust is attached.

"In view of the enlargement of the board of trustees it was decided to authorize either the trustees or the secretary and any other trustee to make decisions regarding the posting of bail in emergency situations."

Signed "Frederick V. Field, Secretary."

I direct your attention now to the group of initials on the lefthand side of the page, and ask you if it appears that the initials "D. H." appear at the point I have indicated? A. It does, sir.

Q. Those are handwritten initials? A. Yes.

Q. Are they your initials, Dashiell Hammett? A. I decline to answer the question on the ground that the answer might tend to incriminate me.

The Court: I direct you to answer.

The Witness: I decline to answer for the reasons given.

Q. Now, Mr. Hammett, I direct your attention, finally, in this minute book, Exhibit 6, to the Minutes of the bail fund of the Civil Rights Congress of New York, October 28, 1949. You are following along with me? A. Yes.

Q. "The board of trustees instructed the treasurer at the earliest possible day to arrange for an audit of the bail fund books at the earliest possible date."

Signed "Frederick V. Field, Secretary," and I again direct your attention to the group of initials in the lefthand margin; do you see there what purports to be initials "D. H."? A. I do.

Q. You recognize them as such? A. As D. H.

Q. You say you recognize them as D. H.; do you recognize them as your handwritten initials? A. I decline to answer the question on the ground that the answer may tend to incriminate me.

The Court: I direct you to answer.

The Witness: I decline to answer for the reasons given.

Q. Now, Mr. Hammett, I show you a group of four recognizances in the cases of Henry Winston, Robert Thompson, Gilbert Green and Gus Hall, and I state to you that these are Exhibit 1 in evidence; will you please examine them and tell me, tell the Court whether or not any of those documents bear your signature (showing)? A. Do you want all of this first?

Q. You can examine them one at a time.

The Court: You are showing the witness what paper?

Mr. Saypol: I am showing him now the recognizance in the case of Henry Winston and am directing his attention particularly to the attached so-called trust agreement.

The Court: That is the recognizance which has been forfeited by the Court?

Mr. Saypol: Yes, if the Court please—

The Court: And the question is?

Q. Will you see whether any of those documents bear your signature? A. (No response.)

Q. I likewise show you—one paper at a time. A. When he said "these documents," I took it for granted that—

The Court: Well, I don't want any confusion about it. Look first at the bail bond pertaining to the bail bond of this man Henry Winston. Those are the papers you now have in your hand.

Q. Do you recognize them as such? A. I decline to answer on the ground that—

Q. First, do you recognize those as the bail bond papers relating to Henry Winston, or the bail papers? A. Yes.

Q. Now, will you see whether any of those documents, particularly the trust agreement attached to that group of documents, contains your signature? A. I decline to answer on the ground that the answer may tend to incriminate me.

The Court: I direct you to answer.

The Witness: I decline to answer for the reasons given.

The Court: Now, pay particular attention to what appears to be a handwriting there on page—

(To Mr. Saypol) What page is that?

Mr. Saypol: It is page 2 of the attached paper labeled "Agreement and Deed of Trust."

The Court: Pay particular attention to the signature which appears to be or purports to be the writing of one Dashiell Hammett. Will you look at that?

(Witness examines document.)

A. I decline to answer on the ground that—

The Court: Well, will you look at it?

(Witness examines paper.)

The Court: You don't decline to look at it, do you, Mr. Hammett?

The Witness: No, your Honor.

The Court: Have you looked at it?

The Witness: Yes, your Honor.

The Court: Have you seen a certain writing which purports to be a signature of Dashiell Hammett?

The Witness: Yes.

Q. Is that your signature? A. I decline to answer on the ground that the answer might tend to incriminate me.

The Court: I direct you to answer.

The Witness: I decline to answer for the reasons given.

The Court: Now will you take up the next bond?

Mr. Saypol: Just one moment, if I may, your Honor.

Q. Mr. Hammett, I refer again to this minute dated October 3, 1949, and I direct your attention to the sentence which reads as follows:

"A copy of the new deed of trust is attached."

Is the deed of trust attached to the recognizance of Henry Winston the deed of trust which was referred to in that minute? A. I decline to answer on the grounds that the answer might tend to incriminate me.

Mr. Saypol: Will your Honor make a direction?

The Court: No, not on that. It is a conclusion.

Q. I show you a group of papers, a part of Exhibit 1, comprising the recognizance in the case of the fugitive Robert Thompson, and I direct your attention particularly to the paper labeled "Agreement and Deed of Trust," the second page thereof, and I ask you to examine it, and having examined it, tell us whether or not it bears your signature, Dashiell Hammett?

The Court: Or whether or not it is a photostat of your signature?

A. I decline to answer the question on the ground that the answer might tend to incriminate me.

The Court: I direct you to answer.

The Witness: I decline to answer for the reasons given.

Q. You still decline? A. Yes.

Q. I show you a group of papers constituting the recognizance in the case of the fugitive Gilbert Green, and I direct your attention particularly to the paper labeled Agreement and Deed of Trust, the second page thereof, and ask you to examine it and having examined it tell me whether on that photostat appears a replica of your signature Dashiell Hammett? A. I decline to answer on the ground the answer may tend to incriminate me.

The Court: I direct you to answer.

The Witness: I decline to answer.

Q. Similarly I show you a group of papers in the case of the fugitive Gus Hall, which are part of Exhibit 1, and direct your attention to those papers described as Agreement and Deed of Trust, the second page thereof, and ask you whether there appears a replica on the photostat of your signature Dashiell Hammett? A. I decline to answer on the ground the answer may tend to incriminate me.

The Court: I direct you to answer.

The Witness: I decline to answer for the reason given.

Q. In each of the group of four sets of papers I have shown you, I show you in the group relating to the fugitive Gus Hall a replica of what appears in the other sets and which is described as a certificate of deposit of the bail fund of the Civil Rights Congress of New York, and I direct your attention particularly to the lower lefthand margin where the following appears, trustees, and then there are a group of six names, the first of which is Dashiell Hammett, Chairman. Will you examine that and tell me whether or not you are the Dashiell Hammett who was chairman of that fund? A. I decline to answer on the ground that my answer may tend to incriminate me.

The Court: I direct you to answer.

The Witness: I decline to answer.

Mr. Saypol: It seems to me at this stage, if the Court please, between the minutebook and these documents on the strength of which the Court entered into an agreement of bail with these trustees of whom Mr. Hammett is one—

The Court: Does it appear that Mr. Hammett is the chairman of this fund?

Mr. Saypol: So it indicates on this certificate of deposit, and on the basis of the indication so far from Exhibit 6, the minutebook indicating the participation of Dashiell Hammett in the activities of this Fund, Mr. Hammett is a representative so that his answers are not tolerable under the White case, and I ask Mr. Hammett now whether he is familiar with the record keeping practices of this fund particularly the record of receipts in the form of stubs which are attached originally to each certificate of deposit and retained by the fund evidently as a record of receipts which have been issued.

Are you so familiar, Mr. Hammett?

The Witness: I decline to answer on the ground that my answer may tend to incriminate me.

The Court: I direct you to answer.

The Witness: I decline to answer.

By Mr. Saypol.

Q. Mr. Hammett, the Court is desirous here of obtaining for its examination records of the bail fund of the Civil Rights Congress of New York of which you are one of the trustees and the chairman of the fund, and those records which indicate the deposit of money and the sources of those deposits, and I ask you whether you are willing to produce those? A. I decline to answer the question on the ground that the answer may tend to incriminate me.

Q. I take it then that you are unwilling to do so. A. Is that a question?

Q. Well, I ask you are you willing or unwilling? A. I decline to answer the question on the ground the answer may tend to incriminate me.

The Court: I direct you to answer.

The Witness: I decline to answer for the reasons given.

Q. Well, is it the question you decline to answer or the production that you refuse to make on the premise that it would be incriminating you?

Mr. Saypol: I am trying to be clear. I don't know whether the witness refuses to answer the question or refuses to produce the records.

The Court: The witness gives every indication of understanding the question. However, he may answer the question.

(Last question read.)

The Court: Suppose you ask him again.

Q. Mr. Hammett, I ask you whether or not you were willing to produce the records including the record of deposits in the form of receipts, receipt books of this bail fund of the Civil Rights Congress of New York? A. I decline to answer on the ground that the answer may tend to incriminate me.

The Court: I direct you to answer.

The Witness: I decline to answer for the reason given.

The Court: Mr. Hammett, I direct you to produce as chairman and trustee of the bail fund of the Civil Rights Congress of New York all books, records, papers and documents pertaining to that fund which are in your possession or under your control. Will you comply with such a direction?

The Witness: May I consult with counsel?

The Court: Yes.

(Witness left the stand and conferred with counsel and thereafter returned to the stand.)

The Witness: Without conceding that I have the ability to or can produce such documents I must decline to produce them.

The Court: I direct you to produce them.

The Witness: I must decline for the same reason.

The Court: For the reason that the production will tend to incriminate you?

The Witness: Yes and without conceding that I have any ability or can.

By the Court.

Q. I will ask you this specific question: Have you now in your possession or under your control any books, records and documents of the bail fund of the Civil Rights Congress of New York? A. I must decline to answer that question on the ground the answer may tend to incriminate me.

Q. I direct you to answer. A. I decline to answer.

Mr. Saypol: I think I need not ask any more, and I ask the Court adjudge this witness in contempt.

The Court: Mr. Rabinowitz and Mrs. Kaufman, I will give you an opportunity, if you desire to avail yourselves of it, of asking this witness any question that you feel may assist the Court in determining the merits of this claim which he has asserted to the various questions and directions which have been asked of him and made to him. Do you desire to ask this witness any question, Mr. Rabinowitz?

Mrs. Kaufman: May we confer a moment?

The Court: Yes. Is the marshal present in court?

A Deputy Marshal: Yes.

Mr. Rabinowitz: I have nothing.

The Court: Mrs. Kaufman, do you desire to?

Mrs. Kaufman: I have no questions, your Honor.

The Court: Step down, Mr. Hammett, before the bar of the Court.

(The witness stepped down from the witness stand.)

The Court: Mr. Hammett, I find you guilty of contempt of court for your failure and refusal to comply with the directions of the Court and to make answer to questions asked of you, and to directions of the Court made to you to produce books, documents and records the bail fund of the Civil Rights Congress of New York.

The minutes of this proceeding in which you committed contempt and in which your contumacious conduct has occurred have not as yet been transcribed. The hearing has not yet been concluded. I direct the stenographer forthwith and without undue delay to transcribe these minutes, and I commit you now to the custody of the marshal, to be incarcerated by him until 8 o'clock this evening, at which time you will be arraigned before me, and I will impose sentence and make such certificate as is required by Rule 42-A of the Federal Rules of Criminal Procedure, Title 18, of the United States Code. The marshal will have custody of this man.

Mr. Rabinowitz: May I make a motion for reconsideration and argue it, or would you prefer that that be done tonight?

The Court: It may be heard now, if you desire, or I will hear you later on at half past seven, if you want to be heard then, or at 8 o'clock.

Mr. Rabinowitz: I prefer to be heard then.

The Court: Whatever suits your convenience, counsel.

Mr. Rabinowitz: All right.

The Court: That will be in this room. At that time the marshal will then bring this man Dashiell Hammett before the Court. That will be at 7:30 instead of 8 o'clock.

Mr. Hunton—

Mr. Rabinowitz: Your Honor, may I suggest that the witness be paroled in my custody until 7:30 tonight? There doesn't seem to be any advantage in taking him into custody now. No gain can be served by it.

The Court: The advantage is that perhaps there will be some respect for the dignity and authority of this Court.

Mr. Rabinowitz: Well, I doubt whether—

The Court: I have endeavored to be most patient, counsel, with these various witnesses who have appeared before me, and they have consistently and repeatedly flaunted the jurisdiction and defied this Court. I think the dignity of the Court and the majesty of its process requires immediate commitment.

The application to parole the man further is denied.

At the 7:30 session:

The Court: Samuel Dashiell Hammett, will you stand, please?

(Defendant Hammett arises.)

The Court: Samuel Dashiell Hammett, I have found you guilty of contempt of this court by reason of your refusal to answer questions, and by reason of your refusal to produce or give evidence of the location of certain books, records and documents in your possession, or under your control, relating to the bail fund of the Civil Rights Congress of New York, and more specifically as is set forth in the certificate which I have made, and which I am about to sign under Rule 42(a) of the Rules of Criminal Procedure, and I will sign the certificate.

Counsel, you have seen a copy of it.

Mr. Rabinowitz: Yes, your Honor.

The Court: Do you waive, on behalf of this man, the reading of this paper?

Mr. Rabinowitz: Yes, your Honor.

The Court: I have signed the certificate as was required by Rule 42(a) of the Federal Rules of Criminal Procedure. I give it to the clerk to file and make part of the records of this case (handing to clerk).

Samuel Dashiell Hammett, have you anything to say as to why judgment should not be pronounced upon you by this Court?

Defendant Hammett: Not a thing.

The Court: I adjudge and order that you, Samuel Dashiell Hammett, be committed to the custody of the Attorney General or his authorized representative for imprisonment for a period of six months or until such time as you may purge yourself of the contempt of this Court. I certify the certificate on file.

Mr. Rabinowitz: Now, your Honor, I would like to make a motion.

The Court: Very well. You may.

Mr. Rabinowitz: Your Honor, I would like, at this time, to make a motion that the execution of the sentence be stayed and that the contemnor be released in reasonable bail to be set by your Honor.

Now, I know that similar motions were made in the other two cases, and that your Honor denied them, and the ground for denying them was that a granting of such an application would be an admission on your Honor's part.

The Court: It might be construed as such.

Mr. Rabinowitz: It might be construed as an admission on your Honor's part.

The Court: I don't like the word "admission." Acknowledgment, if you will.

Mr. Rabinowitz: Very well, your Honor. That there were substantial questions of law involved. I submit, your Honor, that there are in this case more, perhaps, than in the others, very substantial questions of law involved, and that it would be grossly unfair to have this contemnor placed in custody pending an appeal which, in the nature of things, cannot be heard until the fall, when there are certainly substantial questions of law. If it were not for your Honor's ruling, I think that the questions were not even substantial, that they were all on the side of the defendant here, but evidently I am wrong in that respect.

The Court: I think your advocacy blinds your judgment.

Mr. Rabinowitz: Well, I don't think it does always; sometimes I turn out to be right.

The Court: Not always, but that frequently happens to counsel.

Mr. Rabinowitz: Well, perhaps it does and perhaps it does not. Only time will tell.

In any event, in this case, your Honor, I request, and I submit that there is a very substantial question involved, and that therefore it would be appropriate for your Honor to set that aside and—

The Court: Your application is denied. I see no reason why this man's case should be treated any differently from the others. In fact, I was inclined, counselor, at first, to impose a longer sentence upon him because he had seen an example of what happened to Field, and he knew what was going to happen or had reason to believe that some punishment would be visited upon his co-trustee, Hunton, and he occupies the important position, not only of trustee, but he occupies the important position of chairman of this fund, and in addition I felt that his claim of privilege was especially unwarranted and unjustified, either in law or in fact, because he had executed a paper to be submitted to this Court at the time bail was accepted, in which he represented himself to be a trustee of this fund.

On the stand he refused, on his claim of privilege, to admit or state that he was a trustee of this fund. I feel that I have dealt with him extremely leniently.

Mr. Rabinowitz: Well, your Honor, I think that while recognizing the way your Honor feels—

The Court: Well, I am glad that you appreciate my position, counselor.

Mr. Rabinowitz: The moral feelings of your Honor on this subject have nothing to do, or have very little to do with the legal question that is involved, and—

The Court: Well, except by way of punishment, I wanted you to know just how I felt about it, and I am glad that you appreciate my position.[2]

N O T E S

CHAPTER 1

[1] Genealogical information and facts about land transfers, family wills, and other related transactions are from the records of Saint Mary's County on file in the Saint Mary's County Courthouse in Leonardtown, Maryland. The Saint Mary's County Historical Society has information on early Hammett genealogy in the county. Two genealogists, Doris Jones and J. S. Guy, have compiled family genealogies of the Hammett family in Maryland.

[2] Interviews with Jane Yowaisky, J. S. Guy, and Mildred Norris by Richard Layman, November 1-2, 1978.

[3] The long-standing debt was probably the price Samuel Hammett agreed to pay his sister for her share of "Hopewell and Aim."

[4] Jane Yowaisky, Dashiell Hammett's second cousin.

[5] Hammett's birth certificate is on file at Saint Michael's Catholic Church, near Lexington Park, Maryland.

[6] Richard T. Hammett, "Mystery Writer Was Enigmatic Throughout Life," *Baltimore News-American*, August 19, 1973.

[7] Philadelphia city directories, 1900 and 1901; Baltimore city directories, 1902 and following years.

[8] For a description of Hammett's Baltimore neighborhood, see Fred Worden, "Gooseberries and Dashiell Hammett," *Baltimore Sunday Sun Magazine*, June 11, 1978, pp. 26-27.

[9] Walter C. Polhous, Sr., to William Godschalk, May 6, 1974, and May 12, 1974.

[10] Mrs. Charles Rashleigh to Godschalk, May 30, 1974.

[11] Information about Hammett's schooling is from Melvin J. Bordlen, Office of Reports and Records, City of Baltimore Department of Education, to R. L., November 16, 1978.

[12] Richard Hammett, Jr., to Godschalk, April 1, 1974.

[13]Richard Hammett's share of the estate was $150.83. In the May 1909 term of the Superior Court of Baltimore, J. Wesley Freeman brought action to recover a debt of $84.13 from Richard Hammett. That debt was honored by the Saint Mary's County Probate Court, which paid Freeman from Richard Hammett's inheritance at Samuel Hammett's death.

[14]Richard Hammett, Jr., to Godschalk.

[15]R. L. interview with Norris.

[16]Lilian Hellman, *An Unfinished Woman* (Boston & Toronto: Little, Brown, 1969), p. 271.

[17]Army medical records.

CHAPTER 2

[1]The date of Hammett's first employment with Pinkerton's has been give variously as 1915 to 1917. The date cited here, based on his sworn testimony before the United States Court of Appeals for the Second Circuit in the case of Hammett against Warner Brothers Pictures, Inc., is believed to be the most reliable evidence.

[2]For information about Pinkerton's National Detective Agency, see, among other sources, Richard Wilmer Rowan, *The Pinkertons: A Detective Dynasty* (Boston: Little, Brown, 1931) and James D. Horan, *The Pinkerton Story* (New York: Putnam's, 1951).

[3]Veteran's Administration file on Hammett.

[4]Hammett, *Dead Yellow Women*, ed. Ellery Queen (New York: Spivak, 1947). See Queen's note, pp. 94-95.

[5]William Linn to R. L.

[6]Hellman, *Scoundrel Time* (Boston & Toronto: Little, Brown, 1976), p. 47.

[7]Information about Hammett's army career is from his army medical records, his Veteran's Administration files, and from facts provided by the department of the army in letters to R. L., October 10 and November 1, 1978.

[8]Information throughout about the circumstances of Hammett's disability are from medical reports in his Veteran's Administration files.

[9]Interview with Mrs. Dashiell Hammett and her daughter Mary by David Fechheimer, October 12, 1975.

[10]The story about Tony the gandy dancer and Blackjack Jerome are from an interview with R. G. McMaster by R. L., March 9, 1979.

[11]All anecdotes except those attributed to McMaster are from Hammett, *From the Memoirs of a Private Detective, Smart Set*, March 1923, pp. 88-90.

[12]Unidentified clipping, ca. 1934, in a scrapbook kept by Joseph Shaw now in the collection of Nils Hardin.

[13]Hospital for ex-servicemen is opened in Tacoma, *Tacoma Sunday Ledger*, September 19, 1920, B6.

[14]Mentioned in "Tulip" and in an unpublished, untitled story among Hammett's manuscripts at the Humanities Research Center (HRC), University of Texas at Austin.

[15]Fechheimer interview with Hammetts, October 12, 1975.

[16]Hammett papers at HRC.

CHAPTER 3

[1]Information about Hammett's marriage is based on the marriage certificate and the Fechheimer interviews with Mrs. Hammett.
[2]See *City of San Francisco*, November 4, 1975, p. 34. Other information about Pinkerton's in San Francisco is from Jack Kaplan.
[3]Fechheimer interview with Hammetts.
[4]*New York Herald Tribune*, November 12, 1933.
[5]See *Black Mask*, October 15, 1923, p. 127; Elizabeth Sanderson, "Ex-Detective Hammett," *Bookman*, January-February 1932, p. 517. For a history of the Arbuckle case, see David A. Yallop, *The Day the Laughter Stopped* (New York: St. Martin's Press, 1976).
[6]See Sanderson, p. 517; "Name Master Mind in Great Bond Plot," *New York Times*, February 21, 1920, p. 1.
[7]"Trap U.S. Thief Ring," *San Francisco Call-Bulletin*, March 10, 1922; "Hammett Traps Gem Holdup Suspects," *San Francisco Call-Bulletin*, January 26, 1934, p. 7; "Jewel Bandits Trapped By Hammett," *San Francisco Call-Bulletin*, November 23, 1934.
[8]See Sanderson, p. 517; "$125,000 in Gold Coin Stolen on S. F. Liner," *San Francisco Examiner*, November 23, 1921, p. 1; "Dream Bares Hiding Place on S. F. Liner," *San Francisco Examiner*, November 29, 1921, p. 1.
[9]VA files and Fechheimer interview with Hammetts.
[10]Fechheimer interview with Hammetts.
[11]Fechheimer interview with Hammetts.
[12]VA files.
[13]Fechheimer interview with Hammetts.

CHAPTER 4

[1]See *The Smart Set Anthology* (New York: Reynal & Hitchcock, 1934), edited with an introduction by Burton Rascoe. Racsoe's introduction is a history of the magazine and a description of its editorial policies.
[2]Hammet's manuscripts, including drafts of published and unpublished stories, are at HRC. Josephine Hammett refers to Hammett's writing method in her interview by Fechheimer.
[3]Two of Hemingway's short vignettes that were later included as interchapters in *In Our Time* (1925) appeared in *The Little Review* in Spring 1923, and with Hammett's interest in little magazines, he may have seen that issue.
[4]*The Smart Set*, March 1923, pp. 10-12.
[5]See, for example, Howard Haycraft, *Murder for Pleasure* (New York: Simon & Schuster, 1940), and Julian Symons, *Bloody Murder* (London: Faber & Faber, 1972).
[6]*N. W. Ayer and Sons American Newspaper Annual and Directory, 1922* (Philadelphia: Ayer, 1922).
[7]For a history of the pulps, see, for example, Frank Gruber, *Pulp Jungle* (Los Angeles: Sherbourne Press, 1967); Tony Goodstone, *The Pulps* (New York: Bonanza Books, 1970); Ron Goulart, *Cheap Thrills* (New Rochelle: Arlington House, 1972).

[8]Carl Bode, *Mencken* (Carbondale: Southern Illinois University Press, 1969), pp. 70-71.

[9]Fechheimer interview with Hammetts.

[10]Issues of the magazine are rare and there is no known copy of the November 1922 issue. Hammett's story is assumed to have been published in that issue on the basis of an inventory of his work prepared by Muriel Alexander.

[11]"Our Readers' Private Corner," *Black Mask*, June 15, 1923, pp. 126-127.

CHAPTER 5

[1]See William F. Nolan, "Carroll John Daly: The Forgotten Pioneer of the Private Eye," *The Armchair Detective*, October 1970, pp. 1-4; G. A. Finch, "A Fatal Attraction," *The Armchair Detective*, Spring 1980, pp. 112-124.

[2]Raymond Chandler, "The Simple Art of Murder," *Atlantic Monthly*, December 1944, pp. 57-58.

[3]"From the Author of 'Arson Plus,' " *Black Mask*, October 10, 1923, p. 127.

[4]"Dashiell Hammett, Author, Dies; Created Hard-Boiled Detectives," *The New York Times*, January 11, 1961, p. 47. The original interview, quoted here, is unlocated.

[5]Letter to the editor, *Black Mask*, March 1, 1924, pp. 127-128.

[6]Chandler, p. 58.

[7]Hammett, *The Continental Op*, ed. Steven Marcus (New York; Random House, 1974), pp. 4-5.

[8]Ibid., p. 146.

CHAPTER 6

[1]Fechheimer interview with Josephine Hammett.

[2]"Our Own Short Story Course," *Black Mask*, August 1924, pp. 127-128.

[3]*Dead Yellow Women*, p. 107.

[4]Hammett, *The Big Knockover*, edited with an introduction by Lillian Hellman (New York: Knopf, 1966), p. 65.

[5]Besides *Black Mask*, there were *Action Stories*, *True Detective Stories*, *Detective Story Magazine*, *All Detective Mystery Stories*, *Mystery Magazine*, *Real Detective Tales*, and *Detective Fiction Weekly*, among others.

[6]*The Big Knockover*, p. 229.

[7]Ibid., p. 195.

[8]Ibid., pp. 28-29.

[9]There are some thirty unpublished stories and fictional fragments among Hammett's manuscripts at HRC. A small number of other manuscripts are known to be in private collections.

[10]"In Defence of the Sex Story," *Writer's Digest*, June 1924, p. 7.

[11]"The Cabell Epitome," *Forum*, December 1924, p. 159. Hammett also reviewed *Balesand*, by Joseph Hergesheimer, in the November 1924 issue of *Forum* and *Everyman's Genius*, by Mary Austin, in the August 1925 issue.

[12]"Vamping Samson," *Editor*, March 1925, p. 41.

[13]Ibid., p. 43.

CHAPTER 7

[1]Interview with Albert Samuels by Nolan, date unavailable. See Nolan, *Dashiell Hammett: A Casebook* (Santa Barbara, Cal.: McNally & Loftin, 1969), p. 19. Though Nolan dates Hammett's job with Samuels as beginning in 1922, that date is quite impossible and the best evidence points to Spring 1926 as the starting date for his job.

[2]R. L. interview with Albert Samuels, Jr.

[3]R. L. interview with McMaster.

[4]*San Francisco Examiner*, July 11, 1926, p. 11cc.

[5]*San Francisco Examiner*, June 6, 1926, p. 12ss.

[6]R. L. interview with McMaster; Fechheimer interview with Hammetts.

[7]Birth certificate of Josephine Rebecca Hammett.

[8]Mrs. Hammett. In *City of San Francisco*, p. 39.

[9]"Advertising Art Isn't ART—It's Advertising," *Western Advertising*, December 1927, p. 47.

[10]"The Advertisement IS Literature," *Western Advertising*, October 1926, p. 35.

[11]*The Hard-Boiled Omnibus*, edited with an introduction by Joseph T. Shaw (New York: Simon & Schuster, 1946), pp. v-ix.

[12]Ayer, 1929.

[13]*Editor*, December 1928.

[14]See, for example, *Writers Review*, February 1934, p. 28.

[15]*Saturday Review*, January 15, 1927, p. 510.

[16]*The Big Knockover*, p. 279.

[17]John G. Cawelti, *Adventure, Mystery, and Romance* (Chicago & London: University of Chicago Press, 1976), p. 152.

[18]"Yes," *Stratford Magazine*, March 1927, p. 30.

[19]*Bookman*, September 1927, p. 75.

CHAPTER 8

[1]"The Professor and the Anaconda," *New Republic*, March 8, 1919, p. 170.

[2]"The Issue in Butte," *New Republic*, September 22, 1917, pp. 215-216.

[3]"Troops Go to Butte to Guard Workers," *New York Times*, April 23, 1920, p. 17.

[4]"Sanity and Enthusiasm in Western Mining Empire," *New York Times*, January 11, 1920, VIII:7.

[5]Shaw, Introduction to "The Cleansing of Poisonville," *Black Mask*, November 1927, p. 9.

[6]Lurton Blassingame, "The Trinity—And a Dog," *New Yorker*, August 21, 1926, pp. 15-17.

[7]Hammett's correspondence with Knopf is in the Knopf Archive at HRC.

[8]*Red Harvest* (New York: Knopf, 1929), p. 197.

[9]Ibid., p. 149.

[10]Ibid., p. 27.

[11]Ibid., P. 39.

[12]Ibid., p. 43.

[13]Ibid., p. 200.

NOTES

¹⁴Ibid., pp. 198-199.
¹⁵Ibid., p. 205.
¹⁶See Layman, *Dashiell Hammett: A Descriptive Bibliography* (Pittsburgh: University of Pennsylvania Press, 1979).
¹⁷*Bookman*, March 29, 1929, p. 62.
¹⁸*Outlook and Independent*, February 13, 1929, p. 274.
¹⁹*Boston Evening Transcript*, April 6, 1929, p. 3.

CHAPTER 9

¹Sanderson, p. 518.
²Hammett, *The Dain Curse* (New York: Knopf, 1929), p. 214.
³Ibid., pp. 254-255.
⁴Ibid., p. 270.
⁵Ibid., p. 210.
⁶Hammett to Harry Block, April 2, 1929. This letter is in a private collection.
⁷Hammett to Block, March 8, 1929. This letter is in a private collection.
⁸Ernest Hemingway, *Death in the Afternoon* (New York: Scribners, 1932), p. 228.
⁹*Dashiell Hammett: A Casebook*, p. 51.
¹⁰*Outlook and Independent*, July 31, 1929, p. 552.
¹¹*New York Herald Tribune*, August 11, 1929, p. 11.
¹²*New York Times*, August 18, 1929, p. 16.
¹³See *Dashiell Hammett: A Descriptive Bibliography*.

CHAPTER 10

¹Hammett to Block, July 14, 1929.
²Hammett, introduction to *The Maltese Falcon* (New York: Modern Library, 1934), p. vii.
³Hammett, *The Maltese Falcon* (New York: Knopf, 1930), p. 64. This clue was first pieced together by Godschalk.
⁴E. W. Schermerhorn, *Malta of the Knights* (London: Heinemann, 1929), pp. 34-35.
⁵*The Maltese Falcon*, p. 153.
⁶Ibid., p. 214.
⁷Ibid., P. 78.
⁸*New Republic*, April 9, 1930, p. 226.
⁹*Outlook and Independent*, February 26, 1930, p. 350.
¹⁰*Judge*, March 1, 1930.
¹¹Hammett, *The Glass Key* (New York: Knopf, 1931), dust jacket blurb.
¹²*New York Herald Tribune*, February 23, 1930.
¹³*St. Louis Post-Dispatch*, March 21, 1930.
¹⁴Franklin Pierce Adams, *The Diary of our Own Samuel Pepys*, Volume 2 (New York: Simon & Schuster, 1935), p. 961.
¹⁵William Curtis, "Some Recent Books," *Town & Country*, February 15, 1930.
¹⁶R. L. interviews with Marjorie May, 1978.
¹⁷James H. S. Moynahan, "Dashiell Hammett Confesses," unidentified

268

clipping of a 1936 syndicated interview in Shaw's scrapbook, collection of Hardin.

[18]James Cooper, "Lean Years for the Thin Man," *Washington Daily News*, March 11, 1957.

CHAPTER 11

[1]Letter in Hammett collection, HRC.
[2]*The Glass Key*, p. 276.
[3]Ibid., p. 127.
[4]Ibid., pp. 275, 276.
[5]Ibid., p. 282.
[6]Sanderson, p. 518.
[7]*New York Times*, May 3, 1931, IV:23.
[8]*New York Herald Tribune*, April 26, 1931, p. 13.
[9]*Outlook*, April 29, 1931, p. 601.
[10]*New Yorker*, April 25, 1931, p. 91.
[11]*New Yorker*, March 7, 1931.
[12]*New York Evening Post*, June 7, 1930, p. 54.
[13]*New York Evening Post*, July 3, 1930, p. 55.
[14]Affadavit of Jacob Wilk, United States Court of Appeals for the Second Circuit, in the case of Dashiell Hammett against Warner Brothers Pictures, Inc. Affadavit sworn to by Mr. Wilk, October 22, 1948.
[15]From the same case, see Exhibit A, the agreement of Hammett and Knopf with Warner Brothers.
[16]*Memo from David O. Selznick*, ed. Rudy Behlmer (New York: Viking, 1972), pp. 26-27.
[17]Interview with Rouben Mamoulian by Nolan, date unavailable. At HRC there is an eleven-page typescript titled "The Kiss-Off": "City Streets Paramount '30 or '31." "The Kiss-Off" is another title for "After School."
[18]Hammett to Hellman, April 30, 1931, HRC.

CHAPTER 12

[1]Hammett to Hellman, April 30, 1931, and Friday (1931?), at HRC.
[2]VA files.
[3]*New York Evening Post*, September 6, 1930, p. 55.
[4]David Thompson, *A Biographical Dictionary of Film* (New York: Morrow, 1976), p. 546.
[5]R. L. interview with McMaster.
[6]Appendix to Brief of Defendant-Appellee, Hammett against Warner Brothers, Appeal. Harrison Carroll, "New Film to Expose Private Sleuth Racket," unidentified clipping, April 1931, in Shaw's scrapbook, collection of Hardin.
[7]See Hammett to Hellman, March 4, 1931, and Hammett to Blanche Knopf, December 5, 1931, at HRC. In a letter to Hellman dated only "Fri-

day," Hammett refers to his "Bancroft story," referring to actor George Bancroft. This is possibly a reference to *Blood Money*, released in November 1933. The script, based on a story by Rowland Brown, has very slight similarities to Hammett's related stories "The Big Knock-Over" and "$106,000 Blood Money."

[8]Joseph Blotner, *Faulkner: A Biography* (New York: Random House, 1974), pp. 740-743.

[9]The original *Thin Man* and Hammett's note were published in *City of San Francisco*, November 4, 1975, insert pp. 1-12. The original manuscript note and typescript fragment are at the UCLA library.

[10]Ben Wasson's correspondence with H. H. Bromley is in the Berg Collection at New York Public Library.

[11]Wasson correspondence, Berg Collection.

[12]*New York Times*, May 30, 1931, p. 9.

[13]Margaret Case Harriman, "Miss Lilly of New Orleans," New Yorker November 8, 1941, p. 22.

[14]See *An Unfinished Woman*.

[15]R. L. interview with William Glackin, February 16, 1979.

[16]*An Unfinished Woman*, pp. 258-259.

[17]Ibid., p. 259.

[18]Wasson correspondence, Berg Collection.

[19]Sanderson, p. 518.

[20]William Roughead, *Bad Companions* (Edinburgh: W. Green, 1930), pp. 111-146.

[21]Harriman, p. 26.

[22]The Hellman Collection at HRC includes notes and multiple drafts for her plays, in addition to correspondence. See Manfred Triesch, *The Lillian Hellman Collection at the University of Texas* (Austin: University of Texas, 1966).

[23]See *Writers at Work* (New York: Viking, 1967), p. 136. The interviewers are John Phillips and Anne Hollander.

[24]"Actress Gets Damages from Writer," *New York Times*, July 1, 1932, p. 10.

[25]Hammett to Blanche Knopf, January 30, 1931 (perhaps misdated, actually 1932), HRC.

[26]Hammett, *The Adventures of Sam Spade* (New York: Spivak, 1934), p. 106.

[27]*Esquire*, Autumn 1933, p. 34.

[28]Wasson correspondence, Berg Collection.

CHAPTER 13

[1]FBI file. FBI interview with desk clerk at Hotel Pierre.

[2]Jay Martin, *Nathanael West: The Art of His Life* (New York: Farrar, Straus & Giroux, 1970), pp. 158-160.

[3]The contract is in the Berg Collection, New York Public Library.

[4]*Publishers Weekly*, June 29, 1935.

[5]Joyce Haber, "Lillian Hellman Takes a Look at Today's Theater," *Los Angeles Times Calendar*, November 2, 1969, p. 15.

[6]*The Thin Man* (New York: Knopf, 1934), p. 8.

[7]Ibid., p. 251.

[8]Ibid., p. 5.

[9]Martin, p. 159; R. L. interview with McMaster.

[10]*The Thin Man*, p. 97.

[11]John Brady to Hellman, January 5, 1970. Her reply is dated February 19, 1970.

[12]*The Thin Man*, pp. 141-143.

[13]Ibid., p. 192.

[14]*New York Times*, January 30, 1934.

[15]This advertisement is a four-page leaflet distributed by Knopf. (The copy I saw is in a private collection.)

[16]*New York Evening Journal*, Summer 1934. Undated clipping in Shaw's scrapbook, collection of Hardin. This is the only indication that Hammett spent his summers in Port Washington.

[17]*New York Herald Tribune*, January 7, 1934.

[18]*New Republic*, January 24, 1934, p. 77.

[19]*Times Literary Supplement*, June 14, 1934, p. 426.

[20]Cooper.

CHAPTER 14

[1]*An Unfinished Woman*, pp. 271-272.

[2]Jack Kofoed, "Days of Hammett and Hellman Were Good Old Days Indeed," *Miami Herald*, May 23, 1978.

[3]"The Films Now Know Miss Hellman," *New York Herald Tribune*, July 7, 1935, V:3.

[4]*New York Times*, June 30, 1934, p. 18.

[5]*San Francisco Call-Bulletin*, January 27, 1934, p. 8.

[6]Ron Goulart, *The Adventurous Decade* (New York: Arlington House, 1975), pp. 77-81. The *Secret Agent X-9* strips are collected in two volumes as *Secret Agent X-9* (New York: John Day, 1934). These first book collections are scarce; the books are worth about $1,000 on the rare-book market.

[7]"This Little Pig," *Collier's*, March 24, 1934, p. 10.

[8]Ibid., p. 69.

[9]Hammett's drafts for "On the Make" were examined in 1978 at Serendipity Bookshop in Berkeley, California, where they were for sale.

[10]William F. Nolan made a copy of the final story for *Mister Dynamite* available.

[11]This and following references to Hammett's dealings with MGM, his employment record, and his assignments, are, unless otherwise noted, based on correspondence and script materials in the MGM archive at Culver City.

[12]Hammett to Hellman, October 31, 1934. All Hammett's correspondence to Hellman referred to here is from the collection at HRC.

[13]*New York Times*, December 24, 1936, p. 21.

CHAPTER 15

[1] James B. Mellow, *Charmed Circle* (New York & Washington: Praeger, 1974), pp. 407-408. The Ehrman Guest book is in the collection of Robert Wilson, described in a letter to R. L., February 19, 1979.

[2] Haber, p. 15.

[3] Municipal Court of Los Angeles, Plaintiff and Defendant indexes.

[4] MGM files.

[5] Martin, p. 268.

[6] Nathanael West, *The Day of the Locust* (New York: New Directions, 1950), dust jacket blurb.

[7] Hammett's thank you note to Blanche Knopf, January 31, 1936, HRC.

[8] J. Florence Rubin to Hammett, February 14, 1936, HRC.

[9] HenryDan Piper to Godschalk, July 16, 1974.

[10] Hammett to Hellman, March 13, 1937, HRC.

[11] *Writers at Work*, p. 135.

[12] "Dashiel [sic] Hammett Flees Night Club Round Succumbing to Rustication in New Jersey," *The Daily Princetonian*, November 11, 1936, pp. 1, 4.

[13] Interview with Albert Hackett and Frances Goodrich by Matthew J. Bruccoli, July 8, 1980.

[14] Bruccoli interview with the Hacketts.

[15] VA files.

[16] Mrs. Hammett statement, VA files.

[17] Bruccoli interview with the Hacketts.

[18] MGM archive.

[19] Bennett Cerf, *At Random* (New York: Random House, 1977), p. 206.

[20] Letter to "Nat," MGM archive.

[21] *At Random*, p. 206.

[22] *New York Times*, November 24, 1939, p. 29.

CHAPTER 16

[1] Carlos Baker, *Ernest Hemingway: A Life Story* (New York: Scribners, 1969), pp. 311-316, 621.

[2] *An Unfinished Woman*, pp. 66-69. Hellman mistakenly dates the incident in 1938.

[3] Ibid., pp. 70-72.

[4] *Daily Worker*, April 8, 1938, p. 4.

[5] *Daily Worker*, April 28, 1938, p. 4.

[6] Collection of Matthew J. Bruccoli.

[7] FBI files.

[8] *An Unfinished Woman*, pp. 263-264.

[9] Leo C. Rosten, *The Movie Colony* (New York: Harcourt, Brace, 1941), pp. 306-327.

NOTES

CHAPTER 17

¹FBI files.
²Interview with William Glackin by R. L., March 10, 1979.
³*Variety*, September 6, 1939, clipping in MGM archive.
⁴"An Open Letter to All People of Good Will," undated leaflet. Collection of
     R. L.
⁵"Committee on Election Rights," *New Republic*, October 21, 1940, p. 560.
⁶FBI files.
⁷*John Huston's The Maltese Falcon*, ed. Richard J. Anobile (New York: Avon,
     1974), pp. 5-6.
⁸*New York Times*, August 28, 1943.

CHAPTER 18

¹Hammett's assignments and ranks referred to throughout this chapter are
     from his army record, provided by Lt. Col. James S. Miller, Depart-
     ment of the Army.
²Hammett described his army experiences in a series of letters to Hellman,
     "Maggie," and "Nancy." There are thirty of these letters at HRC.
     They are noted here only when the reference in the text is not
     obvious.
³Interview with Robert Colodny by R. L., 1977. Colodny was also assigned to
     Camp Shenango.
⁴R. L. interview with Glackin.
⁵R. L. interview with Glackin.
⁶Hammett to Hellman, January 2, 1944.
⁷The only complete run of the *Adakian* located is in a private collection.
⁸R. L. interview with Glackin.
⁹Al Weisman, "Hammett of Alaska," *Yank*, 1945.
¹⁰*$106,000 Blood Money* (1943), *The Adventures of Sam Spade (1944), The
     Continental Op* (1945), and *The Return of the Continental Op* (1945).
¹¹E. E. Spitzer, "With Corporal Hammett on Adak," *Nation*, January 5,
     1974, pp. 6-9.
¹²R. L. interview with Glackin.
¹³R. L. interview with Colodny.
¹⁴*The Battle of the Aleutians* (Adak, Alaska: Intelligence Section, Field Force
     Headquarters, Adak, Alaska, 1944), p. [8].
¹⁵R. L. interview with Colodny.
¹⁶R. L. interview with Glackin.
¹⁷*Wind Blown and Dripping: A Book of Aleutian Cartoons* (NP, 1945). The copy
     examined is in a private collection.
¹⁸R. L. interview with Glackin.
¹⁹Leonard Lyons, "Tales about Hammett Told," *Hollywood Citizen News*,
     January 19, 1961.

CHAPTER 19

[1]"The Adventures of the Thin Man" ran from July 2, 1941, until 1942 and from 1946 until September 1, 1950. It was broadcast on NBC in 1941 and 1942, on CBS from 1946 until 1948, and on ABC from 1948 until 1950. Nick Charles was played by a succession of readers, including Lester Damon, Les Tremayne, Joseph Curtin, and David Gothard. Scripts were by Milton Lewis, Eugene Wang, and Robert Newman.

"The Fat Man" ran from January 21, 1946, until 1950. It was broadcast on ABC in 1946 and 1947, by the Norwich Company from 1947 to 1949, and on ABC again in 1949 and 1950. The cast of six readers included J. Scott Smart as Brad Runyan, The Fat Man, and Ed Begley as Sergeant O'Hara. Scripts were by Robert Sloane.

"The Adventures of Sam Spade" ran from July 12, 1946, until 1951. It was broadcast on CBS from 1946 to 1949, and on NBC from 1949 to 1951. Spade was played by Howard Duff and later by Steve Dunne. Scripts were by Gil Doud and Bob Tallman.

See Frank Buxton and Bill Owen, *Radio's Golden Age* (n.p.: Easton Valley Press, 1966) and *Dashiell Hammett: A Descriptive Bibliography*.

[2]Hammett against Warner Brothers Appeal.

[3]For a listing of radio performances based on Hammett's work, see *Dashiell Hammett: A Descriptive Bibliography*, pp. 169-170.

[4]Hammett to Hellman, February 14, 1950, HRC.

[5]R. L. interview with Mrs. E. E. Spitzer, 1980.

[6]R. L. interview with Rose Evans, October 22, 1980.

[7]Jefferson School of Social Science catalogue, Winter 1965, p. 4.

[8]J.S.S.S. catalogue, 1954, p. 27.

[9]*Daily Worker*, May 2, 1946, p. 13.

[10]Samm Sinclair Baker letter to Joe Gores, October 9, 1975.

[11]For a summary of the case see *Copyright Decisions, 1951-1952*, civ. no. 8265; and *Copyright Decisions, 1953-1954*, no. 13457.

CHAPTER 20

[1]Fred T. Newbraugh to R. L., January 19, 1979.

[2]R. L. interview with Mrs. Richard T. Hammett, 1979.

[3]Hammett to Margaret Kober, April 16, April 23, and May 1, 1951, HRC.

[4]R. L. interviews with Muriel Alexander, 1979 and 1980.

[5]Hammett to Hellman, January 27, February 8, and February 14, 1950, HRC.

[6]"Dashiell Hammett Has Hard Words for Tough Stuff He Used to Write," *Los Angeles Times*, June 7, 1950.

[7]*An Unfinished Woman*, pp. 267-268.

[8]*The Autumn Garden* (Boston: Little, Brown, 1951), pp. 133-134.

[9]*An Unfinished Woman*, p. 268. See also *Pentimento* (Boston & Toronto: Little, Brown, 1973), p. 200, in which Hellman reports she told Hammett Norman Mailer told her *The Autumn Garden* was good, but that she had lost her nerve. Hammett responded: "Almost everybody loses their

nerve. You almost didn't, and that's what counts, and what he should have said."

[10]United States of America against Dashiell Hammett, United States Court of Appeals for the Second District, 1951, exhibit 1.

[11]FBI file.

[12]There are two letters from Hammett to his daughter Josephine dated November 3 and November 27, 1951, at HRC.

[13]R. L. interview with Rose Evans.

CHAPTER 21

[1]FBI files.

[2]For Hellman's account of these events see *Scoundrel Time*.

[3]FBI files.

[4]State Department Information Program, Proceedings of Permanent Subcommittee investigation of the Senate Committee on Government Operations, March 1953, pp. 83-88.

[5]*The Big Knockover*, p. 269.

[6]Ibid., p. 274.

[7]FBI files.

[8]VA files.

[9]See Cooper.

[10]VA file; Estate of Dashiell Hammett as presented before Surrogate's Court of the County of New York, 1961.

[11]"Lillian Hellman Gives Eulogy at Hammett Funeral," *New York Herald Tribune*, January 13, 1961, p. 20.

[12]R. L. interview with Yowaiski.

[13]FBI file.

EPILOGUE

[1]Hammett disliked Cowan. Hellman has written that Hammett said of Cowan "for the first time in my life I've met a crazy man who is pretending that he is crazy and wondering why you never see danger." *Pentimento*, p. 251.

[2]All information about the probate of Hammett's estate is from the Probate Proceedings before the Surrogate's Court, County of New York, file P419, 1961-1963.

[3]See *Dashiell Hammett: A Descriptive Bibliography*.

INDEX

King Features Syndicate, 16, 25, 114, 152, 153, 165
Klopfer, Donald S., 168
Knopf, Alfred, 90–91, 131, 145, 168–169
Knopf, Blanche, 98, 131, 163, 165, 239
    Dain Curse and, 100, 104
    Red Harvest and, 91–92
Knopf publishers, *see* Alfred A. Knopf publishers
Knox, Monsignor Ronald, 34
Knudsen, Carl, 26
Kober, Arthur, 129, 134, 157, 179, 235
Kohler, Fred, 125
Kossman, Dr. Charles E., 235
Koussevitzky, Serge, 131
Krasna, Norman, 140
Kronenberger, Louis, 179

Ladd, Alan, 183
Ladies' Man, 126
Lake, Veronica, 183
Lally, John A., 21
Landi, Ellissa, 160
Lardner, Ring, 79, 113
Lariat, The, 85
Latimer, Jonathan, 183
Latin American Confederation of Labor, 210
"Laughing Masks," 48
League of American Writers, 192
Leavenworth Case (Green), 33–34
Leigh, W. Colston, 136
Lenin, Nikolai, 198
Lenox Hill Hospital, 163, 215, 235
Leonardson, Daniel, 130
Levant, Oscar, 144
Lewis, Sinclair, 29
Liberty, 79, 136, 138
Life, 178, 189
Lincoln Brigade, *see* Abraham Lincoln Brigade
Lipper, Aaron, 179
"Literature of Advertising—1927, The," 77
Little Caesar (Burnett), 107
Little Foxes, The (Hellman), 136
Little, Frank, 13, 89
Lodger, The (Lowndes), 34

Loeffler, Al, 189
Loew, Andrew W., 178
Loos, Anita, 161
Los Angeles Mirror, 216
Lowe, Edmund, 154
Lowndes, Mrs. Belloc, 34
Loy, Myrna, 152
Luce, Henry, 178
Lukas, Paul, 126, 184
Lux Radio Theater, 183
Lynch, Eugene, 21
Lyons, Eugene, 208
Lyons, Leonard, 199

MacDonald, John Dennis, 217
MacDonald, Philip, 34
MacLeish, Archibald, 164, 171
Magic Mountain, The (Mann), 131
"Main Death, The," 85
Malaret Mystery, The (Hartley), 80
Malloy, Doris, 154
Malraux, Andre, 164
Maltese Falcon, The (Hammett), 7, 82, 96, 100, 106–115, 116, 147
    dedication of, 114
    earlier Hammett works and, 48, 55, 68, 69, 81, 108
    Flitcraft parable and, 112
    Hammett on, 106, 107–108, 128
    Hospitalers of Saint John and, 108, 110–111
    lawsuit over, 212–213
    Modern Library edition of, 106, 107–108, 168
    publication of, 115, 184, 238, 239
    radio version of, 183, 203, 212–213
    reviews of, 112–113, 121–122
    revision of, 107
    sales of, 113, 121
    serialization of, 107
    stage adaptation of, 135
    third-person narration of, 108
Maltese Falcon, The (movie):
    Bogart version of, 183
    first version of, 133
    rights to, 125
    second version of, 162
Maltz, Albert, 179
Mamoulian, Rouben, 126